MY LIFE OUTSIDE THE RING

Hulk Hogan

H

HODDER &
STOUGHTON

First published in Australia by Hodder & Stoughton in 2009
First published in Great Britain in 2010 by Hodder & Stoughton
An Hachette UK company

First published in the US by St. Martin's Press in 2009

1

Copyright © Eric Bischoff Group, LLC

A CIP catalogue record for this title is available from the British Library

ISBN 9781444704273

Printed and bound in the UK by CPI Mackays, Chatham ME5 8TD

Hodder & Stoughton policy is to use papers that are natural, renewable and
recyclable products and made from wood grown in sustainable forests. The
logging and manufacturing processes are expected to conform to the
environmental regulations of the country of origin.

Hodder & Stoughton Ltd
338 Euston Road
London NW1 3BH
www.hodder.co.uk

To Brooke and Nick, for accompanying me on this
journey from old life to new.
I love you.

To Jennifer, for helping me realize how beautiful life is.
I love you.

To Linda, I pray that you find peace and joy in life.
I love you.

CONTENTS

Acknowledgments   ix

Introduction   1

PART I: GROWING UP   9

Chapter 1
From the Beginning   11

Chapter 2
Finding Faith   28

Chapter 3
Working Out   37

Chapter 4
Fighting My Way In   50

Chapter 5
Backing Away   61

PART II: WRESTLING MANIA   69

Chapter 6
On the Road   73

Chapter 7
Just When I Thought I Was Out . . .   80

Chapter 8
Hulking Up   94

Chapter 9
Livin' the High Life   109

Chapter 10
The Perfect Family   122

PART III: TRIALS AND TRIBULATIONS   131

Chapter 11
Pain   133

Chapter 12
Behind Closed Doors   157

Chapter 13
Something New   168

Chapter 14
Season of Change   185

PART IV: THE UNRAVELING   195

Chapter 15
Cruel Summer   197

Chapter 16
The Vigil   210

Chapter 17
The Downward Spiral   227

PART V: TURNING THE PAGE   241

Chapter 18
A Secret Revealed   243

Chapter 19
Coincidence or Fate?   258

Chapter 20
Revelations   288

Afterword: *Expect the Unexpected*   301

Index   305

ACKNOWLEDGMENTS

This book could not have been written without the support of great friends—some old, some new—and I'm grateful for all of them.

Thanks to Eric Bischoff for being there every step of the way. Jason Hervey for bringing me relief when the chips were down. Henry Holmes for seeing me through the last twenty-five years. Scott Hervey for taking on my new burdens. Also Peter Young, my agent, who has become my blood brother. David Houston for absorbing the attacks of the last two years while turning into a real friend and guiding light in the process. Also, to Michael Bernard Beckwith and James Arthur Ray for awakening the Spirit of Christ that has always been in me. I know now I am responsible for my own joy and happiness.

Nothing would be possible without the support of the Hogan Hit Men—the guys who would lay down their lives for me (as I would for them)—Jimmy Hart, Brian Knobs, Brutus, and Big Todd "Yeah-Yeah-Yeah." And, of course, the man who'll take our antics to the grave and who's always there no matter how heavy it gets, Bubba the Love Sponge. (No, Linda, we are not gay lovers.)

I would also like to thank Elizabeth Rosenthal for always watching my back, not to mention making the connection that sparked this book in the first place. Joel Kneedler at Alive Communications and Kathryn Huck at St. Martin's Press for making it possible that my words actually land on the bookshelves. Steve Chapman for being such a good friend and holding down the neighborhood! Finally, thanks to my personal shrink—Mark Dagostino—for helping me write one hell of a book!

I'm heading into the second half of the game now; I'm especially grateful to Nick, Brooke, and Jennifer for moving forward with me—present and aware in every moment.

I bless those who curse me and pray for those who have spitefully used me. I am sorry, I *had* to leave them behind.

INTRODUCTION

Three pounds. I remember thinking, *Three pounds of pressure is all it takes to pull this thing.* Do you know how easy that would've been? I'd been staring at myself in the bathroom mirror for two days straight. *Two days.* A gun was in my hand and my finger was on the trigger and I was thinking, *It would just be so easy.* I felt like a snake charmer. I was headed down this dark road convincing myself it was a road I wanted to take. The weird thing was, I didn't even remember bringing that gun into the bathroom. *When did I pick* this *up? Was it in the safe? Did I have it in the car with me the other night?* I bought that gun years ago to protect my family. A last resort. Was I really gonna use it for this?

I popped half a Xanax and took another swig from the big bottle of Captain Morgan's I'd set on the counter.

The house was empty. Too quiet. I don't do well alone. My kids were gone. My wife was gone. She had left before, but this was different. She didn't want to fix things. She'd filed for divorce—actually went to a lawyer and filed papers after twenty-three years. My mind kept running through it all, over and over. *My daughter thinks I'm the reason Linda left. There's so much I want her to understand, but she won't talk to me. She won't hear my side of the story.*

My thoughts drifted to my son, Nick. Nearly four months had passed since he got into that terrible car accident. And every day since, the details of that August night played over and over in my mind.

It's not often that a man can pinpoint the moment when life as he knew it began to unravel. For me, it was just after seven thirty on the night of August 26, 2007.

After a long day out on the boat, I'd grabbed a quick shower and hopped in my black Mercedes to head to dinner. Nick and his three buddies had gone just ahead of me to grab a table at Arigato, this Japanese steak house a few miles away. I assumed they'd all gone together in my yellow pickup.

I was wrong.

The fast-moving thunderheads that passed through that afternoon left the roads soaking wet. I remember my tires splashing through puddles as I left the big house on Willadel Drive. Just as I left, Nick's friend Danny drove up in my silver Viper with his pal Barry in the passenger seat. Their windows were down, and they looked a little panicky as they pulled up beside me.

"Nick got in an accident!" they said.

Great, I thought. *This is all I need,* thinking that it was just a fender bender.

"Where?" I asked.

They told me on Court Street near Missouri Boulevard—not much more than a mile from where we were.

For some reason it didn't occur to me that it might be a life-threatening situation. With all the stoplights on that road, I thought they meant that Nick had rear-ended someone, or maybe someone rear-ended Nick. I was a little confused as to why Danny was driving my Viper, but I still thought Nick was in my yellow truck.

So off we went. I turned east and headed down Court Street with the sun getting ready to set behind me. All the lights were green, so I was cruising along when all of a sudden I saw flashing red-and-blues up ahead.

What the hell?

I couldn't have left the house more than three or four minutes after Nick. But as I looked toward the intersection of Court and Missouri there were police cars in the middle of the road blocking traffic in both directions.

That's when I saw it: a yellow vehicle smashed up into a palm tree in the center divider.

Oh my God. Nick!

I panicked. I needed to get closer. Traffic was stopped, so I turned into the oncoming lanes and raced down Court Street the wrong way.

As I hit Missouri I just stared at this mangled yellow wreck on the tree, thinking, *Holy shit*. It didn't look like my truck at all. I was confused for a moment. I had this weird little flash of relief. *Danny and Barry got it wrong. That's not my truck. Phew! Nick's okay.*

Then all of a sudden it hit me. *Oh my God. That's my yellow Supra!*

My stomach clenched up in a knot. I pulled the Mercedes up on the curb, got out, and started running toward the car. "Nick? Nick!?" A cop tried to hold me back, but there was no way. "That's my son!" I yelled as I pushed past him.

The yellow Supra was the car Nick loved most. I had no doubt he was behind the wheel. But I couldn't see him.

I could see his best friend, John Graziano, slumped over in the passenger seat. Nick was nowhere to be found. I thought he'd been thrown from the car, so I'm looking up in the tree, on the ground, across the street. By this time another police car is pulling up, and I hear sirens from the fire trucks coming up the road.

The car had spun around somehow and hit the tree backward. As I reached the front of it a policeman pulled John back. I saw his head. His skull was cracked open at the top of his forehead. It was awful. I almost fainted. It buckled me. John was like a member of my family. And the bleeding was bad—like it wasn't gonna stop.

I was right there leaning on the side of the car with my hands when I finally saw Nick—my only son—folded up like an accordion with his head down by the gas pedal. "Nick!" I yelled. I could see he was alive. He turned his head, stuck his hand out, and gave me a thumbs-up. For a second I was relieved. Then the chaos set in. The sound of engines. Sirens. A saw. Paramedics pulling John from the passenger seat. So much blood.

I can't even describe to you how panicked I was. The police and firefighters seemed panicked, too. The Supra's removable targa top was off, and you could see that the cockpit of the vehicle was pretty intact, but the rest of the car was just mangled. The fiber-glass shell on this thing had crumpled like a toy.

All of a sudden the firefighters started cutting the side of the car to try to get Nick out, and I was standing right there when I heard my boy screaming, "No, no, no, stop! Stop! You're gonna cut my legs off. Dad! Just unbuckle the seat belt. I can get out!" So I reached in and pushed the button on his seat belt, and Nick just crawled right out. His wrist was broken. His ribs were cracked. None of that mattered. He was gonna be okay.

But not John. John wasn't moving.

I pressed the gun to my cheek. I tried not to look in the mirror.

In between flashbacks I kept obsessing about Linda. *How could she leave in the middle of all this? How could she?*

I even turned the pity party on myself. *I'm a mess. I'm in so much pain. My hip. My knees. I don't even know if I can wrestle anymore. What the hell am I gonna do? My back hurts so bad I have to sit just to brush my teeth. In this damned chair. Right here.*

I can't get out of this thing.

My God. Look at me. . . .

As the paramedics tended to Nick, I called Linda. She was out in L.A., where she had been living for months. No one knew we were separated then. No one knew how bad things were between us. But she was my wife, and she was still my first call.

"Linda, you're not gonna believe this, but Nick wrecked the Supra," I said, expecting her to ask if he was okay. Instead, she lost it.

"What the fuck!? What the hell was he doing?"

I tried to get her to listen, but she just kept screaming. When the cops came up to try to ask me questions and she wouldn't let me get a word in, I had no choice but to hang up on her.

I called Brooke instead, who was off in Seattle working on her music. Nick's her baby brother. They've always been close, and she broke down crying just listening to the sound of my voice. She was happy to hear that he was okay, of course, but when I told her that John was in real bad shape, she started bawling. She hated being so far away. I told her to get on a plane, and she said she would be there as soon as she could.

I was pacing like crazy at this point, just freaking out about the whole situation. For all I knew Linda still didn't understand how serious this accident was, so I called her back, and she started screaming at me again for hanging up on her the first time.

By now a couple of medevac helicopters were landing on the scene. I couldn't hear a thing. So I hung up again and turned my attention to Nick. He really seemed fine, and he kept telling the EMS people that he was okay, but they wouldn't budge: They insisted he get into one of the helicopters—and told me I couldn't ride with him.

I lost it. I was woozy. The whole thing played out in this weird way, like slow motion and all sped up at the same time. I looked over and saw John laid out flat, strapped to a gurney as they lifted him into a chopper. I turned and saw firefighters pulling that mangled, cut-up car away from the tree. The press was there. There were video cameras and flashbulbs going off. It was all just crazy.

As the helicopters took off I called Linda back, and she finally calmed down enough to ask if Nick was okay. I told her, "He's walking around. He's talking to me. They're flying him to Bayfront Medical Center to check him out, but I think he's fine."

Then I told her about John. She couldn't take it. I could hear her break down right over the phone.

"Linda," I said, "just get on a plane and get back here. Nick needs you."

At this point I was running back to my car, but a cop stopped me before I could get in. I guess he saw me all wobbly and pacing and didn't think it was safe for me to drive. He offered to take me to the hospital instead. I was glad. I'm not sure I would've made it in that condition.

I climbed into the back of that police car, and he just took off. We were flying down all these back roads with the lights going and the siren blaring, running red lights, blasting through stop signs. The world was a blur. And as I sat in the backseat of that cop car, alone, the whole thing started to hit me.

What if Nick has internal injuries? What if he's in shock? Is he hurt more than he's letting on? How had this happened? And what about John? I've never seen someone's head busted open like that.

I felt sick to my stomach. John had to pull through. I prayed to God that he'd be okay. And I prayed to God for my son.

Here I was, nearly four months later, consumed with thoughts of John Graziano, who was still barely clinging to life in a hospital bed.

What if he never recovers?

I took another swig from that bottle of rum. I got angry at the cops and the media and everyone who blamed my son for hurting John. *It was an accident. A horrible accident. Nick didn't set out to hurt anybody. He feels so guilty. I wish I could help him.*

Slowly that anger gave way to pain and this feeling of helplessness.

Why can't I make this all stop?

I could feel the life draining out of me. I could feel myself bleeding. That's what it felt like: bleeding. Not from a cut on my body, but a wound somewhere deeper. It had me curling my index finger on the trigger of a loaded handgun and putting it in my mouth.

For all my strength, my will, my ability to excel and be the best, I couldn't control that feeling. That depression. Whatever you want to call it. I couldn't control it any more than I could control the craziness that seemed to be crushing my family.

I hit bottom, bro. And I stayed there for two straight days. I even slept with my head on that counter. If I got up to go to the bathroom once or twice, I sat right down again and stared at myself like some fool looking for answers that weren't coming.

And that voice in my head would not stop.

Maybe I should just do it. Only cowards commit suicide. My family would be better off without me. What about the kids? I'm gonna do this. Just pull the trigger. Why not end it? Just do it, Hogan. Do it.

That could have been the end of me right there—that night in early December 2007, in the bathroom at the big house in Clearwater that everybody'd seen on *Hogan Knows Best.*

I could picture the crime scene. The news stories. The whole thing.

Obviously I didn't kill myself—but I came damn close. And if it weren't for a completely unexpected phone call that snapped me out of that stupor, I might have followed that dark road all the way to its end, and I might not be here writing this book today.

In the days after I sat there with that gun in my hand, I realized something: I was sick and tired of feeling sick and tired. If I was gonna keep living and breathing, I had to change things. I didn't know how I would do it. Maybe I'd have to change everything. I just couldn't take it anymore. I wish I didn't have to sink that low to get to that point, but that's what it took.

Slowly but surely in the weeks and months that followed, I opened my eyes to a whole new world. And it worked. I'm choosing to live life differently in the second half of the game.

That doesn't mean everything's perfect. Far from it. As I'm sitting down to write this, my soon-to-be ex-wife is dragging the divorce into a second year. Hell, she's spending time with a nineteen-year-old boyfriend—in the house that I pay for. Not to mention I'm facing a civil suit from the Graziano family that seeks more money than I've made in my whole career. So no, not everything is perfect. The difference now is how I handle this stuff; how I look past those things to see the bigger picture; how I'm actually grateful that these things are happening because I know that something greater is right around the corner. If that doesn't make a lot of sense to you right now, I'm hoping it will by the end of this book.

The main thing I want you to take away from this is simple: If I can get through everything I've been through in the last couple of years and be happier and stronger than ever, then you can get through whatever terrible things might happen in your life, too.

Despite what some people might think, I'm not writing this book to make excuses for anything I've done or to try to change anyone's opinion of me or my family. All I want to do is tell the truth and clear the air so you'll be able to understand where I'm coming from, and where I'm headed. 'Cause believe me, once you breathe clean air, you never want to go back to breathing anything else. That's how I'm living now, and that's why I want to use the lessons I've learned to help other people. I hope that doesn't scare you off. In fact, I hope that you'll be one of the people I help—even if it's just in some small, unexpected way.

If not? Well, that's okay, too. I'm ready to open up about everything in my life. And there's plenty to tell! So I promise to be as open and honest in these pages as I possibly can—occasionally about some heavy stuff that I'm sure you never expected to hear from the Hulkster. I don't know, maybe you'll laugh at me. Or maybe you'll see a little bit of yourself in me. Either way, if you want to read this book for the sheer entertainment value of it, that's fine by me, too. Let's face it, brother: My life's been one hell of a trip, and I'm more than happy to take you along for the ride.

PART I

GROWING UP

CHAPTER 1

From the Beginning

I hate confrontation. I've always hated confrontation. The thought of a truly violent physical confrontation scares me more than just about anything else in life. I know that sounds strange coming from the most famous professional wrestler that ever lived—but it's the truth.

It's a truth I need you to understand because it cuts to the core of who I am as a man.

I was born Terry Gene Bollea in Augusta, Georgia, on August 11, 1953. I certainly don't think of myself as a Georgian because I was only one or one and a half when my parents moved to Florida. To get specific, we moved to Paul Avenue in Port Tampa, Florida—two blocks south of Gandy Boulevard.

Many years later I'd realize that living south of Gandy makes you an official "SOG" in Tampa-speak. S-O-G, for "South of Gandy." The perception is that's where all the poor people in Tampa live, that it's full of football players and wrestlers and all kinds of redneck tough guys. That's not a negative thing. If you're from Port Tampa, there's a certain mystique about it. So people always assumed that I was a whole lot tougher than I really was—just because of where I grew up.

In many ways, Port Tampa was like its own small town. Most of the big roads in the area were dirt back then, and there were red brick streets between the rows of houses. They still exist, actually, which is a pretty unique sight to see.

Like it or not, you knew your neighbors. You couldn't help it. The houses were no more than a stone's throw from each other on any street. I drove back through there a couple of times in recent years, and I'm surprised how small everything seems. As a kid, it really was my whole world.

My father, Pete, my mother, Ruth, and my older brother Alan and I all lived in a little white two-bedroom home. You probably wouldn't believe it if you saw it. It was very humble. I'm not saying it's like the house that Burt Reynolds and those guys walked up to in *Deliverance*. But when I watched the movie *Ray*, about Ray Charles, and they showed him growing up in a little wooden house? It's kind of like that. Just a little square box. When Alan and I were teens we had to sleep catty-corner on the floor because we couldn't fit two twin beds in the room that we shared.

My dad was a pipe fitter, and he was great at it. I remember he did big jobs—installing drainage systems for the malls and high-rises that were being built around Tampa. After a few years he was promoted to foreman. When the road was all dug up and they were laying big six-foot pipes and messing up traffic, he'd be the guy standing in the sun with his arms folded overseeing all that work—then jumping in to do it himself when it wasn't coming out just right. He wasn't a real big guy, maybe five foot eleven, but he was real strong, with strong hands and a good grip. That seemed to be common among the Bollea men, going back to my grandfather.

Now, my grandfather was a real old-school Italian guy who lived in New Hampshire and worked in the forests. Legend has it that one time he picked up an eight-hundred-pound rock—just rolled it right up onto his thighs into a squat. Years later I'd think about that when I bodyslammed André the Giant at WrestleMania III. André was the biggest he'd ever been. He was pushing seven hundred pounds that night—a hundred pounds *less* than my grandfather had lifted—and it still tore the muscles in my back to shreds.

Of course, when it came to life in Tampa, being strong didn't pay much. I remember asking my mom how much dough Dad made. I think I was twelve when I first got curious about money, and she told me straight up: $180 a week. When he got his promotion, which was a huge deal, he went up to $200 a week. That was it.

My mom was a housewife, so that's all the money we ever had, but it never seemed to me that we didn't have much money. Everything seemed normal. Heck, every Friday my mom would pull out these little frozen minute steaks for dinner. So every Friday we'd get to eat steak!

Life was good. Life was simple.

I remember playing in the dirt in the backyard, just pushing these little toy trucks around while my dad tended to his grapefruit and tangelo trees. I had this weird habit of stuffing rocks up my nose. Little rocks that I'd find in the dirt. I'd just stuff my nose full of them until my parents made me blow 'em out. It's weird the stuff you remember.

I've never been very good at comparing my life to other people's lives. I've always just lived in my own world, I guess that's what you'd call it. For instance, I remember my childhood being really happy even though there wasn't a lot of outward affection at home.

Put it this way: Many years later, just before I got married, the first time I met Linda's mom she gave me this huge hug—and it shocked me. I just wasn't used to being hugged like that by anyone in my family at all.

I think about how Linda always hugged Nick and Brooke when they were kids, just over the top with all kinds of affection, and how my mother wasn't like that with me. Maybe there was a kiss on the forehead when she came in to tuck me in at night. I probably hug her more when I go to visit her now, as an adult, than I ever did when I was a kid.

As for my dad, I don't remember him saying that he loved me. He was just old-school New Hampshire Italian, like his father. I know that he loved me, though, and he was there for me. He took me to baseball games and always came to watch my games and threw the ball around whenever I wanted—all that stuff. Again, it's not a bad thing that my parents weren't all lovey-dovey. That's just the way it was.

Even without that outward affection, we were tight. My parents' marriage seemed really strong, too. They stuck together through some really rough times, especially as my brother, Alan, grew older and got into some major trouble.

SIGNS OF STRENGTH

Some of my earliest memories of childhood involve getting bullied by the older boys in my neighborhood. Especially by this one red-haired kid who was meaner than a snake: Roger.

Roger lived maybe three houses down from us on Paul Avenue. I remember one day, I was six or seven, and I was out in the yard collecting caterpillars from the trees and putting them into glass jars. All the kids used to collect those yellow caterpillars. It was a big deal for some reason. I put my jar down for one minute, and next thing I know, Roger has taken all my caterpillars and put 'em in his jar.

That was it for me. I got all pissed off. I just wasn't gonna let that happen. So I stormed over to pick up his jar, and as I was trying to turn the cap off he came up from behind and pushed me down. Smash! The broken glass nearly cut my index finger clean off. When Roger saw my finger hanging there and the blood gushing out, he got real scared and started running home. So I bent down and picked up a rock, like David and Goliath, and I threw it so hard—I just launched it all the way down the street and hit him right in the back of his head. Dropped him right there on the pavement. Blood was everywhere.

I was shaking like crazy after I did it. I felt horrible. In the end he was fine, and I was glad I didn't hurt him too bad. I tell you one thing, though—I never got bullied again after that. And for that I'm thankful, 'cause I get real emotional just thinking about that kind of confrontation.

Alan liked to get in fights all the time—brutal fights, just for the fun of it—and I could never understand it. I'm not afraid of getting hurt. I'm not afraid of pain. It's the aggression that leaves me shaking. I mean, if wrestling wasn't fake, I never would have done it. Seriously, if wrestling wasn't predetermined and was some kind of actual fight, I wouldn't have gone anywhere near it. I was only attracted to it after I discovered that it was entertainment.

In the years after my run-in with Roger, I learned to put my throwing arm to much better use—primarily in baseball and bowling.

Yes, you heard it here first: Hulk Hogan used to be a bowler. I had a friend named Vic Pettit who lived in the neighborhood and whose dad owned the local bowling alley. That made it pretty easy to find practice time. So Vic and I became partners and got really into it. From ages eight to twelve, Vic and I were state team bowling champions. Even back then, when I was into something, I gave it my all, but Vic was the real reason the team won. I've seen that kid bowl three back-to-back 300 games. That's thirty-six strikes in a row!

Vic played baseball with me, too. When it came to playing ball, I had a natural advantage over everyone: my size. I was six feet tall at twelve years old. There's an old team photo where you can see it clear as day. Not only was I taller than the other kids, I was taller than the coach. Combine that with my expert throwing arm (sorry, Roger), and I jumped to the front of the Little League ranks.

Every time I got up to bat it was like a special occasion. I hit the first home run over the electric scoreboard. I hit the first home run over the lights. We went to the Little League World Series, where I got up to bat fourteen times—and I went ten for fourteen. I had a .714 batting average in the finals of the Little League World Series! It was unheard-of.

I'm not sure if it's still there, but for many years there was a plaque hanging at the Interbay Little League baseball fields down near the entrance to MacDill Air Force Base noting that Terry Bollea had the most home runs in a single season.

Don't get the wrong impression, though. I wasn't a jock or a big-man-on-campus type. In fact, I didn't get along with the jocks at all, and when I say I was big, I don't just mean I was tall. I mean I was fat.

I loved playing baseball. Loved to pitch. Loved to play third base. Unfortunately, I couldn't run to save my life, and more embarrassing than that was my gigantic head—and I'm not talking about my ego. My head was so big that there was only one helmet on our Little League team that fit me—this bathtub-sized helmet that nobody wanted to wear. The team only had four helmets to begin with. So if the bases got loaded and somebody else had that helmet, or if the coach left the helmet in the trunk of his car when it was time for me to get up to bat, we'd have to stop the whole game just to make sure I got that special helmet.

The issues with my big head went all the way back to first grade. It was the first day of school and I was scared to death, and my tablemate, Sarah, looked at me funny and said, "Has your head always been that big?" That's the first thing a girl said to me on my very first day of first grade. Poetic justice being what it is, Sarah had her sweater tied around her waist, and she pissed on it before the first day was over.

Even people I considered friends made fun of my big head. Butch Smith, whom I liked, used it as a nickname. "Hey, Fat Head, you wanna play baseball? Hey, Fat Head, you wanna come over? Hey, Fat Head, you wanna go to the movies?"

By the time I was twelve it wasn't just the head. I was six feet tall and weighed 196 pounds. Sure, I made the All-Star baseball team. Sure, I could hit home runs. But do you think any girls would be interested in *that* guy? I was an outsider. Even with the abilities I had, I couldn't run worth a damn—so PE class was always embarrassing.

PE

The two things I remember most about fifth and sixth grade at Ballast Point Elementary School are first, the day that Kennedy got shot—I was sitting in Mrs. Crittaball's fifth-grade class when they told us—and second, just how much I dreaded PE class on Fridays.

The class was taught by Coach Hatch, who wore a big lift on one shoe to compensate for his one short leg. The legend was that he got shot in the war—whichever war that may be, probably World War II—as he was coming down on a parachute. That was the story, anyway. He was a big, mean-looking guy, but that wasn't why I dreaded going to his class. I dreaded it because he'd make us dance.

Coach Hatch had a big wooden rolling cart with a record player on it, and he'd set up speakers on the basketball courts outside, and we'd all have to do a circle dance, or skip as we danced to "Skip to My Lou" and all of those old songs. I hated it! The only upside was there were always more girls than guys in Hatch's class, and it was up to the girls to pick the guys they wanted to dance with. I would just pray that I wouldn't get picked. The majority of the time, that prayer was answered. Like I said, I had a big head, I was fat, and girls didn't like me—but my feelings weren't hurt by it at all on those days. Those of us who didn't have a partner would get to go out on the football field and kick a ball around instead of dancing.

Coach Hatch made everyone run around the goalposts, from one end of the field all the way down and back. I was so slow, he would start me at the far end and make me run back just once. The other kids would go all the way down the football field and round the goalpost and come back and pass me before I'd covered one lap.

PE was even worse once I got into high school. First of all, because of my size, everybody wanted me to play football. I actually played a little, but when they put me on the varsity team in tenth grade, I hated it so much after two games I quit. All the football players hated me for that. So did the coach. This big, mean, three-hundred-pound guy named Coach Mann. He never forgot it and never let me forget it, and I swear he had it in for me the rest of my high school years—me with my hippie long hair.

Coach and the football players weren't the only ones who hated me. The wrestlers hated me, too. Believe it or not, I wanted nothing to do with high school wrestling. Coach Mann never let me live that down, either.

Maybe it was just my bad luck, or maybe it was Coach Mann's doing, but when I got to senior year, I got stuck in seventh-period PE class—the class with all the jocks in it. It was the end of the day, so it was basically like an early start to football practice and basketball practice and wrestling practice—all the jocks would just keep practicing after the bell rang, you know?

One day, Coach Mann brought this kid in who had graduated the year before, Steve Broadman. Steve was the wrestling champion of all champions. He was a hero to all these guys, and a heavyweight. Just to teach me a lesson, Coach Mann said to me, "Boy, get your ass over here," and put me on the mat to wrestle Steve. This wasn't out in the gym, it was in the locker room. I was scared. I thought for sure Mann had brought him in there to kill me, or at least hurt me real bad. So I did everything I could to end this thing fast—and wouldn't you know it, I pinned him! I pinned Coach Mann's number-one guy right there. With zero training, I just did it out of pure fear.

Boy, was Mann pissed. Coach threw his hat down, and he was mostly bald-headed with these weird patches of hair. He had some disease. I think it's called alopecia. But he threw his hat down and threw his clipboard, and he was just steaming.

"All right, Bollea, try me!" Coach Mann actually got down on all fours, in position. "Get on top of me! Come on!"

So I got on him, and I hooked him right away, just pulled his arm out from under him and took his weight right with me. I chicken-winged him, and I pinned him, too! Right there in front of the whole PE class.

Everyone started laughing and hollering. Except Coach Mann.

Dude, I went runnin' for my life! I ran right out of the building, and big Coach Mann chased me all the way down the street in front of Robinson High School. I was sure he wanted to kill me!

My parents went and talked to the principal the next day, and they let me out of PE class for the rest of the year.

So I wasn't in with the football players or the wrestlers or any of the jocks. Not at all. I had all kinds of heat with everybody.

MY ESCAPE

Those school years were pretty tough on me, but not nearly as tough as they would've been if I didn't have an outlet to take me away from it all.

That outlet was music.

We always had a piano in that tiny house of ours, and my mom was always playing. So I developed an ear for music without even trying.

For some reason, right before junior high, I suddenly got really interested in guitar, and I remember asking my parents if I could take lessons.

Even though we didn't have much money, my parents were always real supportive of stuff like that. So they hooked me up with a teacher, and as soon as I showed some talent my dad bought me my first guitar. Not a cheap department store guitar, either. It was a Guild, and it cost like three or four hundred bucks. Looking back on it now, I have no idea how they afforded it. It was a real nice electric guitar, and I certainly got every penny's worth out of it.

Music just made sense to me for some reason. I was always real good at math, and music was kind of like math to me. So I picked it up pretty quick, and had several guitar teachers, and before long I started playing in bands.

My very first band was called the Plastic Pleasure Palace. Very '60s, right? We never played anywhere, but it was good practice.

We had a drummer named Chet and a guitarist named Danny. Danny and I both had such big egos that neither one of us wanted to give up the guitar to play bass. So the band was just two guitars and drums. We were the greatest garage band that never got out of the garage.

Just a few months after joining up with those guys, I stepped out on my own and joined a real band, with real gigs.

Infinity's End looked like a professional group, but we were all just a bunch of kids. (I was still in junior high!) Still, we were a pretty slick organization. The keyboard player was named Gary Barris, and his father, Bob Barris, would drive us all around in this station wagon with a trailer off the back to haul all of our equipment. Mrs. Barris used to paint peace signs and daisies on our pants with black-light paint that would glow onstage. She also made us wear socks with our penny loafers, and if we didn't we'd get fined five dollars. It was a big deal to her for some reason.

I remember Mr. Barris was a real stiff kind of guy and took the whole thing real seriously. Whatever the gig was, we would play forty minutes, then take a twenty-minute break. We couldn't be late; we couldn't break too early. He kind of took some of the fun out of it with all that discipline, but the thing was, we were junior high kids and we were actually making money at this on the weekends. We played all the local rec centers and a lot of high school dances, and we'd drive up to Gainesville or wherever to play fraternity parties at colleges. We even had gigs in the clubs attached to some of the Big Daddy liquor stores down here, which was a real big deal.

I don't remember what those gigs paid, but I do know that every once in a while we'd play a private party or some corporate gig and we'd pull in like five hundred dollars. It wasn't much after you split it all up and took out the expenses, but it was still good money in junior high.

I guess it was right around this time when I first started to notice that my family didn't have as much money as some other families. Even my friend Vic Pettit—his parents had a big color TV in their living room and always seemed to be getting new cars every few years. Other kids seemed to have cooler clothes or newer clothes than I ever did. They certainly had more clothes. I remember wearing the same pair of pants to school over and over. Maybe it was because I was a teenager now and hyperaware of peer acceptance, but it really started to bother me thinking that other kids would notice.

So having that extra money coming in from the band was a godsend. It allowed me to go out and buy a new shirt or a new pair of pants, to help me feel like I fit in a little better, you know? I loved having the freedom to do that with my own money instead of always having to ask my parents for something.

Don't get the wrong impression and think I was turning into some cool rocker dude just because I was in a band playing gigs so young. It's kind of like how I wasn't a jock even though I could play baseball. Infinity's End was just a bunch of nerds. We were these totally nerdy guys in our black-light pants and penny loafers doing synchronized dance moves with our guitars while we played Iron Butterfly and Steppenwolf songs. We were like a live jukebox. People loved the music. But we didn't get any attention from young girls.

So that whole notion of "sex, drugs, and rock 'n' roll" didn't really exist for me. If we looked like hippies with our long hair, trust me—we were hippies who didn't smoke pot. I didn't so much as see a joint back then. I don't even think I saw one in high school. I was oblivious to that stuff. Even with my older brother, Alan, I didn't understand what he was into at the time. I just thought he was crazy. Years would go by before I realized what kind of drugs he was taking. I'm sure everybody else was doing it, but I didn't know anything about drugs. I didn't know anything about sex, either.

For the most part, I was way too nervous to make a move on a girl. A girl like Sherry Mashburn. Man oh man! I was in love with her all the way back in the sixth grade. I would ride my bike all the way to her house just to see her. She had long dark hair, like Cher, and these long legs like a pony. She was just gorgeous.

As we got into high school she started to hang out with all the cool kids, you know? She wasn't a cheerleader because she didn't have to be. She was more like an Angelina Jolie type. She would play harmonica before school in the mornings, and I just couldn't take my eyes off her. She was so gorgeous. But the idea of ever asking Sherry out was just way beyond anything I could've handled back then.

Sue Clark was another girl who was a little more approachable, and I was crazy about her, too. I totally blew it with her, though, because I tried to kiss her one time, and I had no idea that you were supposed to open your mouth and use your tongue. It was so embarrassing. And this wasn't in junior high or something—this was high school! I was a slow learner in that department.

In fact, not a mile away from Sue's house there was this other girl, I can't remember her name, but we used to sit on her couch after her parents would go to bed, and we would just kiss and make out for hours and hours. No sex. No nothing. Just kissing. When I stood up to go, I couldn't figure out why I'd have a wet spot in my underwear. I didn't have a clue. I didn't know anything about masturbation, none of that shit. There wasn't any sex ed in those days, and no one ever talked to me about it.

For some reason my friends figured it out. My buddy Ed Leslie, later known in the wrestling world as Brutus "the Barber" Beefcake, was having sex all the time—and he's younger than me! But not Terry Bollea.

I lost my virginity so late, I'm not even gonna reveal it in this book. It's just too embarrassing.

What can I say? I was naive. I was just too focused on other things. In those days, baseball and music were just about all I could think about.

BROTHER, BROTHER

My brother Alan, whom I shared a room with in that little house on Paul Avenue, was about eight years older than me. So he was a big kid, even a teenager, by the time I start having real memories of him. While nothing stood out much in the early years—we were like normal brothers, I guess—the thing I remember most is him putting our parents through so much crap in his teen years.

Alan was always drinking, and always fighting. It's nothing to brag about, but he had a reputation in Port Tampa of being a crazy motherfucker. He was a big guy, like me, but he didn't hide behind the perceived "SOG" persona like I tried to. He was a real tough guy. And while I didn't do any drugs, Alan and his buddies were into everything.

I didn't realize it all at the time, but what they liked to do was drop acid, get drunk, and then fight. That was their deal. Every Friday and Saturday night, that's what they did: get drunk, drop acid, and go out looking for fights. Alan was always getting put in jail, always getting in trouble. It just drove my parents crazy. It was a nightmare for them.

At seventeen, Alan up and married this girl named Martha Alfonso, and they moved from Paul Avenue like two streets back and six blocks down to a house on the corner of Ballast Point Boulevard. They ended up having three kids, and even that didn't slow Alan down. Only now, instead of him bringing his trouble directly to our house, Martha would come over to tell us the news: "Well, he's not home!" "He's drunk." "He's down the road and he's in a fight and the guy's eye got knocked out!" So we'd all go down to wherever he was, and it was always just a drunken mess with all kinds of cussin' and blood. I mean just over and over, every weekend it was something.

It seemed to me like Alan loved the drama. Like he somehow fed off of that craziness. Like Alan needed that anger in his life to keep living.

I remember when I was about sixteen years old, he almost sucked me into it. I was at the house, and out of nowhere Alan came crashing through the front door. It looked like a movie scene. His eye was swollen shut and blood was everywhere, and he was really selling it. "Oh, my eye! Look what he did to me. You need to come with me!" I was a real big kid by then, right? So Alan tried to rope me into helping him go fight back. "This guy down here at the Trophy Room hit me in the eye with a cue stick!" he said.

Because he's my brother, and I didn't know any better, I hopped in the car and drove down there. The two Bollea brothers go power-walking into this bar with our chests all pumped up. I'm sixteen looking for some guy that hit my brother in the eye with a cue stick at a bar!

By the time we got there, the guy and his buddies had all taken off. Thank God. But it was stuff like that all the time.

Somehow we all just knew that it would end real bad for Alan someday.

It almost happened before I was out of high school.

I went to school with a kid, Kenny, whose mother owned a honky-tonk bar called the MacDill Tavern, on the corner of Interbay and MacDill Avenue.

One night toward the end of high school, I'm pulling into my parents' driveway in this Dodge Mopar Road Runner I had at the time. It must have been near midnight. Before I even turned off the ignition someone comes pulling up in a car and starts shouting at me. "Your brother's just been shot! Your brother's just been shot at the MacDill Tavern!"

I couldn't believe it. I backed the car out of the driveway and hauled ass down MacDill Avenue goin' eighty, ninety, a hundred miles an hour. I got there within two or three minutes—and I could see all the cops standing outside. I thought that was it for my brother, you know?

But my brother was nowhere to be found.

From what I could piece together, Alan had been down at the Silver Dollar, one of these real hard-core bars by the docks. He had gotten in a fight, like usual, and beat up a couple of people real bad. He and his buddies were high as kites, doing that LSD and drinking thing they always did. As soon as they left, someone at the Silver Dollar called Kenny's mother at the MacDill Tavern and warned, "Alan Bollea's headed your way, and he's really, really messed up."

When Alan walked into that bar and asked for a drink, Kenny's mother refused to serve him. So he grabbed her by the back of the head and threatened her. And when she told him to get out of the bar, he pushed her head down on the counter. Now, I don't know if he "pushed it" or "slammed it" down. There were different accounts of what happened—there are always different accounts in heated situations like that—but everybody that I talked to agreed that her face hit the bar.

So as Alan started walking out, Kenny's mom pulled a gun from under that counter and shot him twice in the back.

My brother, tough guy that he was, took two bullets, fell facedown in the dirt, picked himself up, brushed himself off, and drove himself to the hospital before the cops even arrived.

Like I said, Alan was one crazy motherfucker.

The doctors managed to get one of the bullets out, but they couldn't remove the second one. It was too close to his spine. So it stayed in Alan's back the rest of his life.

That didn't slow him down, though. A few months later, right when he was getting ready to go to trial, Alan disappeared. I found out later that he'd moved to Houston, Texas, where he hung out for a while and held down different jobs. He changed his name, but he didn't change his attitude. He got in all kinds of trouble there, too.

The fighting just never stopped. He kept in touch with my parents, and I'd hear from him every now and then, but I never really saw Alan again until my wrestling career was in high gear.

I didn't see my other brother, Kenny, until my wrestling career took off, either. I realize I haven't mentioned Kenny until this moment. I guess it's because I barely ever knew him.

Kenny is my much older half brother. My mom was married once before she married my dad. By the time I was born, I guess

her Kenny had moved out or was living with his father or something, because I don't remember him living in that house on Paul
Avenue at all. I heard about him from time to time, though.

My mom was real proud of Kenny. He got into the air force
and went to the Virginia Military Institute—if I'm remembering
this right—and he graduated as a lieutenant. By the time I started
wrestling with the WWF in late '78, '79, he was working in the
budgeting department at the Pentagon, and he was a full-blown
major, or a colonel, or whatever his rank was—he'd done real well
in the air force.

When things really got going with the WWF, I wound up
wrestling at the Capital Centre in Maryland about once a month,
not far from his place up there, and we started to get in touch
with each other. I'd even stay at his house when I was in town.
This went on for about two years. It was nice having some other
family to connect with in another part of the country like that. It
was a nice break to staying in hotels night after night, too.

Then this one time Kenny asked to borrow some money from
me. I don't remember what he needed it for, but it was something
pretty urgent, as I recall. He came down to MacDill Air Force
Base in Tampa on a government plane, and the amount he wanted
to borrow was five thousand dollars.

At that point it could have been fifty thousand dollars or more
and I wouldn't have said "no." He's my brother. He's family. But
he was real insistent. "I'm gonna pay you back in 30 days, don't
worry," he said.

I said, "Okay, no problem." And that was that.

Well, thirty days went by, then sixty days, then ninety days. I
remember my mom asked me if Kenny had paid me back yet. I
don't remember if I told her about the loan. I'm pretty sure he
didn't. Anyhow, one way or another, she knew, and I guess she
kinda called him on it. He said to her, "Oh, don't worry, I'm gonna
get the money to Terry."

But it never happened. Instead, he quit communicating with
me. Just quit. Basically to this day we don't talk, over that small
amount of money. I mean, if we're not talking anymore he might

as well have gone to half a million, you know? That was a cheap lesson for me in the long run. Money does weird things to people.

If Kenny had told me he couldn't pay me back, that would have been fine, but I just never heard from him again. I had a real problem with that for a while. As years went by and Hulkamania started taking off, there must have been a dozen occasions when some random fan would come up to me and go, "Hey, you got a brother named Kenny?" I was so freaked out by what happened between us that I'd usually just say no.

"Oh, you know, your brother—he works in the Pentagon. He says his brother's Hulk Hogan, the champ!"

I'd just go, "No, I don't know him." I went on with that ridiculous crap for ten or fifteen years before I finally got over it.

Many years later, when my father was dying, Kenny came down to Tampa with his whole family. We were all gathered at Tampa General, and they took my dad outside in the wheelchair—so he could get out and see the water there—and I remember when I tried to say hi to Kenny's wife, Susan, she just turned her head. I don't know what I ever did to her. But the whole thing's just strange. Except for a few words right after my dad passed away, Kenny and I haven't spoken at all. He's based in Dayton, Ohio, now. He must be sixty-seven, sixty-eight years old. And it hasn't changed.

I basically learned to let it go. But here I am writing about it. So I guess maybe it still bothers me. I just don't understand how a little bit of money could rip a hole like that in what's supposed to be one of life's strongest bonds—the bond of family.

CHAPTER 2

Finding Faith

While Alan was getting high and throwing punches, I actually turned my attention in a whole different direction.

I had gone to Ballast Point Baptist Church off and on since about the first grade. The church sat catty-corner to the elementary school, and my parents (more likely my mom) would sometimes bring me on Sundays. Now and then I'd go with Vic and his parents—the ones who owned the local bowling alley. Then later on I'd go with these two junior high football buddies of mine, Don and Ron Satterwhite—two brothers who coincidentally enough are both ministers now.

Church never had much of an impact on me as a little kid. My dad was really hit-or-miss with the whole religion thing, and I think that probably rubbed off on me. We would go on Sunday, then come home and never talk about God or religion during the week at all. I asked about going to Sunday school a few times, mostly because I saw all the other kids going and making things out of clay and painting them, and it looked kinda fun. But my parents were always "No, no, no." Dedicating an hour a week to church was enough of an inconvenience already.

Things changed when I was about fifteen. I had just gotten my learner's permit, and I already had my first car: a 1965 Ford Galaxy. Green with red interior. It looked like a Christmas tree. But instead of the regular shifter it had this three-speed Sparkomatic in it that some previous owner had installed. So it was almost cool! (Almost.)

I don't remember if I was still playing football at that point or if I had quit already, but I remember it being just after football practice that the Satterwhite brothers finally convinced me to come with them to the Christian Youth Ranch. They'd talked about it ever since junior high. But they finally suckered me into coming by saying they needed someone to play guitar so everybody could sing along. They knew that music was my sweet spot.

I had a wooden box guitar and could play your standard three-chord progression, which is all most of those church songs were. So I went. And all the kids sang along. It was just a real nice peaceful environment.

The meetings were every week. I forget if they were Mondays or Tuesdays, but I didn't have anything better to do at that time, so I kept going. And in between the songs each week I'd listen to the lessons of the Rev. Hank Lindstrom—especially the one verse that Rev. Lindstrom would beat into everybody's heads, week after week:

> For God so loved the world that he gave his only begotten Son, that whoever believes in him shall not perish but have eternal life.   —John 3:16

When Rev. Lindstrom was done he'd say, "All right, now how many of you here accept Christ as your savior? Close your eyes, everybody. Raise your hands." Everybody would be peeking with one eye open to see who was raising a hand and who wasn't.

In the beginning I wouldn't raise mine 'cause I didn't understand it. But it didn't take long for it to all sink in.

Growing up, I always believed there was something more to us than just the flesh—something more than just this meat suit that we're running around in, you know? Other kids would say things like, "Oh man, I don't ever want to die." And even early on I remember saying, "I'm not afraid to die because I think I'm going to heaven." I never really understood the whole religion thing, but I just had a feeling there was a God.

Now I realize that people follow a lot of different faiths. Whether it's Allah or the "higher self," every religion has a name for what they believe to be the higher spirit or higher energy or higher being. But simply "God" made sense to me for some reason.

I also had my own sort of moral code as a kid. "Well, if I'm good, if I get good grades, if I don't get in trouble"—it was more like a checklist, like Santa has—"if I'm a good person, then I'll get into heaven."

It wasn't until I met Hank Lindstrom that I came across a barrier to that basic belief. He told me, "You know what, man? You can't get into heaven like that."

I said, "What do you mean?"

"You have to accept Christ as your savior," he said. "You have to accept that we're all sinners, you know? And that God gave his only begotten son—he sacrificed his son to pay for your sins."

I took a real interest in what he was saying for some reason, and I kept asking him to read me different passages from the Bible. What they all seemed to be saying is that you don't necessarily have to do good, the way I had been doing things. All you have to do is believe. And that didn't make much sense to me. I mean, after seeing what my brother Alan had gotten into, I definitely knew I wanted to go down the right path and do the right thing. I didn't quite agree with the idea that you could go out and murder people and all of a sudden, "Oh, I believe in Jesus Christ," and all would be forgiven and you'd walk through the pearly gates.

But that didn't negate the idea that if you believe in Christ, you'll have eternal life after death. To me, it just felt like acknowledging what I already knew in my gut—that everything wasn't just surface level. That everything wasn't materialistic. There was something more.

Why did I believe in God? Maybe I was just too scared not to: *I don't want to say I don't believe in God 'cause, oh my God, what will happen then?* You know? But when you really stop and think about it, the Bible's been so consistent, and handed down over thousands of years. How can you not put some kind of stock in it? Even if you're just reading the words and going, "Oh, I don't know if I can believe this." Look at it from a different angle: If there's nothing to it, if it's a hoax, if it's folklore, if it's an urban legend, it's a pretty good one to have survived all those years.

All I know is that I could tell the difference between my human flesh and what I felt inside. Call it a spirit. Call it whatever you want. But if you believe in that, and you believe in John 3:16, which is the foundation of Christianity and what I believe in, well, then all of a sudden you're not afraid to die anymore.

And the amazing part is, once you're not afraid to die then you're not afraid to *live.*

I didn't fully understand the power of that when I was fifteen, sixteen years old, but I did feel something shift in my life at that point. I followed that feeling, knowing that I'd been saved; knowing that I would have eternal life if this meat suit I'm walking around in ever got wrecked.

Once I accepted Christ, I just stayed on the path that I was instinctively following before. It was mostly commonsense stuff—this overwhelming feeling of just wanting to be good instead of bad.

Looking back on that Christian Youth Ranch, it really helped lay the foundation of strength and resolve I would need to accomplish everything in my life—and certainly the foundation that helped get me through the rough times that were to come all these years later.

I remember the moment, maybe five or six weeks after I first started playing my guitar there, after listening to Rev. Lindstrom hammer away at the Bible, when I first raised my hand with the rest of the kids. It was pretty simple. I said to myself, "You know? I think Christ *did* die on the cross for our sins."

So when I say I was "saved," it wasn't some big evangelical moment. It wasn't some over-the-top thing. It wasn't like I joined some sort of cult or something. It just meant that I accepted the basic tenet of Christianity.

I kept going to that Youth Ranch pretty much every week right through the rest of high school. And I kept those teachings in the back of my mind long after Port Tampa was disappearing in my rearview mirror—when Sundays were spent in the ring and not in some pew.

I kept in touch with Rev. Hank Lindstrom, too. We would call each other now and then. It was always good to hear his voice.

A DIFFERENT TEMPLE

If somebody asked me if I'd ever had a "religious experience" in my early years—one of those mind-blowing, life-altering, shake-your-whole-world moments of elation where you just want to raise your hands to the heavens and shout, "Thank you!"—the answer would be yes: the first time I sat in an arena and watched live wrestling.

Vic and I used to love to watch wrestling on TV. *Florida Championship Wrestling* was the bomb! Every Saturday morning.

There was no other wrestling on here in Tampa. There was no WWWF on TV at all. (Not many people remember that it was three *W*'s and an *F* when it first started—for World Wide Wrestling Federation. Later it became WWF, and then WWE.) There was no cable with Ted Turner and the WCW. Nothing. *Florida Championship Wrestling* was it, and we were addicted to it.

Back in the '60s and early '70s they had a wrestler called the

Great Malenko (whose kid wound up working with Chris Benoit and Chris Jericho years later) and a great champion named Buddy Colt. There was Jos LeDuke, "the Canadian Freight Train." Eventually Superstar Billy Graham was on there. And of course André the Giant was in and out.

But the guy that we really would watch every Saturday, and if he didn't talk, or if he wasn't on TV that week we'd be all pissed off, was a guy named Dusty Rhodes. "The Great American Dream, baby!" He was the first guy we ever heard trash-talk. This big, strong, powerful-looking dude with a white afro and this twangy voice, and he'd get that weird lisp going, "The man of the hour, man of the power, the man too sweet to beat! The American Dream, Dusty Rhodes!"

Dusty Rhodes was the be-all end-all. He beat *everybody* up. There was a promoter here named Eddie Graham, and his son Mike Graham was a wrestler who would eventually take over the business from him. I didn't understand anything about the "business" back then, but what they would do, since Dusty Rhodes was like their Hulk Hogan, their hero, is they would bring in bad guys to feed to him. Like Superstar Billy Graham or the Russian Bear, Ivan Koloff. These guys would show up down here and they were scary, these three-hundred-pound wrestlers out of New York.

I guess all the promoters were friends from wrestling together in the '60s, so the WWWF up at Madison Square Garden would send out wrestlers as a favor to these other territories. One of the places that Vince McMahon Sr. used to love to send wrestlers was to Florida, so they could disappear for a while and the audience up north wouldn't get bored with them. Then six months or a year later they'd come back to New York, and the fans would go nuts, you know?

As a kid I didn't know any of that, and I didn't care. All I knew was there was this cast of bad guys that would come through Florida trying to dethrone my hero, Dusty Rhodes. And he would beat every one of them with the Bionic Elbow. He'd be down and bloody, but no one could stop him. He'd get up and make the comeback with that elbow, *bang!* and then put the Figure Four on 'em, like the Ric Flair Figure Four Leg Lock—that was his finish.

We got so addicted to watching wrestling that we finally talked Vic's dad and my dad into taking us down to the armory. I think we were about nine or ten years old the first time we went. I remember Vic's dad got us really good seats, in the second or third row. We were right in the thick of the action.

The Fort Homer Hesterly Armory wasn't a big building, and I remember there was a guardrail up on the top level. Sitting in the crowd, you could look up and see the wrestlers looking over that guardrail, watching what was happening in the ring. I thought it was so cool to be there and see what you could never see on camera.

On one side was the good guys' dressing room, and on the other side was the bad guys'. Every once in a while a bad guy would come out and look over the rail, then he'd go in. Then a good guy would come out. You'd see them at that guardrail, and then they'd disappear. Even though there was this big set of stairs off to the side that came all the way down to the main floor, when it was time for their match, the wrestlers would disappear and then come out through the bottom of the arena for their big walk out to the ring.

I was just totally blown away watching wrestling live.

On that very first day we saw all of these matches, one after the other, and I was just ready to burst out of my seat I was so excited. Vic and I were just dying to see Dusty Rhodes. Then all of a sudden, the time for the main event hits, and Dory Funk Sr. comes fighting down the stairs with Dusty Rhodes!

There was blood everywhere before the match even started. It was the wildest thing I'd ever seen.

When Dusty finally climbs into the ring and the match really starts, instead of locking it up or doing arm drags or hip tosses or body slams, the bad guy just kicks him and starts beating on him. My hero got jumped by the bad guy! He's down on the mat. We're all standing up trying to see what happened, and he's down in the fetal position getting his ass kicked.

This goes on for what seems like forever. Then all of a sudden Dusty gets free. The bad guy backs off for a second, and Dusty Rhodes rises up from the canvas. By now he's just a crimson mess. His white hair's filled with blood. He regroups and gets his strength back and out of nowhere hits a Bionic Elbow on his opponent, and the whole place explodes. It sounded like a cannon. *Boom!*

Every time he'd do an elbow, *boom!* He'd throw it nice and slow so everybody could see it comin', and when it hit the whole arena would go, "Oh!"

Once he was on his feet it was *boom! boom! boom! boom! Ding-ding-ding-ding.*

And it was over.

I was reeling! "Oh, man!" The whole match lasted about three minutes, and that was the main event. Not two seconds later Vic and I were begging our dads, "We gotta come back! We gotta come back!" It was unbelievable. And I got totally hooked.

Vic and I went back with our dads probably three or four times a year from then on. Once I was in high school and got my license, I would sometimes skip school on Wednesdays to go watch them film wrestling at the Sportatorium on Albany. My mom would even write notes claiming I was out sick. She was real cool like that. Just like with music, my parents supported whatever I was into.

As much as I loved to watch wrestling, though, it was way too violent for me to even remotely consider doing myself. It never even crossed my mind. I mean, we used to mess around and fake-wrestle in high school. Me and my buddies would go outside in the parking lot during shop class and pretend to ram each other's heads into a door, or fake bodyslam someone on the hood of one of our cars. We'd ham it up like we were really gettin' hurt.

In reality, I had this weird John Lennon/Yoko Ono peace-and-love type attitude about fighting. Even if I was playing a gig and a bar brawl broke out, which happened all the time, I wouldn't go anywhere near it. Maybe it was some kind of a knee-jerk reaction to seeing what happened to my brother Alan, but I just hated the thought of participating in anything violent at all.

So despite my passion for it, it would take years—and one very big revelation—before I'd even think about getting into wrestling myself.

CHAPTER 3

Working Out

One day during junior year, this friend of mine I'd known since elementary school, Scott Thornton, asked me if I could give him a ride to the gym. His car had broken down, and I had nothing better to do, so I said, "Sure."

I drove him to Hector's Gym, downtown on Platt Street, and as he got out of the car Scott said, "Why don't you come in?"

Now, I don't know why I went into that place. I had no interest in lifting weights whatsoever. The last thing I wanted to do was hang around a bunch of muscle-heads. But as soon as I walked in that door, something real cool happened. Instead of all those weightlifter guys going, "Hey, what's that fathead doing in here?" or giving me that kind of outsider treatment that I was used to getting everywhere I went, they welcomed me with open arms.

As soon as we walked in, this big hairy bear-looking guy with that perfectly V-shaped bodybuilding physique came over and said, "Hi there. Want to come in and work out with us?" My normal reaction would have been to come up with every excuse in the world not to do something like that. But this guy was so nice I thought, *What the hell.*

I don't know what their deal was, but every guy in that place seemed to want to help me. They put me on the bench press and put up a bar with two 45-pound plates on it, which is 135 pounds, and they stayed right there to spot me and said, "Just try it out." I didn't know how to bench-press. I didn't know anything. I did it like five or six times, though, and they said, "That's pretty good. You look like you could be good at this!"

Brother, that's all I needed.

With that little bit of encouragement, I knew that I could walk in that gym and feel safe. Hector's wasn't full of jocks or PE-Coach type guys going, "Hey, you fat piece of shit, what are *you* doin' here?" like I expected.

If any of that negative shit happened, I'd have never gone back, but because they were nice to me, I said, "Okay. I'm gonna start workin' out!" From that summer right through the whole last year of high school I found myself hitting Hector's Gym at least twice a week.

It was a little disappointing at first. I expected results right away, and I'd look in the mirror and not much would change from week to week. Of course, later I would realize that big changes don't happen to your body until you change everything and you're real consistent—your diet, your attitude, everything. I did notice that I was getting stronger. My grip felt better, and instead of doing a few reps of 135 I got to the point where I could put up 225 pounds and take it off the bar without any help.

Since I wasn't obsessed with going every day, it took about a year, I guess, before I noticed that I'd put some muscle on where the fat used to be.

It may not seem like much, but that little physical change filled a void in me. I started to feel better about myself. I'd take my shirt off at the beach. I still had that big head, and I was starting to go bald at eighteen or nineteen, but going to that gym was like a buffer. It helped give me the confidence to forget all that and actually talk to an attractive girl now and then.

Looking back on it now, that confidence, that buffer, that little extra-icing layer of safety, did a lot more than help me talk to girls. It gave me the extra push that would help me accomplish everything I wanted in life.

But back then, I couldn't figure out what the hell that was.

LOST

If there was one thing I thought I knew for sure before I graduated from high school, it was this: I didn't want to die a Port Tampa Death. That whole idea of staying in Port Tampa your whole life, working construction, working on the docks, roasting in the sun all day until they put you in a grave, just didn't appeal to me.

Part of the reason was that music had shown me so clearly that there were other options in life.

Back when I quit the football team for good, around the same time I started going to the Christian Youth Ranch, I hooked up with the Jeannie Conroy Show. This lady, Jeannie Conroy, was like a local celebrity who had a summer replacement TV show on the air, and one of the ways she capitalized on her name recognition was to put together a fourteen-piece show band and play dinner clubs. They needed a bass player, and by that time I'd switched over to playing fretless bass more than guitar. The old ego I had in my first band slipped away, and I found that I actually liked being in the back instead of out front.

Her band had a horn section that played all this Tower of Power stuff. We also played themes from *Oklahoma!* and this fluffed-up music for the senior crowd. I just did it because it was good money. We got paid big bucks to play that stuff.

I also hooked up with a couple of other bands my junior and senior year—these bands with guys in their twenties who were playing the really hot clubs in the area and making some real dough. And it dawned on me: Here I was, in my teens, and I could make more money playing music two nights a week than my dad made working all week in the sun.

That was a huge wake-up call for me. My parents never had any new cars, and all of a sudden, my senior year of high school, I go out and buy a new Charger for like three grand. I was actually living in a hotel part of my senior year, for free. It was part of the deal with this band that played at the Islands Club, where I was playing all this new dance music and had to wear the platform shoes and the whole deal. It was the 1970s, man, and we had to look the part.

Playing music clearly meant that you could avoid working a real job and still live fine. But it also meant you could avoid the real world in general by staying out late and going to bed when everybody else gets up to go to work. I loved the escape. That's part of the reason wrestling would eventually appeal to me—I just wanted to do anything to avoid that boring, routine 9-to-5, you know?

With music there was always that possibility that you're gonna break through and become a national or even international act, and I had a real ear for it. I could jump in and play with almost any band, and I would do that: just drop in and fill in when some band at the Holiday Inn needed a bass player for the night. For a while I wound up playing with a guitarist who'd toured with Todd Rundgren—the guy who wrote that song "Hello, It's Me"? Like a huge hit! He got tired of life on the road and moved down to the area, and we worked together. And I just loved the possibility of "making it" someday.

It wasn't that I was lazy. I was willing to work real hard. It just seemed to me that with most jobs there was already a period on the end of the sentence. Why would I even think about working a regular job that had a cap on top of it—a job in which you could only go so far, and that was it? But growing up in a place like Port Tampa, the draw to get one of those steady, secure jobs was always there, and I really struggled with that. For years.

When I graduated from Robinson High School in 1971, I moved out to North Tampa and enrolled at Hillsborough Community College. I was the first Bollea to ever go to college, which was a big deal—even though it was only a two-year school. I picked up a liberal arts degree, which basically meant I avoided making any kind of a decision about what I was going to do with my life.

From there I went to the University of South Florida and

majored in business with a minor in music while still playing gigs on the weekends. Business got to be too hard, so I switched to a major in mass communications, but that didn't stick, either. I probably quit four or five times to travel around with these different rock 'n' roll bands until I finally just didn't go back. So I never received a real degree of any kind.

The rock 'n' roll thing wasn't a perfect fit, though. Even though I loved music, part of me was getting sick and tired of going down to the same clubs every weekend, and playing the same songs, and going through the same routines. I wanted to break into the big time, you know? After three years at the same club you might get a two-hundred-dollar raise—and that's split between five guys! It just wasn't enough for me.

Plus, the thing about working with those bands was it seemed like as soon as we'd get a break or a chance to start makin' real big money, the guys would start bitching about having to work too much, or one guy would go off and get married and then wouldn't want to travel. It was like banging my head against a wall sometimes. Like no one was willing to give it their all to get to that next level they all said they dreamed about gettin' to, you know? I certainly couldn't be a solo act. I couldn't sing worth a damn, and I didn't have that leading-man look.

So part of me was starting to wonder if my music career had a cap on top of it, too. Here I was in my early twenties and already starting to give up. In between bands, I wound up falling back on that old Port Tampa mindset and trying to land a regular job—the thing I swore I'd never do.

One of the first places I applied was Tampa Electric Company. The general feeling around town was, man, if you worked for the electric company? What a job to get. That was security for life! But I never heard back from them.

Another time I applied at Honeywell, an electronics company that was another big-deal employer in Tampa. I never heard back from them, either.

Finally I applied at Anheuser-Busch. They had a big plant between Tampa and St. Pete, and I thought if I could get in there and start unloading the beer off the trucks, I could work my way up. That's what everyone always told me: "You could wind up driving one of those trucks, and then get promoted to supervisor, and then you can be a district manager," and on and on, "and if you do that, if you put in your twenty-five, thirty years at Anheuser-Busch you'll be set!" Guess what? I never heard back from them.

The one place I did find work was on the docks off the Twenty-second Street causeway. I was around 250 pounds in those days, and a lot more cut than I am today. You could actually see my stomach muscles back then instead of this one big ab I've got now. And the time I'd spent at Hector's Gym made me strong enough to do some big lifting.

Anthony Barselo, one of the lead singers in one of the seven or eight bands I was in, helped me out. His dad was in the laborers' union, and he got my name on the books. So every time I'd get sick of a band, when the guys were bitchin' and complainin', I'd go back and put my name on those books as a way to change gears and make money.

At first they sent me out on construction jobs or pouring concrete or helping electrical workers. Then one day they sent me out to the docks to help load and unload ships.

I took to that real quick. I was good at anything to do with math, and figuring out how to load these ships the right way was all about math and balance. It was important, too: If you had a big ship going to Singapore or Tokyo and that ship wasn't loaded correctly, you could sink it. No joke.

They threw me down in the hole, and I worked real hard, to the point where they invited me to join the longshoremen's union. I was the first white guy ever to get into the longshoremen's union in Tampa, believe it or not. And the more I worked, the better I got at figuring out how to load these ships with these big containers of meat and fertilizer or whatever the product of the day was. I'd always do it just the right way.

So they kept me on these twelve- to fourteen-hour shifts for about six months until I was so good at it they invited me to join the stevedores' union. That was a really big deal. Stevedores were the guys on the deck of the ship telling everybody where to put the load.

So there I was, the big man in charge, up on deck, roasting in the hot sun.

But I just kept picturing that Port Tampa Death. I didn't want to live and die on those docks. I wanted something different for my life. I was still young. I couldn't give in. Not yet. I knew I had to walk away.

Music wasn't perfect, but at least I was having fun looking out on a crowd full of beautiful girls and not sweating it up on a container ship all day.

Had I landed one of those other jobs I applied for, who knows what would've happened?

If somebody had called me back and hired me at Tampa Electric, and all these friends started congratulating me on landing a great job, I'd probably still be working there today. I might even be retired by now. I'm sure I would've been a linesman with my own crew; a foreman, like my dad. I would've grown my goatee. I'm sure I would've lifted weights and taken steroids and been a legend in my own mind, standing on the side of the road all buff and tan with my hard hat on, posing as everybody drove by—being that guy that everybody wanted me to be.

I have friends who took those gigs, who turned a temp job unloading trucks into a twenty-year career. And I'm sure if I'd had the opportunity, making four, five, six hundred bucks a week, that big union money, I would have done it, too. I just thank God that it never panned out.

Honestly, at that point in my life, I was nothing more than a 250-pound piece of putty. I had no skill. I had no trade. I didn't have a degree in accounting or business. I never even thought about becoming a doctor or a lawyer or a dentist, let alone a marine biologist or something really interesting like that. Coming out of Port Tampa, that mindset was just never there, you know? It wasn't something you even dared to think about.

I was lost. I was just looking for someone to point me in the right direction.

THE REVELATION

By 1976, this pattern of moving between rock 'n' roll and hard labor was gettin' real old. But things started to click with this band called Ruckus.

Finally all the elements came together. We had all these good local musicians working in the same group, including Anthony Barselo, the heartthrob lead with feathered-back hair and a really great voice, and that kick-ass guitarist I mentioned before who had worked with Todd Rundgren. We had top-notch equipment. We were playing big gigs and sounding really good. We even had some original songs that the crowds seemed to love.

More and more people started coming to see us wherever we played. Word spread everywhere that Ruckus was the "next big thing."

Even though I wasn't the front guy, I developed a major knack for interacting with the audience at this point and became sort of the voice of the band. Whenever there was a break between songs, I'd be the one to step up to the mike and get everyone fired up. "How's everyone doin' tonight?! We're Ruckus, and we're gonna be rockin' ya straight through to midnight!" I just had a rapport with the audience. I could kind of read their mood, and if we were having a lull I'd come up with something crazy. "Hey! It's time for a beer chuggin' contest!" Whatever it took to get everyone involved and having a great time. I had zero stage fright, and I actually enjoyed that part of the show as much as any of the music we played, if not more.

I'll never forget this one night in late '76, when I looked out from the stage and saw this towering blond guy walking through the crowd. It was Superstar Billy Graham! One of the top wrestlers from New York. This massive figure I'd been watching on TV for years.

I can remember the first time I saw him on TV, climbing up to the second turnbuckle and facing the crowd with his arms up, and those massive twenty-two-inch biceps. He looked inhuman. I remember thinking, *I want to be just like* that *guy some day!* He looked like this golden god, you know? And here he was in the club, listening to my band.

He had his manager with him, too, who I also recognized—this red-haired Humpty Dumpty–looking guy named Sir Oliver Humperdink.

Next thing I know, two nights later, four or five other wrestlers come in. Jack Brisco, the world heavyweight champion, comes in with his brother Jerry. Then Dusty Rhodes himself, my childhood hero, comes walking into the bar to hear *our* band.

Over the next few months, all these wrestlers started following Ruckus around, just like the rest of the crowd, to wherever our next gig was. Before I knew it, I found myself talking to these guys—these behemoths who had always seemed larger than life to me.

And guess what? After a while, it started to seem like they were just normal people. The more I talked to 'em, the more their mystique wore off. Once I wasn't intimidated or awestruck, I told them all about this passion I had for watching wrestling when I was younger. I wasn't afraid to talk about being a big fan.

The more I talked about it, the more pumped up it got me about the sport of professional wrestling. I started going to see live matches again. I started asking them all about their training and how they built muscles.

I started going to the gym a little more myself—where word was just beginning to get around about steroids and what they could do for your performance.

I remember sitting at a club one night drinking with Superstar Billy Graham and asking him, "Hey, man, you know anything about steroids? You ever taken steroids?"

"No, brother," he said. "Never taken 'em."

(Yeah, right. If you know anything about the history of steroid use in wrestling, Superstar Billy Graham was one of the first guys to take steroids. He was a pioneer! Many years later he would openly admit it, but he certainly wasn't gonna admit it to this no-body bass player who kept talking his ear off at these clubs.)

Once I started to look at these guys as just regular human beings instead of these larger-than-life figures, I started watching what happened in the ring with a whole new set of eyes.

That's when the revelation came—a revelation that would change my life forever.

If you're a wrestling fan, you're probably familiar with Randy Orton. Well, Randy's father, Bob Orton, was a big wrestler here in Florida. He was a real aggressive guy in the ring.

So I was at this match one day with a seat close to the ring, watching Bob Orton do his thing. He's on top of this other wrestler and gettin' ready to pummel him, and I read Bob Orton's lips, as plain as day.

"Hit me."

All of a sudden the guy reaches up and hits him!

I went, *What*? Had I really just seen that? I kept my eyes glued to Orton's mouth until it happened a second time. "Hit me again," he said. And the guy hit him again!

After all this time, nobody'd ever smartened me up to the notion that wrestling was fake, let alone that the ending of the match was predetermined. Even as kids we all had moments where we wondered about it. It seemed like common sense that if I'm beating some guy up and I throw him against the ropes, I'm not gonna just stand there and let him bounce off the ropes and come back and knock me over, right? Why did they do stuff like that?

But I'd never seen anything as clear as this.

"Again," Orton says. "Again, again!" And the guy keeps hitting him. I can see it's not a one-off thing. I recognize that Orton is creating this tension in the ring where it looks like he's about to get beat, so that he can suddenly turn it around and make a comeback. And he does. And the crowd goes nuts!

My whole world changed. Right in that moment I thought to myself, *I can do this. I can do this!*

Once I knew that these guys weren't trying to kill each other for real, that no matter how crazy it looked in that ring it wasn't a real confrontation, I knew in my gut that I could get up there and do it as well as any of those guys I'd idolized, if not better.

I instantly went from being a pumped-up fan, from just being proud to hang out and have a beer with some of these wrestlers, to wanting to be one of them.

That's when I started pestering them. "Hey, man, you know, God, I'd sure like to be a wrestler someday."

When I wasn't getting any assistance from the wrestlers themselves, I turned my attention to the only manager I knew: Oliver Humperdink.

Humperdink's role was to bring all the bad guys in to try to dethrone Dusty Rhodes. So I thought I'd try to be a bad guy for him and have him bring me in, too. I had the build and had already been trying to get even more of a bodybuilder look, just to look better in the band. Diet sodas had been introduced around that time, and most days I'd go to Burger King and eat a Whopper with a Diet Coke or a Diet Pepsi and fries, and that would be the only meal I had all day. I got down to like 240 on that Burger King diet, which actually looked rail thin on me at the time.

I just kept bugging Humperdink until finally one day he told me to meet him at his apartment over in Clearwater at noon. I was pumped. I was there right on time, but he didn't show up until four or five o'clock. He had been down in Palm Beach for a match the night before, and wrestlers pretty much kept musicians' hours. So I shouldn't have been surprised he was so late.

There are two things I remember about our meeting that day. One, Humperdink wasn't wearing socks, and when he took his penny loafers off I got hit by a stench like nothing I'd ever encountered in my life. The smell of that Humpty Dumpty guy's feet will haunt me for as long as I live, no matter how much I try to block out the memory.

The second thing I remember, even though I had never set one foot in a wrestling ring, is what I swore to Humperdink that afternoon. "If I can get into the wrestling business," I promised him, "I'll be the greatest wrestler who's ever lived."

There was something about being in a band and being onstage and having that interaction with the crowd, combined with this newfound knowledge that wrestling was more of a show than a fight, that made me absolutely confident I could do it.

I thought about Dusty Rhodes and how he could pump up the crowd, and the bad guys yelling at the ref, and the boos and the ire they'd inspire, and I knew I could do it. I just knew it.

I had spent so much time watching Dusty and Superstar and all of the other great wrestlers that I had this vision of just stealing a little something from all the best wrestlers and rolling it all into one character. I didn't know what that character would be called, or how it would all play out, but I could see it in my mind.

So with absolutely nothing to back up my words except my own gut feeling, I sat in front of that smelly-feet Humpty Dumpty just begging and bragging my ass off. "I swear to you, if you help me, I'll be the greatest wrestler who ever lived!"

You know what Humperdink said? "Terry, my brother—I think you will be."

That was the beginning of my demise.

The thing I didn't realize about Oliver Humperdink was that he wasn't really in control of anything. He was just an employee of the organization, you know? So when he invited me down and I started hanging around the matches, rolling my sleeves up, anxiously waiting to be a part of his stable—thinking I would jump right in as one of his big blond bad guys right next to Superstar Billy Graham—I had no idea that I was barking up the wrong tree.

It turns out that Mike Graham and some of the other guys wouldn't let him put me in the ring. Humperdink wasn't from Tampa. He didn't have that small-town mindset that so many of these Floridian wrestlers had. He saw that I had some charisma. He saw how big my arms were. He saw that I was six foot seven!

But the more I hung around and begged him to put me in the ring, the less he talked to me. He started to just plain avoid me. I didn't get the subliminal message that none of these local wrestlers wanted me around, and I guess he didn't have the heart to tell me.

It's like I had blinders on. I was so confident that this wrestling thing would be my ticket, I suddenly became that guy I hated in the rock 'n' roll band—the one who gave up just as things were getting good.

Ruckus got booked for a major out-of-town tour. When the guys told me it was locked I said, "Sorry. No. I can't go."

The guys looked at me like I was nuts. "What do you mean?" they said. "We've been trying to get this booking forever!"

I said, "Nope. I'm gonna be a wrestler."

Dude, they died laughing. They knew how much I loved wrestling and how obsessed I'd become with it lately—but they also knew I hadn't stepped foot in a ring.

It didn't matter. That was it. I just fuckin' quit. I knew what I wanted to do.

CHAPTER 4

Fighting My Way In

In 1976, I started going down to the Fort Homer Hesterly Armory for the matches every Tuesday night. I'd hang around the backstage door afterward like some groupie just to see everyone. Then every Wednesday they'd tape matches during the day at the Sportatorium, and I'd show up there. I got to be real friendly with this guy Charlie Lay, who was like seventy, an old ex-wrestler himself who worked at the front desk and always let me in.

I had no idea how obnoxious I was. I have fans now who come up to me all the time and say, "Hey, Hogan! I've been working out for three years. I want to get into the ring. Look at me! I could be the next Hulk Hogan!" I just roll my eyes and can't wait to get away from some of these people, you know? In the business we call these guys "marks." They're pretty much looked at as fools you can put a beating on if you're so inclined. And here I was showing up saying I was gonna be the next Superstar Billy Graham, every single day.

I didn't feel like a mark, though. Like I said, I was following my gut. I knew I wasn't necessarily the toughest guy in the building, but I knew that if it had to do with smoke and mirrors, showmanship, calculating and planning, if it had anything to do with strategy, I could be really good at it.

I could see that wrestling was as much show business as anything else. I didn't even know what the word "entertainment" meant back then, but it turns out I had an innate understanding of what it means to entertain. In many ways, I understood the meaning of that word better than a lot of people who'd been in the wrestling "entertainment" business their entire lives.

Only no one believed me.

After weeks of my not shutting up, telling everyone in town that I was gonna be a wrestler, Mike Graham finally pulled me aside. I knew Mike in high school and never liked the guy. He was older, and didn't think much of me. He made that clear from day one. His father, Eddie Graham, was a wrestling promoter, and by this time Mike liked to think of himself as a bona fide wrestler. He was all muscled up and thought he was big news on the local wrestling scene.

So we're outside the Sportatorium on this roasting hot day, and Mike Graham takes me to his van. It must be 120 degrees in that thing. He sits me on the floor, and he's sittin' on the hump between the front seats talking down to me.

"So you want to be a wrestler," he says. "You've been telling everyone you want to be a wrestler. Well, I'll tell you right now, the first thing you oughta know is that you shouldn't be telling people you want to be a wrestler."

Mike made it perfectly clear that no one talked about the secrets of wrestling. If somebody said wrestling was fake, he'd get punched out. That's no exaggeration. You have to remember, it was the 1970s. It was barbaric. There were no lawyers, no PC police; there wasn't anybody suing anybody. So if you said to a wrestler after a match, "Hey, that was a great show!" the wrestler would just flatten you. Put you in the hospital if he could.

I'm listening to this guy who never thought much of me, and who I still didn't like, and he's taking this authoritative tone—he's lecturing me like he's my dad or something.

Then something surprising happened. Instead of sending me away, he invited me to come back and get some training.

"I'm gonna set you up with a guy named Hiro Matsuda," Mike said. "Be here tomorrow."

Finally! I was beyond thrilled. *Oh my God, he's really doing me a favor, setting me up with Hiro Matsuda!*

I'd seen Matsuda wrestle at the armory a bunch of times. He was a mid-card guy, and I never paid much attention to him, but it turned out he was the baddest sonofabitch around. In a real fight, Matsuda could've easily kicked any of the top-tier main-event wrestlers' asses.

It also turned out that he was one of the partners in the promotion end of the local wrestling business with Eddie Graham. He owned part of the company, he was partially a promoter, and he did big business booking wrestlers in Japan—a whole other side of the wrestling world that I knew nothing about at that point.

So I went down to the Sportatorium thinking I was gonna get a workout from Matsuda, maybe learn a few things. What I didn't realize was that the word he had gotten from all the other wrestlers was "Get rid of this guy. We never want to see him again."

I didn't find any of this out till much later, of course. Eddie Graham, Mike Graham, all of them had decided I'd become too much of a nuisance to have around anymore. That lecture in Mike's van was just a setup to do me in. They all teamed up and gave Matsuda the task. "Just get rid of this motherfucker," they told him, "and while you're at it, make an example of him."

From the moment I walked in the door that day, they exercised me till I was about to pass out. Matsuda's guys were ragging on me for my long hair, calling me a hippie, pressing me so hard that I was ready to puke. The whole stadium started to go white. I got light-headed and couldn't even see—that's how close I was to fainting. But I walked in there willing to do whatever it took. So I didn't stop.

Just when I was about ready to keel over, these guys said, "All right, now get in the ring and wrestle!"

I was so out of it by then they practically rolled me into the ring. Suddenly Matsuda comes out of nowhere and jumps on top of me. I hit the canvas. He drops down, puts an elbow down in the middle of my left leg, grabs my foot, and wrenches it as hard as he can—in the opposite direction than your leg is built to go. *Crack!* He broke my leg in half, right in the middle of my shin.

It hurt like a bitch. I'd never broken a bone before, let alone a huge bone against the grain like that.

I was done. I couldn't move. Matsuda didn't even say anything to me. He just left me rolling around in agony on the canvas.

I'm sure they all thought that was the last they'd see of Terry Bollea. What fool would come back for more of that?

The most embarrassing part was I was driving this big Econoline van at the time—a standard, with a clutch on the floor. There was no way I could drive it home. So I had to call my mom, who had to call my dad at work to come pick me up. Man, he was pissed. It wasn't that long ago that I'd told him I was quitting college to play music full-time, and just a few weeks earlier, I had told him I was quitting music to go wrestle. And this is the first thing that happens?

I got reamed out all the way to the hospital and all the way home. For about the next ten weeks, I nursed my leg back at my parents' house, which I hadn't slept in really since senior year. I never heard the end of it, either. Every single day my dad laid into me for being a quitter and thinking I could do something as stupid as wrestle to make a living.

I don't want to make it seem like he was a bad guy. Not at all. Years later, my dad was about as proud of me as any dad could be. He was so thrilled by what I'd accomplished in the wrestling business, and he constantly let me know it. And I'll never forget that.

Honestly, at that moment, he had every right to be pissed.

He just had no idea how resolved I was to make this wrestling thing work.

At the end of those ten weeks, when the leg was feeling good, I headed back over to the Sportatorium and walked up to my friend Charlie Lay.

"Mr. Lay, I'm here to see Mr. Matsuda."

The guy about fainted. "Damn, kid, they told me they were getting rid of you and you would never be back here!" He goes, "Are you sure you want to see Matsuda again?"

"Yeah, I want to see Matsuda again."

The thing was, over those ten weeks my whole mindset had moved away from that crazy, naive "I want to be a blond-haired Superstar Billy Graham!" thing. Now my whole mindset was "Never give up."

I knew I wanted to be a wrestler, and there was no way they were ever gonna take advantage of me again.

Before I showed up, I cut my long hair completely off. No more hippie taunts. They'd have to work harder to find a way to break me down. As far as I was concerned, they couldn't get rid of me.

I wound up in the ring with Matsuda again that day. Only this time, when he tried to take my leg, I blocked him. I didn't know anything about wrestling other than what I'd watched on TV and seen in the ring, but I was physical enough and had been working out long enough to have a real good grip. It served me well.

When he got my arm, instead of letting him break it, I knew enough to get it away from him. Whenever he tried to hurt my neck, I knew enough to get my head away. I wouldn't let him take anything.

Matsuda was more pissed than ever. It was his mission to try to break me, but he couldn't. I walked out of there alive and unbroken, and vowed to come back the next day.

Word got around that I was back, and now all of a sudden the other wrestlers started coming down during the day just to watch me get tortured. Matsuda and the other guys would just beat on me and beat on me, and I wouldn't give in—until one day, it finally turned a corner.

Matsuda started smiling when I fought back. It got to the point where he started liking me because I wouldn't give up. I mean, he'd choke me or put me in a submission hold like you see in the UFC—the Ultimate Fighting Championship, where they do mixed martial arts—and I would not tap.

He made me pass out. I still wouldn't quit. I was crazy.

Finally Matsuda invited me to come down to his gym on a daily basis. "Okay, now we're really gonna get serious," he said. What more could he do? I was thinking, *Oh my God.*

What he did was set out to make me as fit as I possibly could be.

Every day he'd set me into a routine of jumping, squats, jumping, squats, jumping, squats—for an entire hour! He had a Japanese kid there named Lance that used to watch and count so I couldn't cheat. After that, he'd make me run.

I'd go out the front door, and he'd get in his station wagon and follow about ten feet behind me. He made me just run forever, all the way down and around Tampa Stadium, and once I'd circled the stadium I'd get to run back.

Remember back in middle school and high school, how I was the guy who could barely run between two goalposts? Nothing had changed! For all the weightlifting I did, I never ran a day in my life. But he'd get in that car, and I swear to God I thought he would run me right over if I stopped. He had me so psyched out that I'd just keep going and going.

All told it was about two and a half, three miles a day.

This went on for nearly a year. The whole time, I noticed other wrestlers coming in and joining the ranks. Paul "Mr. Wonderful" Orndorff, who had played football for the University of Tampa and been drafted by the New Orleans Saints, decided he wanted to be a wrestler, came in, got some training, and was out getting matches in something like eight weeks. I thought, *Is something wrong with me? What has he got that I don't?*

Brian Blair came in, worked out for a while, and the same thing happened. I thought, *Damn, why am I still here?*

What I didn't realize was that Matsuda liked having me as his boy. Whenever a new mark would show up wanting to get into the wrestling business, I was the one who'd go down and work them and exercise them until they went away. I was in such good shape that I could usually work them until they puked or fainted and left. If I couldn't run them off, Matsuda would come in and take care of them the same way he tried to take care of me that first day. I never hurt anybody or broke anybody's leg or anything like that. That was his job. But he was really happy to have me there, and he didn't want to let me go.

Finally, over a year into this, Jack and Jerry Brisco came in to see me. They always liked me from back when they'd come to see Ruckus at the clubs, and for some reason, they finally decided to break ranks with the guys who still thought of me as a mark. They decided to bring me into the fold.

"I have a present for you," Jack said as he handed me a brand-new pair of wrestling boots. "Terry, you're having your first match next week."

I'd been so focused on getting strong and just hoping and praying that this day would come, I almost couldn't believe it was finally here.

And all of a sudden I was scared to death.

The thing was, for all the hard work I'd put in—the training, the exercise, getting in this unbelievable shape I was in—no one had given me any of the inside scoop on wrestling yet.

I heard terms like a "work," which meant when you were faking it, and you'd make it look like you were twisting somebody's arm when you really weren't hurting them at all. Then there was a "shoot," which means you're really doing the deed and hurting them, like a real fight. That's a "shoot." But I didn't know when to work or when to shoot. I still didn't even know for sure that the outcome of the matches was predetermined. No one taught me any of that.

I just thought I'd get in there and something in between a work and a shoot would happen and we'd improvise in the ring from start to finish. I still thought the outcome of the match was something real, you know? I knew it didn't involve trying to kill each other, but I thought that somehow the better wrestler would win. I would have to figure it out on my own—and it would all have to get clear real fast.

The thing I didn't realize was that some of the other wrestlers were still planning on having a few laughs at my expense.

HAZY DAYS

When I first got into the business, I had no idea that there were gay wrestlers in wrestling. I just never thought about it. It's not unlike the whole gays in the military issue, I suppose. It was sort of "don't ask, don't tell" back then for the most part. It's just the way it was.

There was this one wrestler named Pat Patterson who was wrestling in Florida who was openly gay, though, which was kind of shocking to me then. Just because I had never really encountered that before. I love the guy to death, and he's a great guy, but he's one of these guys who'll rib you about stuff. He's always joking, and I didn't know this at the time.

His pal Buddy Colt was the Florida heavyweight champion, and I don't know if he's gay or not. There were always rumors. As it turned out, the way things went down before that first match of mine, it really didn't make any difference.

It was August of 1977. I'm gearing up for my very first match, with no idea how the whole thing's gonna go down. I truly didn't know if I was gonna get killed in that ring or what. For all I knew, someone else would try to break my leg the way Matsuda did in the beginning. I had no idea what would happen, and nobody told me a thing.

The day before the big match, Pat Patterson stops by Matsuda's gym. "Hey, Terry," he says, "why don't you come down to the Sportatorium tomorrow and we'll ride down to Fort Myers together."

I didn't care one way or the other about the fact that he was gay. I was just psyched that a big wrestler like that would reach out to me.

So I get into a car with Pat and Buddy the next day, and Pat says, "Hey, you know, this is a big night for you."

"Yes, sir, it is, Mr. Patterson."

"Well, this is your initiation night."

"Oh man, this is gonna be great, I can't wait!" I acted all pumped, but like I said, I was really scared. I was so worried about getting beat up, or what I'd have to do to win, or if I'd wind up losing my first time out.

"Well, you know what?" Pat says. "We got you in the car 'cause we've been chosen to initiate you tonight."

I said, "What do you mean?"

"Well," Pat says, "we've got about a hundred and fifty miles to go, and before you get to the arena you have to give one of us a blow job."

"*What*?" I said. "What do you mean?"

"You have to give one of us a blow job before you get to the building, 'cause that's your initiation before you wrestle," he says.

I was completely taken aback. "Well, I can't do that, you know, I'm—I've never done nothing like that. I'm not gay. I can't do that!"

They both got real serious. "Well, you have to do it."

"I'm not gonna do it!" I was horrified. I was so upset. All this time I've done nothing but prepare for this night and they're telling me I have to do this thing that I can't possibly do or they won't let me wrestle my first match? It was seriously fucked up. I didn't have the slightest clue that they were ribbing, you know?

"I can't do this. This is fucked up," I said. I just wanted to wrestle, and they took advantage of how serious and focused I was. They tortured me.

It was the longest car ride of my life. On top of worrying about the match, how I'd do, if I'd look like a fool in front of a stadium full of people, they put this fear into me that they wouldn't let me wrestle at all if I didn't do this horrible thing. As we got closer and closer to the stadium, I just refused, over and over. Finally we were pulling into the parking lot, and they still wouldn't let up.

"Okay," they said. "Since you didn't give one of us a blow job before your match, we're gonna have to tell all the other guys that you failed your initiation. So after your match, in the shower in the locker room, everybody's gonna grab you and fuck you in the ass."

Again there wasn't even a hint that they were kidding. This whole wrestling experience had been so barbaric, you know?

With the leg breaking and the pushing me till I fainted and the watching other marks get beat to shit and run out of the business. I was so fucking scared. And now I have to get in the ring and wrestle thinking I'm gonna be fighting for my life in the locker room after the match. Really fighting. The thing I feared most.

So I get in the locker room. It's total silence. No one says a word to me. I get suited up and tie up my new boots, and I go out to wrestle Brian Blair. Now, I knew Brian. He was a friend of mine. He was an amateur wrestler in high school, so he knew a lot more real wrestling moves than I did. What I didn't know was that Brian was under orders to do a twenty-minute "Broadway"—to keep the match going for twenty minutes as basically a time filler that would end in a draw.

No one told *me* that, of course. All anyone told me, right before I hit that ring, was that I was supposed to go out there and win. It was yet another rib.

So off we go. *Ding-ding-ding-ding.* I'm out there trying to pin him, trying to hold his shoulder, and he keeps kicking out. We're fighting. I mean, we're really beating the shit out of each other. I thought I was supposed to win this thing, and he was just following his orders to not get beat.

Brian didn't think it was too funny, but I noticed at one point during the match that all the wrestlers were standing out by the dressing rooms watching us. They weren't supposed to do that. The bad guys and good guys weren't supposed to be seen together at all. Looking back on it, it must've been like the biggest joke to them.

After twenty minutes of this brutal battle, finally I hear *ding-ding-ding-ding-ding.*

I'm exhausted. I'm all bruised up. And instead of basking in the moment of finishing my first match in this arena full of people, I'm only thinking about one thing: *Now I've gotta go back in the dressing room and fight for my fucking life.*

On the way back from the ring, I was so worried and so upset, there were tears in my eyes. I don't think any of the guys saw it, but I was a wreck. I'd thrown everything in my life away for this dream of wrestling. My music career was gone now. I was so fixated on making this thing work, and *this* was what I'd gotten myself into? I was shaking, practically bawling, thinking, *I don't want to be a wrestler anymore.*

I felt like a loser. An outsider. The twelve-year-old fat kid. I was weak, I felt sick, I just wanted to get out of there. I was so scared and so messed up, it was all I could do to gird myself and get ready to face my fate as I pushed through the doors and stepped into the locker room—

Where all of the wrestlers were waiting with beers in their hands. "Congratulations! You made it!"

What the hell? They were cheering for me.

The rib was over. The whole thing had been a big goof at my expense.

They patted me on the back and shook my hand. Someone handed me a beer. They were all so happy that I made it through the match, and everybody was talking about what a good fight I'd given Brian.

Hazing is pretty common in fraternities. I guess it's pretty common in the military, too. I had no idea it was a rite of passage in the wrestling world. In fact, maybe it wasn't all that common. Maybe I was just an unlucky stiff who was too naive for the other wrestlers to pass up.

I was completely dazed. I didn't understand it. I didn't understand why they would do something like that. It's still so weird to think about. Even now, it still upsets me.

But there in that locker room on that August night, for the first time in this whole crazy endeavor that I'd devoted my life to for more than a year now, the other wrestlers stopped treating me like some dumb-ass kid.

For a moment at least, they treated me like one of their own.

CHAPTER 5

Backing Away

Sometimes you've gotta be careful what you wish for. I was so focused on getting into this Florida wrestling circuit, so focused on not letting Matsuda beat me down, so focused on being accepted, that I didn't look at the bigger picture.

I still had blinders on.

After that first match, I expected I'd be able to make a living at this thing. Everybody else—like Brian Blair and Paul Orndorff—was wrestling six nights a week, rotating from West Palm to Tampa to Miami to Jacksonville to Sarasota. Me? I was only getting two bookings: Wednesday in Miami, which is a five-hour drive each way, and Monday in Tallahassee, which is a five-and-a-half-hour drive each way. And I was always the one who had to drive. All of the other wrestlers would pile into my van and drink beer, and then sleep on the way home.

This went on for like three or four months. I was barely making any money. More than that, it started to feel like some kind of a rib again—like I was being taken advantage of.

Finally I mentioned this to my friend Charlie Lay, the old guy at the front desk at the Sportatorium, and he looked at me and said something I must've been just too deaf to hear until that moment. "Kid, don't you get it? They don't want you around here."

I knew he was right. We all know that feeling, when you hear something you know is the truth but it's something you've been dreading and just didn't want to hear. It knocks you in the stomach. And I mean, I had been fighting that truth from day one. Day one.

Even though I'd had my first match, and the matches after that all went really well—I was getting real good in the ring and starting to find ways to really pump up the crowd—and even though I survived Matsuda's training, and even though I'd suffered through that hazing or whatever you want to call that shit they put me through, I was never gonna escape that stigma of being a mark. These Florida wrestlers were always going to treat me like some kid who didn't deserve to be there.

With one last flicker of hope, I met with Matsuda and Jack and Jerry Brisco—people I thought were real friends by that point—to ask about wrestling six nights a week. The solution they came up with was to transfer me to another territory up in Kansas City.

That was that.

No offense to Kansas City, but I wasn't about to be banished off to Hicksville. And I sure wasn't going to sit there and be humiliated any more than I already had been for the last year and a half.

So that was the end. Three, four months into my professional wrestling career, I walked away. I was done.

I called a guy named Whitey Bridges over in Cocoa Beach. He owned a place called the Anchor Club that was part of the rock 'n' roll circuit I used to be in. He was this really built, forty-year-old blond-haired guy who loved to party and always had lots of girls around. I'm not sure why I called him. Maybe I thought I'd go visit him, hang out for a while, blow off some steam while I tried to figure out what the heck I was going to do next. Maybe I just wanted to say hi and see how he was doing. Anyway, when I mentioned that the wrestling thing wasn't really working out, much to my surprise Whitey made me an offer.

"Why don't you come over here and help run my club?"

Done deal, brother. I was gone. Cocoa Beach, here I come!

Not only did I help him run the Anchor Club, but we decided to go into business together and open up a gym.

Everything fell into place real easy, like it was meant to be. In a matter of weeks we unlocked the doors to Whitey and Terry's Olympic Gym—right near the beach, in the middle of town.

Splitting my time between the two places was a lot, and I decided I needed someone I could really trust to work the door of the club and handle the money. Since I hardly knew anybody else in Cocoa Beach, I wound up calling my buddy from Port Tampa, Ed Leslie.

Ed's a bit younger than me, but I went to school with his older sister and always liked the guy. We just hit it off. He wasn't into wrestling at that point, but still he was big enough and had the kind of build that I thought he could easily handle any situation at the door. In case you've forgotten, Ed became better known later in life as Brutus "the Barber" Beefcake.

Over the course of that year, Brutus and I got real serious about two things: working that club and working out in that gym. I mean, I got crazy focused on building my body. Whether it was some kind of a reaction to the whole wrestling fiasco or not, I made up my mind that I was going to get as big as I possibly could.

I had a pretty good starting point—I was already in fantastic shape—but even with the muscle base I'd built, and how fit I was from those Matsuda workouts, and the God-given gift of my natural size, there was no way I could achieve that over-the-top, thick, massive golden god look I was after without help.

The help I needed came in two forms: needles and pills.

WHEN 'ROIDS WERE THE RAGE

By the late 1970s, steroids were everywhere—and I'm not just talking about the wrestling world. You could walk into almost any gym or locker room in this country and find steroids if you had your eyes open. It was a different era. They were legal. Doctors would pretty much hand you a prescription for whatever you wanted—all you had to do was ask. There wouldn't be a federal ban on steroids until the end of the following decade.

In Cocoa Beach, in 1978, I didn't even have to go looking for them. Instead, steroids found me. They just walked right in through the front door of Whitey and Terry's Olympic Gym.

A couple of local weightlifters came through to check out the facility, and before I knew it they were talking like traveling salesmen. "Hey, man, why don't you take Dynabol? You won't believe the results! Just try it and see. And if you really want to see some bulk, you should take this and take that." There was no indication that this stuff could hurt you—or kill you—and anyone who used the stuff was the best spokesperson possible because they all looked great! Brutus and I were sold, right then and there, and when we got into it, we got into it heavy.

We found pretty quickly that it was all about finding the right cocktail that worked for you, and once you hit the correct combo, the results were fast and furious. There was always a base of testosterone—it could be 1 cc, maybe more. You just went by feel. Then there was "Deca," Deca-Durabolin, an oil-based steroid, and you'd take that once or twice a week. Then there were pills, like Anavar and the aforementioned Dynabol, which I know now is actually very toxic—it's like an androgen that makes you hold fluid. All steroids are stressful on your internal organs. But I was young and invincible, you know? I took pills every day and shot up about every third day. The results were incredible, so I just kept going.

In just a couple of months I was seeing that sort of Greek god swell I envisioned.

There was no limit to the amount of steroids we could do. And as much as we wanted, the local weightlifter-dealers could provide. If you wanted to buy a hundred pills, you could; and if you wanted to buy ten thousand pills, you could. The way we understood it—whether this was true or not—if you had a prescription from your doctor, then you were covered because they weren't illegal. Even if you got caught with a thousand bottles from a drug dealer, as long as you had that prescription for that substance in your bag, you were okay.

A local doctor there who was friends with Whitey was kind enough to write down whatever we wanted, so we'd be street legal. Then once we had his prescription for, let's say, one bottle of testosterone, we'd run right out and buy fifty bottles from one of those dealers down the street.

The thing is, I didn't have any second thoughts about pumping my body full of this stuff because everybody said steroids were safe. I guess it's kinda like in the 1950s when everybody said smoking cigarettes was safe. Hell, some people even said smoking was good for you, right? In the '70s, everyone just upped the ante a little. They went around saying it was perfectly safe to smoke pot, and it certainly wasn't gonna kill you to snort some cocaine, and in locker-room circles it was just a given that shooting steroids was safe, too.

It was also sort of a social thing. When you took steroids, you were just like every other muscle-head in the gym. And if you didn't? It was almost like, "Why are you wasting your time in here?"

The convenience and availability just pushed it over the top. Why make an appointment and waste all that time at a doctor's office to get one bottle when I can buy ten bottles of what I want right now, and do it for three dollars a bottle? I remember testosterone was like ten dollars a bottle and had ten shots in it. There was just so much of it, everywhere, it actually made you feel "in place" as opposed to "out of place" to take steroids. Before long, everybody in the gym was doing it, everybody who worked at the bar was doing it, and you could look at the way the top athletes looked and know that they were all doing it, too.

So it wasn't considered a reckless thing. In fact, that whole year I spent in Cocoa Beach was anything but reckless.

Even though I was running the Anchor, I didn't drink. I went all of 1978 without putting a drop of alcohol into my body. Alcohol just wouldn't cut it with the schedule I was keeping.

After working out and running the gym all day, Brutus and I had a pretty standard routine. We'd open up the bar and get everything settled, and then we'd come back and watch David

Letterman's *Late Night* show. Man, we laughed our asses off. While we watched, we'd drink these power shakes. I'd take the most fattening protein there was, called Metabol, and dump it in a blender with half a cube of vanilla Häagen-Dazs ice cream, a banana, and two huge wads of peanut butter. Probably the most fattening shit you can eat. We'd drink two blenders of that crap, watch Letterman, then go back to the bar and stay until closing at 4:00 A.M.

I would have been wrecked the next day if I'd been boozing it up. So alcohol was out.

And pot was in.

I had started smoking pot a little bit in the last couple of bands I was in. The other guys would disappear on me during breaks. I'd put the bass guitar down and ask, "Where the fuck did everybody go?" It's as if they had a secret code to lose me or something. They would come back smelling like weed. I finally asked David, the keyboard player, about it, and he said, "You should try it!"

I never wanted to. I was a pretty clean-cut kid. But then the whole band went on this camping trip down the Withlacoochee River, and I finally smoked a joint. Nothin' happened. So I smoked another one. Nothin' happened. I must've had four, five joints that first time, and I didn't feel a thing. Then all of a sudden when we stopped to pitch the tent I started eating everything in sight— potato chips, Oreos, everything I could get my hands on—and they're all laughing, "Oh! You're stoned! You're stoned! You've got the munchies, man!" It sure didn't feel like I was stoned, but I guess I was.

Maybe that's why those fattening shakes went down so easy in Cocoa Beach—I was stoned!

Part of me could have stayed in Cocoa Beach just living that laid-back life forever, but settling in one spot wasn't in the cards for me. Life has a way of always keeping you in check, doesn't it? Just when things seem to be settled and going great, the rug gets yanked out from under you.

At the end of that year, Whitey decided to get married. He'd had it with the whole beach scene and he decided to sell the bar. I couldn't keep the gym open without Whitey's backing, so that had to close down, too.

Poof! Our little bachelor-party lifestyle was shut down.

The thing was, enough time had passed that I'd started to think about wrestling again. The crap I went through took a backseat in my mind to that amazing feeling of being in the ring with a big crowd of people hollering and oooing and aahing to my every move. Plus, now I had this body on me. I finally looked like those heroes I worshipped as a kid. In fact, I looked better than them!

I started to wonder—if I got out of Florida and away from the stigma they had put on me because of the way I got into this thing, maybe there was a chance that I could make the big time.

I had a newfound confidence that didn't exist back in Tampa, so I called up Superstar Billy Graham.

"Dude, I think my arms are bigger than yours now. I just taped my biceps and they're twenty-four inches!" When Superstar Billy Graham's hit twenty-two inches in the mid-1970s they were considered the biggest guns in the world. Now all of a sudden mine were twenty-four inches around! I couldn't touch my shoulders for like a year I was so bloated up.

Graham couldn't believe his ears. "If you're that big, and you really want to wrestle," he said, "I'm gonna send you to Louie Tillet."

Tillet was this French-Canadian guy who ran the Alabama wrestling territory, which covered Pensacola and Panama City— basically that whole northern Florida panhandle.

I was pumped. I was ready.

I asked Brutus if he wanted to come along. He didn't know a thing about wrestling, but I promised to teach him everything I knew—and I wouldn't torture him like I'd been tortured by the guys in Tampa. He already had the body and the size, and I figured wrestling would be a lot more fun with a partner in crime along for the ride.

He was 100 percent in, and so was I. So we packed up my customized gold Dodge van that I'd bought from Whitey. I said good-bye to Cocoa Beach, and I drove off to Alabama.

It was the start of a whole new adventure.

PART II

WRESTLING MANIA

"Everything happens for a reason."

A lot of people say that phrase. We've all heard it a million times. But I don't think I ever really understood what it meant until this last couple of years.

The thing is, there are lessons to be learned from every moment in your life—the good, the bad, the amazing, the awful, everything. Whether you recognize those lessons or not is up to you, but you can't avoid them. Because of that, everything that has ever happened to you, from the day you were born until this very second, has helped prepare you for the moment you're in right now.

It's kind of mind-boggling when you think about it: Every single thing that's happened, whether you wanted it to or not, has led you to where you are right now.

Unbeknownst to me, all I had done through that point in my life had prepared me to become the biggest professional wrestling superstar the world had ever seen. Just like everything I did in the years that followed would prepare me for the backlash and the wallops I'd suffer in 2007 and beyond.

It's all connected. It's all intertwined. I know that now. I didn't know that then.

CHAPTER 6

On the Road

Brutus (Ed Leslie) and I looked a lot alike after our year in Cocoa Beach. We both had blond hair. We both had mustaches. We were both juiced-up musclemen. So we started wrestling as the Boulder Brothers—Terry Boulder and Ed Boulder—and a lot of people assumed we were really brothers.

We were certainly as close as brothers. Traveling around the Alabama territory was fun at first. We'd get to the arenas early, and I'd take Brutus in the ring to teach him the ropes. I'd grab three or four of the other wrestlers, and we'd show him how to work a match—how to fall without killing yourself, how to make it look like you were wrenching a guy's arm without actually snapping his wrist or breaking his elbow.

Louie Tillet liked us and put us out there seven days a week—but we were hardly making any money. I'd only take home twenty-five or thirty dollars a night. So rather than waste our dough on hotels, the two of us just slept in my van. It was carpeted and had a loft bed where I would sleep. Brutus would settle in on the floor. It was perfectly comfortable for a while.

North Pensacola Beach was central to just about all the venues we hit, so we parked the van right there most nights and basically made that parking lot our home. There were public restrooms, so we had a place to shower, shit, and shave in the mornings. There was a great little all-you-can eat restaurant nearby, too. Man, they were scared when they saw me and Brutus walk in. We'd eat breakfast, lunch, and dinner in one sitting. We'd clean the place out!

There were a couple of other wrestlers who were living out of their van on that beach, too: these Samoan guys named Afa and Sika, who became known as the Wild Samoans. Years later, when we were all on TV, they pretended to be these wild brothers who were pulled right out of a jungle somewhere to wrestle and who couldn't speak English at all. Actually they spoke English just fine, and we all became friends—just parking our vans by the sand.

It was a perfect place for Brutus and me to work on our tans. I remember that feeling of walking out on that sand in the morning, looking out on the ocean, feeling the wind. Not a bad way to live. Between wrestling seven days a week, tanning all the time, and continuing the steroids, I perfected that bronzed god look I was going for. That look gave me just a little something extra in the wrestling ring.

Technically, I wasn't the best wrestler. I wasn't quick. Wasn't athletic. I couldn't jump off the top ropes. On the other hand, I wasn't an old-fashioned thickheaded fat wrestler, either. I was right in between. And the more I wrestled, the more I developed my own style. In fact, it was right during this time that I started using the leg drop to finish off my opponents. The crowds went nuts for it.

A few months into this routine, Louie Tillet made a big mistake. "I'm booking you out this Monday night," he told me. "I want you to go up to Memphis."

By this time I had started to understand the wrestling business a little more. I had picked up on things. I didn't have those blinders on like I did when I first started in Florida, and I knew that Memphis could be a major stepping-stone to wrestling in New York City.

The Memphis territory, run by Jerry Lawler and Jerry Jarrett, was known for doing all kinds of circus stuff. They had tar-and-feather matches, and loser-leaves-town matches, and hang-the-manager-in-a-cage-above-the-ring matches. Crazy stuff. But it was also the perfect place to develop a gimmick—and that was key, because all of the guys who were making the really big money in New York had a gimmick.

There was Sergeant Slaughter, the Russian Bear, the Iron Sheik. There were no Joe Blows, you know? No regular-named wrestlers who just got in the ring and wrestled. Everybody had something extra.

So Brutus and I drove up to Memphis for this one night to wrestle as the Boulder Brothers, and we put on a hell of a show. I know because Jarrett and Lawler pulled me aside immediately after the match and said, "Terry, we want you to come work here."

I told them I couldn't. I was committed to the Alabama territory. Louie Tillet had given me a break when I really needed it, and I couldn't let him down.

Then they asked me how much money I was making.

"Like one fifty, one seventy-five a week," I said.

"Well, we'll give you an eight-hundred-dollar-a-week guarantee."

Now, that was a shocker.

I wasn't as much of a mark as I used to be, but I wasn't totally disloyal, either. So I played real cool and told them I needed to go back and talk to Tillet about it.

And that's exactly what I did. I went back to Alabama and confronted Tillet. "I'm wrestling seven days a week for you. The Boulder Brothers are making a name and drawing audiences. How come I'm only making one seventy-five tops?"

His response? "That's all you're worth and all you deserve."

So I hit him with the eight-hundred-a-week guarantee I'd just been offered in Memphis and said Ed and I were leaving—and Tillet just about shit a brick.

He called Jarrett and Lawler up in Memphis screaming, "How can you steal talent? I did you a favor for one night and this is what happens? How can you do this?!" He was pissed. Didn't matter. Brutus and I already had one foot in the van at that point. We were on our way to the big time, and we knew it.

The offer came at the perfect moment, because just as we were rolling into Memphis the motor blew in that gold van. Not only was that van our home, but it was the only transportation we had to get to wrestling gigs. No one flew in those days, and the matches were all over the place. In the Memphis territory it would be a 200-mile drive to Nashville one night, then 250 miles to Tupelo, Mississippi, the next, followed by Evansville, Indiana—nine hours away. The venues were never lined up in a row to make it easy. Nobody planned like that. So you were literally all over the map.

Imagine if the van had broken down while we were broke and living at the beach. What would we have done?

As soon as we rolled into Memphis, Jarrett took me straight out and bought me a big green Lincoln Continental. I'd pay him back for it, but he was more than happy to front me the money. He treated me like one of his own, right away. And since he was paying me eight hundred dollars a week, I didn't need a van to sleep in anymore.

THE HULK

As I started rising in Memphis, Jarrett asked me to go on TV now and then to promote matches. I could certainly talk the talk, you know? After all those years listening to Dusty Rhodes and interacting with audiences in all those bands, I was a natural. I wasn't saying "Hey, brother" and that real Hulk Hogan–style stuff quite yet, but I could say, "Hey, this is Terry Boulder, and I want you to come down to the Mobile Civic Center, where you'll see the greatest wrestlers in the world!"

One day, I went on a local talk show and wound up sitting on-air right next to Lou Ferrigno. That's right, the guy who played the Incredible Hulk, who was all over people's TVs with his green body makeup at that time. He was a real nice guy, and everyone was so impressed by how huge he looked with those big bulging muscles.

The thing was, sitting next to me at that point in my life, the guy looked kinda small. That blew Jerry Jarrett away. I got back to the dressing room after the show and Jarrett was like, "Good God, Terry! You were sitting on TV and you were bigger than the Hulk!"

From that moment on, Jerry Jarrett started billing me as Terry "the Hulk" Boulder wherever I wrestled.

Now, I don't know if you'd call that fate or coincidence. I didn't think much about it at the time, but what are the odds that Lou Ferrigno would wind up on the same talk show as me, sitting right next to me, in the middle of Tennessee?

It's weird, right? Because if it weren't for that moment, there's a very good chance I never would have acquired the Hulk nickname. And without the Hulk nickname, could "Terry Boulder" (or whatever other name I might have picked up along the way) have conquered the world the way "Hulk" did?

Today I understand a lot more about the law of attraction, and how we have the ability to bring these sorts of powerful "coincidences" into our lives. Back then? I was just rolling along, dreaming of hitting the big time. I had always been a celebrity in my own mind—I had always envisioned a fantasy life with boundless possibilities and had even practiced my way to get there by playing in bands and paying my dues.

But even as I acquired the Hulk nickname, the thought of that dream becoming real kept falling further and further into the back in my mind.

Despite the new name and how popular I was getting on the Memphis circuit, the whole business of wrestling quickly started to become a drag all over again.

WRESTLING WITH WRESTLING

Brutus didn't last very long in the Memphis territory. I guess in some ways there's only room for one big blond wrestler in any given circuit. So he wound up transferring to Portland, Oregon, where he started to become a star in his own right.

He was fine with the move. Brutus has nomad in his blood or something. He just doesn't care where he sleeps, and he'd make the best of any situation. He's up in Oregon for two weeks and I call him and he's got four or five girls in bed with him! He's having the time of his life.

Me? Not so much. Being on the road in the car and in hotels all the time—that whole lifestyle was really draining to me. I missed having a friend on the road. And even at eight hundred a week, it was starting to feel like I was getting ripped off. Again.

The thing is, there's no security in wrestling. I always knew that. I didn't think I cared because at least it wasn't one of those regular jobs with a period at the end of the sentence.

But even at the Memphis level, it was much more of a fly-by-night business than I ever imagined. There were nights when you'd walk into some building to go to work for a promoter, and rather than it being a smart businessman or maybe a former wrestler who wanted to make something of himself, it would just be some guy who owns an electrical supply company who happens to promote wrestling on the side.

Wrestling was my life. I wanted to grow my fan base, sell out bigger arenas, and make more money. I wanted to keep moving forward. How could that happen when I wasn't in charge of my own destiny? And when the men who were in charge were treating it like a side gig or were too small-minded to see anything above and beyond what they were already doing in whatever tiny little territory they considered their domain?

I kept obsessing over it and complaining—mostly to myself—that things should be better. I didn't know how to fix it, though, and I didn't really make any effort to take control. I didn't know how.

Plus, it was just so weird to walk in every night and know that if you got cut or you got hurt, it was up to you to go to the doctor. There was no insurance. There was no retirement plan. None of the stability that a "normal" job has. There was no structure to it. I started to feel like there was nobody there to back me up if I ever needed help.

To be a wrestler meant that everything you had—your future, your health, your sanity, all of it—was stuffed into this little bag you carried with your boots and your tights. You'd put on this costume to go perform like a dancing monkey. Then you'd take the costume off, get paid, and move on to the next town's circus.

To look around at this sold-out arena, to hear them roar and chant your name, to know that they're walking out of there with their buddies reliving every moment of the show you put on—just like Vic and I used to do when we left the armory back in Tampa as kids—and then after all of that, a guy hands you twenty-five bucks and says, "See you next week?" It all seemed like such a let-down.

After a while, the raise up to a hundred bucks or so didn't make it any better. That was still just the price of a few seats in that whole arena. Was that all I was worth? I knew a good portion of those fans were there to see me. I had built a following. I was the one out doing spots on TV and helping to promote this whole thing. I knew I deserved more. I knew I was worth more. So when it was clear that there were no giant raises in my future, I took a step back and tried to reevaluate this whole situation.

My conclusion? Wrestling for no money sucks.

So that was that. Once again, I decided to quit. I drove back down to Tampa, where I'd always return whenever we had a few days off. This time, I really thought I was quitting for good.

CHAPTER 7

Just When I Thought I Was Out...

In the latter part of 1979, I set myself up in a room at the Expressway Inn for eleven dollars a night, and I put my name back on the books at the longshoremen's and stevedores' unions. I was still a member of both. All that time, from Cocoa Beach to Alabama and Memphis, I kept paying dues. I guess in the back of my mind I wanted to have something to fall back on.

I was only back in Tampa for about a week when I stopped into the Imperial Room, this bar where all the wrestlers used to wind up after the Tuesday night matches, and I ran into a wrestler named Terry Funk. He was really surprised to see me, and he said he'd been trying to find me. All of a sudden Jack and Jerry Brisco came over, and they were doing the same thing. "What the fuck happened? Where the hell have you been?" they asked.

I told them, "I quit. I'm not doing this shit anymore."

They didn't seem to want to hear that. "We've been trying to get ahold of you. Where the hell are you living now? Vince McMahon Sr. has been calling us from New York trying to track you down. He heard about what you were doing in Memphis, and how all the arenas were sold out. He wants to see you!"

I was so down on the whole thing, I really didn't care. I said, "Guys, I'm not interested. I'm going back to work on the docks. I'm just gonna stay here in Tampa."

The next day, the Briscos pretty much hijacked me and dragged me down to the Sportatorium. When we walked in, Eddie Graham was there. By now I guess we'd all made peace in my absence, which I didn't quite get. Anyway, they get Vince McMahon Sr. on the phone. Later on his son, Vince McMahon Jr., would take over and help turn the organization into an international phenomenon, but for now, Vince Sr. was still the man, and the New York territory was his.

"You know," McMahon said, "New York's a big man's territory. We've been watching you, and we're real interested in you. We want you to come up here. Why don't you come up here and wrestle on TV, and we'll see if you're as good as everybody says you are, and if the crowds love you as much as everybody says they do."

I told him I wasn't interested. When he asked why, I told him about how much money I was making, and how I couldn't stand driving nine hours just to wrestle three minutes, and that I was pretty much sick of the whole thing.

"You really have been screwed over," McMahon said. "You've never had the opportunity to make the money you need to make, Terry. This is where you belong. Madison Square Garden. New York. The big time. You belong here!"

And he asked me again: "Just come up here and meet me, face-to-face, and see what you think."

The guy was a heck of a salesman. Finally I caved. Sort of. "Okay," I said. "I'll fly up and I'll talk to you. But I'm not bringing my wrestling boots."

So they flew me up north, and I met Vince at a stadium in Allentown, Pennsylvania, where the WWWF shot their TV matches every three weeks. He kept staring at me over the top of his glasses when I walked in, eyeballing me up and down. He couldn't believe how big I was.

I'd just come off this big steroid run, and I'd been wrestling nonstop. I was in my mid-twenties, at my biological peak. No other wrestler looked like me, and I knew that. It's like everything else in life: If I'm gonna work out, I work out. I would either get the biggest arms in the world or explode them trying. I was eating everything in sight, too. I decided that the perfect wrestler should have big arms and a big belly. I just thought that's the way you should look—that a bodybuilder's six-pack wasn't the way to go. It was too unrelatable to the crowd.

I really didn't want to wrestle anymore, but I stuck around that night to watch the match. I was wearing a tie-dyed T-shirt, kind of like Superstar Billy Graham always wore. Graham was at his peak in popularity at that point. I'll be honest; I really did try to emulate his look as I was coming up. Like I said, the idea of stealing a little bit from all the best wrestlers was my whole game plan right from the beginning. In fact, at that moment with my hairline receding and everything, I looked just like the guy—or at least a younger version of the guy. So when I stuck my head out from behind that curtain to see what the crowd looked like, all of a sudden a whole bunch of people thought I was him.

"It's Superstar Billy Graham!" they started yelling.

Vince Sr. saw that and said, "Don't ever wear tie-dye again." But I think the reaction made him realize what he could do with me. It was like starting over with a brand-new Superstar Billy Graham, having a new young superstar that he could build and mold in his organization.

That night he took me to dinner. He'd made up his mind. "I'll set you up in an apartment," he said—in West Haven, Connecticut, where all the wrestlers lived. "I'm also gonna put you with a guy named Tony Altomare, who'll drive you everywhere and take care of everything so you don't have to do that yourself anymore." Altomare was Capt. Lou Albano's tag-team partner, and they wrestled as the Sicilians back in the day. "And I'll give you a guarantee that makes eight hundred a week look like chump change."

The funny thing is, I don't even remember what the number was.

"Come up here and I'll make you a star in New York," he said.

What struck me more than the money was how McMahon seemed to really be bending over backwards to try to get me to come to New York—the place that was the top of the wrestling food chain.

It sure was a world of difference from being treated like a desperate mark down in Tampa, or a replaceable monkey in Alabama and Memphis. Also, compared to most of the promoters I'd ever met, there was just something about McMahon that inspired confidence. Wrestling wasn't a side gig to him. It wasn't just a job. I had a feeling that if I worked with him, the two of us could make great things happen.

I decided to go for it. I shook his hand. I went home and got my wrestling boots. After taping a few matches for the TV cameras in Allentown, I made my debut at Madison Square Garden in December of 1979.

OH, DONNA

Although my wrestling career was starting to take off, my personal life was kind of floundering.

First of all, I was never a girl-magnet type of guy. If I had one of those gorgeous movie-star faces it would have been different, but let's be honest: My body looked good, but I was balding, and about the best thing I would say about my face is I'm "brutally handsome."

Good uniform, bad helmet.

I was also still portraying a bad guy in the wrestling world, so even wrestling-fan women had this misperception that I was some kind of crazy mean dude. That didn't exactly get the girls flocking to me, you know? I didn't get jealous of the other guys who seemed to land a different girl every night, though. That wasn't my style. After all, I had what I thought was a steady girl back home.

I met Donna toward the end of my band days down in Tampa, and she was by far the hottest girl I'd ever been with. We made quite the pair: We both had matching long blond hair!

We started dating and had this thing going on and off for years. She never wanted to come on the road with me. That just wasn't her style. So I would see her in between road trips while I was in Alabama and Memphis and all the way through my start with the WWWF. I wasn't real sure, to be honest, whether she was dating other guys in between or not. I didn't really think about it. Anyway, by 1979, it seemed like the most serious relationship I was probably ever gonna find for myself, so I up and asked Donna to marry me—and she said, "Yes!"

I gave her a nice engagement ring, the whole deal—but something just wasn't right. I could feel it, but I never wanted to admit it, you know? In some ways I was still so naive, I don't think I knew how to have a real relationship.

Once things started to take off for me in New York, Donna seemed to get more and more distant. Even if she didn't want to hit the road with me, I thought she'd want to come see me at Madison Square Garden, at least. Something. Nope. She just was not into the whole wrestling lifestyle. She wanted to stay in Tampa.

I understood that. If it wasn't for McMahon's big push, I had planned on staying in Tampa myself.

I came back on Christmas that year, and Donna basically started a fight with me. (Women have a way of doing that, don't they?) She told me to not even bother coming back for New Year's—so, of course, the first thing I did was make sure I showed up for New Year's. I walked into her apartment and found her sitting on the sofa there with her arm around this guy from the Tampa Bay Buccaneers.

A football player! Of all the guys she could've picked, right?

I walked over, took the engagement ring off her finger, and slipped it onto her other hand. "You're free," I said. "See you later." And I walked out the door.

The whole thing was so weird. I can't imagine actually being married to Donna, yet I was so naive about love and marriage and sex and relationships, I had put a ring on that girl's finger even though we were totally incompatible! What was I thinking? I'm just glad it ended when it did.

On a side note—just to show what a small town Tampa really is—years later Donna worked for the Avis rent-a-car at the Tampa airport. So I would see her every single time I flew in or out of town. Eventually she married the owner of that local Avis spot, they had a kid, and that kid went to the same school as *my* kids. So I saw Donna almost every day! It was spooky.

LEARNING THE ROPES

In some ways, letting go of Donna allowed me to concentrate fully on my wrestling career in New York. I didn't feel that pull to get back to Florida quite so often—even though I still considered it my home.

My early career in the WWWF was fast and furious, and it's all been pretty well documented. You can find Web sites all over the place that list my matches, and who beat whom.

It seems like most people have even heard the behind-the-scenes stories—about how Vince McMahon Sr. changed my last name to Hogan because he really, really wanted an Irish wrestler in his stable and how he even gave me red dye for my hair, which I refused to put in and just flushed down the toilet.

The guy was on a big kick for including all ethnicities and na-tionalities in the ring, so you could draw an audience from all of those various groups. The Italians could root for the Sicilians. The Irish could root for Hulk Hogan, and so on—even though Hulk Hogan was meant to be more of a bad guy.

So I flushed the red dye, but I kept the name. I don't even know if most people think of Hogan as an Irish name, do they? It didn't matter. When McMahon dropped the "Terry," it sounded good. "Hulk Hogan." It just had a nice ring to it.

Again: fate or coincidence?

McMahon followed through on everything he offered. He put me up in a great apartment in West Haven. He paid me real well. He hooked me up with Tony Altomare to drive me everywhere—but Tony did a lot more than that.

Tony was the kind of guy who loved to drink and raise hell. As an older guy who'd been in the business forever, he knew the ins and outs of everything—and for some reason he shared it all with me.

It was almost like that movie *The Sting*, where Robert Redford finally meets a guy who can teach him the ins and outs of the game. Tony taught me all about how the promoters worked, and what percentage of the gate the houses took. He taught me the back doors, which restaurants to hit in each city, which hotel rooms to get. He also taught me how to go head-to-head with some of the old-school barbaric wrestlers who were still on the circuit—the guys who'd bite you just to keep you in your place. (I have a few bite scars to prove it!)

Tony Altomare was my personal crash course in the real business of wrestling, and one of the best gifts McMahon ever gave me.

As for McMahon's promise to make me a star? He didn't follow through quite the way I expected, but I made it work regardless.

One thing he used me for was a foil for André the Giant. André needed a real champion-level wrestler, a worthy opponent that he could fight when he went on the road. He just made mincemeat of the little wrestlers in all the other territories. There was no drama to any of the matches because it was so obvious that André was gonna win. So McMahon figured I could go along with him whenever he went out of town, and the two of us could put on a real show for the crowd. (That also meant McMahon would gain more control over what happened in those other territories.)

McMahon didn't see me as a hero figure. Instead, he kept me in a bad-guy role so an established wrestler like Bob Backlund could come in and defeat me when he needed a boost in popularity.

For those of you who didn't tune in to the whole Hulk Hogan thing until the mid-1980s, this might be hard for you to believe, but I got booed! Wherever we went, they always wanted the other guy to win. Especially André the Giant. He was a much bigger star than I was, and everyone wanted to see him crush me.

The thing was, even if I got beat, I was the blond-haired muscle-bound perfect prototype of a wrestler—so crowds would still come out to see me.

It got to the point where I was booked in one main event after another, and the crowds kept getting bigger and better. We were selling out stadiums everywhere we went.

But it always came back to Madison Square Garden. I wrestled there almost once a month. And let me tell you, brother: Standing in the ring in the middle of that venue was like no other feeling in the world. The piercing roar of that 22,000-deep sold-out MSG crowd was so loud, it actually made my jaws water.

HOMETOWN MENTALITY

Somewhere in the middle of this crazy run I had a chance to drive down to Florida. I rolled into town in that green Continental thinking I'd finally made something of myself. There wasn't a wrestler in town that could hold a candle to what I'd accomplished.

In fact, I was feeling so pumped I decided to go find Sherry Mashburn—that beautiful Angelina Jolie–type girl I'd been in love with since the sixth grade.

I found out that Sherry was working in this really high-end modern furniture store called Scan Design. So I drove over there and walked in real casual like and said, "Hi."

Well, so much for my confidence. Seeing her face-to-face I broke out in this massive sweat. I mean, I was drenched. It was pouring down my back, down my neck, off my nose. My shirt was drenched. Even my underwear was drenched.

We went outside and stood by my car, and Sherry kept asking me, "Are you okay?"

Finally I fought through this crazy reaction I was having and asked if she wanted to go out on a date.

"Oh, I'm already dating somebody," she said.

Great.

Then the conversation started to turn a little bit. "Is this your car?" she asked. "That's a real nice car."

Hmmm. Maybe she's more interested than she's letting on.

She seemed pretty clueless about what I'd been up to, so I told her I was a wrestler now.

And she said, "Oh, like Mike Graham?"

Mike Graham?

"Are you as famous as Mike Graham?" she asked.

Mike Graham was Eddie Graham's kid—the guy who talked to me in the van and set me up with Matsuda as a way to get rid of me. As a fan, I couldn't understand how a guy that small could even get into the business against all these monster wrestlers. As time passed, of course, it dawned on me that anyone whose dad was the promoter could get through the door.

Mike Graham was a *local* hero.

All of a sudden I stopped sweating. Sherry started asking all these questions, like "Have you ever wrestled Steve Kearn?" All these years had passed and Tampa and these high school guys were still her whole world. I was working for Vince McMahon, selling out Madison Square Garden, wrestling the biggest wrestlers in the world—but until that moment, I was still nervous about what Sherry Mashburn thought of me.

The fact is, I was still nervous about what everyone in Tampa thought of me. It was crazy. By this point in my career, I was a main-event wrestler at the biggest venues in the world. When Dusty Rhodes came up to wrestle in New York, they put him in the opening match—before half of the crowd had even filtered into the arena—and here I was, the main event that had everyone up on their seats at Madison Square Garden going wild at the end of the night.

I never went out with Sherry Mashburn. Honestly, even at that age, I still barely would have known what to do with her if I had her in my arms. I found some peace in that moment, though. A peace that had been a long time coming.

Back in New York, the rise of Hulk Hogan just couldn't be stopped. The match people loved to watch most seemed to be the one that Vince always put me on: Hulk Hogan vs. André the Giant, the five-hundred-pound behemoth of the wrestling world.

A lot of people think WrestleMania III was the first time I ever bodyslammed André, but that was just the first time it happened on national television. On August 9, 1980, at a completely sold-out Shea Stadium in front of almost sixty thousand people— that's when I bodyslammed André for the very first time.

It wasn't seen widely on American TV, but it aired in Japan, where wrestling was about the biggest sport in the world. After that, the legend of the power of Hulk Hogan started spreading all over the globe like wildfire.

I'd settled in on the red and yellow colors. I'd perfected the Atomic Leg Drop. I'd just about mastered my sense of crowd control—that ability to time and finesse my movements so all I'd have to do is put my arms out and look at the crowd and I'd incite the loudest roars of "boo" you ever heard.

I also developed a move where I'd pick up three guys in the ring at the same time. I'd get one guy on my shoulders and bear-hug the other two and lift all three of 'em at once and then "Raaaah!" I'd throw them all down.

It wasn't easy. I'd say I probably failed to pull that move off about 50 percent of the times that I tried it.

It only took one time to change my life forever.

MY GUY SLY

The greatest thing about working in New York was being on TV. Every three weeks we'd film down in Allentown, and the matches were broadcast on the MSG Network—MSG standing for Madison Square Garden. This channel hit homes all over the tri-state area and down into Pennsylvania, and you just never knew who was watching.

One night, I think it was early 1980, *Rocky* mastermind Sylvester Stallone tuned in. He was on the lookout for a wrestler to cast in a role in *Rocky III*, and he saw me on a night when I happened to pull off that crazy move—lifting three wrestlers at once and just hurling them to the canvas.

Stallone didn't know how to get a hold of me himself, so he turned to his casting director, Rhonda Young. She didn't know anything about wrestling, or who the heck this wrestler was that Stallone was talking about. So she called her brother, Peter.

"Peter," she said, "Sly's gotta have this wrestler, this guy he saw on MSG. He's a bad guy, and he's done this and that," and Peter knew right off the bat. "Oh, that's Hulk Hogan." (Peter Young became my agent shortly after that and has been my agent ever since.)

So I'm coming out of the ring one night when I get a message that Sylvester Stallone wants me to call him. I thought it was a joke! I had seen *Rocky I* and *II*, and in the late '70s and early '80s there was no one as big as Stallone. He was this all-American hero figure. There was no way he was calling me. *It must be one of the guys pulling a rib*, I thought, and I blew it off.

Around this same time, McMahon sent me over to Japan to wrestle for seven weeks. Now, that was an amazing experience. All these Japanese fans worshipped me like some sort of god. It was really unbelievable to be over there and feel that kind of idolization—even if I couldn't understand a word anybody was saying. The Japanese promoters didn't want me to leave. They were begging me to stay longer. Wherever I went the arenas were packed to the rafters.

I came back to Allentown after that to find a Western Union telegram waiting for me—a certified letter that I had to sign for.

Please call Sylvester Stallone. It's an emergency.

It was getting closer and closer to when they would actually be shooting this film, and Peter and Rhonda were starting to panic that they weren't going to be able to deliver the one guy Sly wanted.

So I called him, and he picked up the phone, and it really was Sly Stallone. It was so weird to hear that familiar voice on the other end of the line.

I wasn't sure how interested I was in being in a movie. I'd

never done any kind of acting (outside of the ring, at least). I told him, "Look, I'm going back to Japan for two weeks, but I'll stop by to see you when I'm back."

We met at a gym. I had blue jeans on and cowboy boots, and my nose was all taped up—it got smashed in a match in Japan, and I hadn't had a chance to fix it yet. I wasn't prepared at all for some kind of audition.

Stallone insisted. "I want to see how you move in the ring." So Stallone starts doing his Rocky thing and starts reaching out to try to punch me.

"What do you want me to do?" I asked.

"Well, see if you can stop me," he said.

"Stop you?" I laughed out loud. He was maybe 170 pounds, and I was pushing 320 at that point.

He stayed pretty serious about it. "When I try to punch you, see if you can get ahold of me," he said.

So in one move I grabbed him and hooked him and pinned him to the canvas. Over in Japan, I had actually learned some real wrestling moves. The Japanese guys taught me hooks and submissions, all this UFC-type of stuff that you could use to survive if anyone really tried to come at you in a fight.

Stallone seemed real impressed by how easily I took him down. So he got right up and said, "Hit me as hard as you can."

"I don't think you want that," I said.

"Well, hit me like how you would hit somebody when you want it to look good but you don't want to really hurt 'em."

I explained that one way to do that would be for him to bend forward a bit and I would hit him with my forearm between the shoulder blades.

"Great," he said. "Do that. Hit me as hard as you can."

I refused. He's not a big guy! I could've killed him. But he kept insisting. "Hit me seventy-five percent then," he said. Finally, "Fifty percent!"

So I bend him over and "Grrrrrr," *bang*! I hit him, and dude, I had no idea he was gonna crumble like he did. The second my forearm hit his back, Sylvester Stallone's face hit my cowboy boots.

Amazingly he popped right up again, this time with blood trickling out of his nose. "You got the job," he said.

I remember walking out of the ring thinking, *This guy's fucking nuts!*

Then all of a sudden he put a camera in my face. "You got the job," he repeated again, all excited and pumped up. "Now tell me how bad you're gonna kick Rocky Balboa's ass!"

I caught on to what he was doing real quick. He wanted to see if I could talk, to maybe cut a promo or something. So I turned on that voice I'd been developing since my first TV appearances back in Memphis. "Okay, Balboa, you're goin' down!" I don't remember exactly what I said. I'd sure love to see that tape. It's probably in a vault somewhere. Anyway, after a few seconds he turned the camera off and said to me one more time, "You got it."

We shook hands. I didn't have an agent at that point and had no idea what you should get paid to appear in a film, but he said, "I'll give you ten thousand dollars to do the movie."

Me, being the smart negotiator I am, thought it sounded a little low. "How about fifteen thousand dollars?" I said.

"Okay, fourteen," he countered. Done. I signed a piece of paper right there on the spot. I couldn't believe that I was going to be in a Rocky movie. Not in my wildest dreams did I ever imagine acting in films, let alone acting with someone as big as Sly Stallone. I knew it would be a huge boost for my career. Heck, a boost to my whole life.

When I got back to New York I told Vince McMahon Sr. that I would be shooting this movie in a couple of months.

"No, you're not," he said.

For some reason I didn't take him seriously. "Okay," I replied, but I never even gave it a second thought. I knew this would be great not only for my career, but for the whole sport of wrestling. To put one of us up there on the big screen in a Rocky movie, which was sure to be a huge hit seen by millions of people? It was a real no-brainer.

Like I said before, I was always looking ahead, thinking about making more money, thinking about how I could make this Hulk Hogan thing bigger and bigger. I thought Vince Sr. thought that way, too. But maybe I was wrong. Maybe he was just like the other promoters. He had control of the number-one territory, his own little kingdom, and maybe that was enough for him. Maybe he just didn't have the vision for how big this could get.

A couple of months later I was wrestling in Fall River, Massachusetts. As I left the arena at the end of the night, I said goodbye to whoever it was that McMahon had running the show that night. "I'll see you guys. I'm gonna go do this Rocky movie tomorrow. It should take like ten days, maybe two weeks to shoot, and I'll call you when I'm done."

They were shocked. "No. We just called Vince. He said you're supposed to leave tonight and drive to Charlotte to be on TV by noon tomorrow."

It made no sense. He knew this film was coming up. So I called McMahon at his home in Boca Raton. There was no way I could make it to Charlotte by noon the next day anyway. It was snowing in Massachusetts that night. So the whole thing was nuts.

"Terry," McMahon says, "you're a wrestler, not an actor. If you go do this Rocky movie, you're fired and you'll never work here again."

"Okay, Vince." I hung up the phone, said good-bye to everyone at the arena, and flew out the next day to do *Rocky III*. I'd come too far to let anyone, even Vince McMahon Sr., hold me down. I knew the ins and outs of the business now. I also knew that Hulk Hogan was already bigger than anything McMahon could envision—especially in Japan.

So I flew out to Los Angeles and shot my scenes with Stallone, playing this over-the-top character named Thunderlips.

When I was done, I rang up my new pals in Japan. "Guess what?" I told 'em. "I'm free to come wrestle whenever you want me now. And I can stay there as long as you want."

CHAPTER 8

Hulking Up

It's pretty wild to imagine a kid from Port Tampa moving to the Far East, but that's exactly what I did in 1981. I basically decided to go where I was wanted most. Stallone wanted me more than Vince McMahon Sr., so I went to L.A. and shot his film. The Japanese promoters wanted me more than the American promoters, so I went to Japan.

It's an awesome thing to feel wanted. But the thing that made my time in Japan *really* memorable was I met and dated this gorgeous Japanese girl. She ran a modeling agency called Folio that was on the level of a Ford Agency or any of the other big modeling agencies here in the States. She spoke perfect English, which definitely helped in the finding-my-way-around department, and because of her business she had hookups for everything.

When the big rock 'n' roll acts came through, from Rod Stewart to the Rolling Stones, she always had backstage passes. And when it came to partying in a country where getting caught with a few ounces of marijuana could mean a lifetime in jail, she had access to every drug under the sun. I even dabbled in a few other substances besides the steroids, and I'll tell you a little more about that later.

The long and short of it is, I was real happy hanging out with her in Japan.

With no exaggeration, I was like Brad Pitt in that country. Everywhere I went was a mob scene. I towered over almost everyone, and the people there worshipped me. Most of all, they were nice to me. That's what I really loved. There was just a respect and sincerity among the people there that I'd never experienced back home.

But it wasn't home.

As some of the American wrestlers came through, they started telling me about this guy named Verne Gagne, a promoter in Minnesota. He apparently wanted to talk to me. So one day when I was feeling a little homesick for the good ol' U.S. of A., I called him up.

"I want you to come wrestle here," Gagne told me. "I've got this guy named Jesse Ventura who I want to put you in the ring with. We've got a real small territory here, which means you'll only have to wrestle four days a week—but I want to pay you a lot of money."

Like I said, at this point I just wanted to go wherever I was wanted the most, and from the numbers he was throwing at me, Verne Gagne wanted me bad.

So I said okay. Just like that, in early 1982, I left Japan, that girl, and that crazy fame, and I went back to wrestle in this tiny Minnesota territory.

There was just one problem. I was supposed to be the bad guy. That always worked before, but after *Rocky III* hit theaters that spring, every time I would step foot in an arena the place would explode. The crowds cheered for me instead of booing. It started to become real clear that my playing the heel wouldn't cut it anymore. That basically ruined all of Verne Gagne's plans to make me the challenger to Jesse Ventura.

In a way, that was the start of Hulkamania right there. It was the audience that made that happen, the crowds that decided Hulk Hogan was someone they wanted to cheer for rather than boo. So I embraced it. I wouldn't fold with one punch. It would take three or four punches to make me fold. I would really play it up, combining bad-guy and good-guy elements all in one: I'd get hit in the head with a chair (which, not surprisingly, hurts like hell), or swiped by a pair of brass knuckles, and it'd just get me mad and I'd shake it off. There was a whole different aura to everything I did, and the audience just started eating from the palm of my hand.

It was in those arenas that I started playing Survivor's "Eye of the Tiger" as my theme music whenever I walked in. Wrestlers never used theme music before that. You can't imagine how loud the crowds roared when they heard that song from *Rocky III*.

I was the main attraction at every arena. Hulk Hogan was the star. No question. Everyone in the wrestling business knew it, too. I could feel the world opening up to me.

THE LINDA FACTOR

During my years in Minnesota, I was still flying back and forth to Japan all the time. The four-day schedule made it pretty easy to do that, and the Japanese audience just couldn't go long without their fix of Hulk Hogan in the ring.

What I'd usually do on my way there or my way back was stop over in Los Angeles. I had become friends with Stallone at this point, and we'd occasionally hit the town together—just stirring up everything and making the girls go wild at the clubs. I also reconnected with an old high school pal of mine named Nelson Kidwell.

One night Nelson took me to this place called the Red Onion, up in the Valley. The place was just swimming with Valley Girls. Blond hair and long pink fingernails everywhere. But this one girl really stood out. Her name was Linda Claridge, and she actually asked me to dance. I still wasn't much on dancing, so I said no, and Nelson went out and danced with her instead.

It was there on that dance floor that I really started to notice her. She was just gorgeous. Built like a racehorse with these muscular legs, and that ass of hers—that's my weakness right there.

When she came back over I bought her a drink, and we just started talking. That was the start of everything.

Linda's personality was so over-the-top. She was real bubbly and happy. I was drawn to that immediately. She didn't have that hard edge to her the way a lot of Florida girls did. After that initial meeting at the Red Onion, she played hard to get and that drove me wild. I kept calling her and calling her.

I liked the fact that she seemed to be successful in her own right, too. She told me she owned this nail salon she worked in, and she drove this brand-new Corvette. She was cool!

Whether I had my blinders on again or Linda hid it all from me, there didn't seem to be any negative side to Linda Claridge at all. She was the most positive, upbeat, happy girl I'd ever met. That over-the-top, fun personality of hers drew me in like a moth to the flame.

I think I was also drawn to the fact that she didn't really know anything about wrestling. Or at least that's what she let on. I think it was two weeks after we'd met that she and her mom went to see *E.T.* at a movie theater near their house. As the story goes, the lines were so long they skipped it and went to see *Rocky III* instead. Once she saw me pop up in that movie she started to connect the dots on how famous I was.

My boy Nelson couldn't understand what the hell I saw in Linda. "There's a million girls out there. She's just a Valley Girl! They're all the same," he said.

She certainly wasn't "the same" to me. Everything about Linda seemed a million light-years ahead of the hard-edged Florida girls I'd dated. To me, she was a blond California dream. I was completely hooked from day one.

In the early days of our relationship, finding time to see Linda was tough because of my schedule. We'd talk on the phone every day, but I'd only be able to catch her in person for a day or two at a time when I hit L.A. between flights back and forth to Japan. I'd asked her to come live with me in Minnesota, but she just wasn't into the whole idea of up and leaving her California lifestyle behind.

The funny thing is, if she had said yes and gone with me to Minnesota, then I probably never would have reconnected with my brother Alan, whom I hadn't seen since he split Port Tampa after getting shot in the back.

Linda and I had only been dating a little while when he suddenly showed up outside of the Gold's Gym on Sherman Way, the gritty main thoroughfare that cuts east to west across the Valley. I'm always kinda slow getting out of the gym—it takes me a little longer than everyone else to quit sweating, get dressed, and come out of the building—but I was finally on my way out that day when Linda came running in with her eyes as big as saucers.

"Terry, there's this real big guy outside. He's bigger than you are! I can't even see his skin he's got so many tattoos," she said. "He's sitting on the hood of the car. He's got a big, black beard and long black hair. He says he's your brother!"

"Yeah, that's my brother," I told her. "Tell him I'll be out in a minute."

I hadn't talked to Alan in years—since he was living in Houston under an assumed name. During that period I heard that he beat a guy real bad and threw him in a dumpster. When I asked him about it over the phone, he said, "Oh yeah, he was cheatin' playing pool!" As if that was a good excuse. It was just ridiculous to me that he was still doing crazy shit like that, so I said, "I don't ever wanna talk to you again." And that was that.

Now all of a sudden he's sitting out on my car. I have no idea how he knew that I was working out at that gym that day. I don't even want to know. But the only reason he stopped by was to say hello, and I have to say: It was great to see my brother again.

Alan was riding with the Hell's Angels at that point. He became vice president of the San Francisco chapter, and after our Gold's Gym hello he started to show up with like twenty or thirty Hell's Angels in tow every time I'd wrestle at the Cow Palace or the Oakland Coliseum.

I can't even tell you how much that would freak the other wrestlers out. These Hell's Angels were huge wrestling fans, but they all treated it like it was real and they wanted to come in and kill the bad guys! Mr. Wonderful and some of the other wrestlers would all hide whenever my brother and his Hell's Angels buddies came around. I think some of them were just as scared of a real confrontation as I'd always been.

Whenever all these Hell's Angels came around and I'd hug them hello, I could feel the metal on them. They were packing guns everywhere. The other wrestlers had a right to be scared. But it was also kind of cool, you know—it was such a macho thing to have a brother who was a powerhouse with the baddest biker gang around. It brought me that old sort of "SOG" respect from some of the other wrestlers. They just assumed that they'd better not mess with me.

Still, it scared me to death. I could tell my brother was high as a kite every time he came to visit me at those arenas—and to think of him riding around like that with these guys and all these guns? It just scared me.

I never really spent much time with him at all. I'd always say hi and then tell him I had to get ready for the match, and once the match was over I'd start saying I had to get ready to go to the next city, you know?

Over the next couple of years he met a lady named Marsha, and they got married and moved to L.A. He had another child with Marsha, David Bollea—who's actually a mixed martial arts fighter now—and they opened a carpet-cleaning business. It really seemed to me like he was getting his life a little bit more on track.

Even though I didn't spend much time with him, it was nice to feel like I had a brother again.

WEDDED BLIP

Linda and I dated for about a year and a half before I finally asked her to marry me. Having learned a few lessons from my failed engagement to Donna, I knew for sure that this was the real deal.

I never felt happier than when I was with Linda, and she seemed to spend every moment with me smiling like I'd never seen a girl smile before. The engagement was enough for her to make the leap, and she moved to Minnesota with me into a brand-new townhouse I'd just bought—the first piece of property I'd owned my whole life.

My schedule didn't let up, of course, and that didn't leave much time for a wedding. So we simply made the best of it. On December 18, 1983, I flew back from Japan for one day, we got married in L.A., and I went back to work the very next night. There was no slowing down.

The wedding was great, don't get me wrong. The party was awesome. The entire crew from Japan flew back with me, and all these wrestlers were there, and it turned into an all-night blowout. As the story goes, I got so drunk that I woke up the next morning still in my tuxedo. So Linda and I never consummated the marriage on our wedding night.

It didn't matter, of course. Linda knew she had me for life. And I guess for her, the Valley Girl, it was a big, big deal. To catch a guy as famous and quickly-becoming-rich as Hulk Hogan meant she'd caught herself a big fish.

In retrospect, Linda and her whole family probably thought they had caught themselves a sucker fish.

My first clue was right there in front of me that night. Apparently the wedding guests ran up a huge bar tab—like twelve or fourteen thousand dollars. So Linda's mom came up to me and asked me to pay the bill. And I did.

The parents of the bride usually pay for that kind of thing, right? I didn't care. I had the money on me, and I was having such a good time, I just handed it over. That's something I would wind up doing a lot of over the course of my marriage.

For the time being, though, Linda and I were off and running. A blissful husband-and-wife team, out on the road and living large. We didn't have time for a traditional honeymoon, but as we traveled around for my matches, staying in different hotel rooms and partying every night, those first few years felt like a honeymoon that never ended.

THE MAN IN PLAID

Verne Gagne had big, big plans for me by the time I got married. Nick Bockwinkel had emerged as the champion in the Minnesota territory, and they started booking me in Steel Cage Matches as his primary opponent in every big city from Salt Lake to Chicago. We were also putting our forces together with all these big wrestlers to buy time on Channel 9 in New York. We knew we had the talent to go head-to-head with the WWF, and with TV time setting us up, there was no telling how quickly we could take over the New York territory.

Oddly enough, that's exactly when I got a surprise phone call from Vince McMahon. Only this time, the call came from a very different Vince McMahon—it was Vince McMahon Jr. on the line.

When I was working for Vince Sr., his son Vince Jr. was acting primarily as a commentator and ring announcer. When André the Giant came out of the ring all bloody from taking a Hulk Hogan beating, Vince was the guy in the suit with the microphone getting the ringside interview. But something sure had changed, because now Vince Jr. was a guy with bigger ambitions than I'd ever encountered in this business.

"Hey, I know my dad fired you," Vince said, "but my dad's gonna retire, and I'm takin' over the business. We've been watchin' how great you're doin' in Minnesota. We want to bring you in and make you our champion."

I was flattered, I guess, but I had also been burned by the McMahons once before.

"Look," I said, "I'm going on three years here and I'm doing really well, I only work four days a week, and I just bought a townhouse—"

He kept interrupting. He didn't want to hear my excuses.

"What I'm saying is we want to give you the biggest push of all," Vince said. "I'm gonna take over this business. I have plans to change the wrestling business and make you the biggest star in the world." The McMahons only controlled wrestling in that New York–Connecticut–Massachusetts corridor, but he was talking about going everywhere. Worldwide!

Vince recognized how popular I'd made this Hulk Hogan character, and he shared the same vision I had—that I could take this character anywhere.

He insisted on meeting me in person, and a few days later he flew into the Minneapolis/St. Paul airport. I had Linda go pick him up. "All I can tell you is you're gonna see a guy in a plaid tweed suit with big shoulder pads," I told her. He was a pretty geeky-looking guy back then.

Sure enough, she picked him right out at the airport. Linda brought Vince back to my townhouse, and we sat around drinking wine and eating pizza, talking about his vision. The idea was to take the WWF to venues all across the country and around the world, with Hulk Hogan leading the charge, and to go national with big TV events. I don't think we talked about it that first night, but Vince Jr. is the guy who spearheaded the whole concept of pay-per-view TV. Before cable was everywhere, he had the idea to simulcast Madison Square Garden events on big screens in stadiums in other markets—instantly doubling, tripling, quadrupling the audiences for every big match.

With all the fly-by-night promoters and even the great promoters I'd worked with in this business, I had never encountered a vision as big as Vince's. It lined up with all I had in my head about how big this thing could become—the monstrous vision I had when I first realized that wrestling was as much a performance as it was a sporting event, when I knew that I could be great at it.

Vince's passion got me so fired up, there was no way I could say no to the guy.

Right around four o'clock in the morning, we shook hands.

Two days later, I locked the door of that townhouse and walked away from Minnesota, knowing I'd never be back.

BEATING THE SHEIK

Linda and I settled into an apartment in West Haven, Connecticut, and I immediately started going back and forth to wrestle again for the WWF TV tapings in Allentown.

There was just one problem: Vince Sr. hadn't retired yet, which meant that he was still calling the shots even as Vince Jr. was starting to step in.

As soon as I arrived I could tell Vince Sr. was a little uncomfortable having me around—partially because of the way things ended between us, I figured, and probably because the other wrestlers were so pissed off about my sudden arrival. They knew this Hulk Hogan thing was about to eclipse whatever fan base they had built for themselves.

Bob Backlund, who was supposed to be my tag-team partner, wouldn't even get in the ring with me. It was all that sort of small-time crap that Vince Jr. and I were ready to put behind us.

In fact, our plan for world domination was already in motion. Just a few weeks after my return, we were gearing up for this massive coup in Madison Square Garden.

Not long before that, the Iron Sheik had won the championship belt from Bob. It was all part of a story line that would have Backlund back in the Garden to win that belt back from him on January 23, 1984. That was Vince Sr.'s plan. Vince Jr. decided to put me in that ring against the Iron Sheik instead, to give Hulk Hogan the world championship belt and start building this thing into something much bigger.

There are lots of rumors about what happened that night. Here's what I know to be true. For one, Verne Gagne, who was furious that I left his Minnesota plans high and dry, called the Iron Sheik and offered him money to punish me in the ring. In one swift move, the Iron Sheik would have landed a lucrative deal to go wrestle in Minnesota while simultaneously eliminating Vince's new star.

I honestly don't think that plan would have worked. Even if the Sheik somehow managed to give me hell, there was so much love for Hulk Hogan among the fans that it would have created this massive wave of sympathy for me. I probably would have blown up even bigger, even faster! And the Sheik would have been so hated that he very well might have faded into oblivion in the Midwest. Plus, I think the Sheik was smart enough to see the bigger picture of what Vince Jr. was trying to set up, which would be worth a hell of a lot more than what Gagne was offering if it all worked out.

The obstacle was Vince Sr. A short time before the big match, he took me aside and said, "You know, Terry, we may have to put this off for a while. We may change our plans."

I couldn't believe it. I knew he was just caving in to Bob Backlund, who had been whining and complaining ever since he heard that I was gonna win the belt. He didn't think it was right that somebody who wasn't a "real athlete" would hold the belt. That was his excuse: that I hadn't been a real amateur wrestler like he had.

He got awful petty about the whole thing. At one point, when he didn't seem to be getting his way, he went to Vince Sr. and said, "By the way, Hulk Hogan smokes pot." That led to all these questions in the locker room, and all kind of problems for me.

So when Vince Sr. pulled me aside to say we might not follow the plan I'd been promised by Vince Jr., I basically told him he could forget about having Hulk Hogan stick around. "Look, Vince, if you're changing your plans, I just burned a huge bridge in Minnesota. I'll go right back tonight and rebuild that bridge," I told him.

Vince Jr. stepped in at that point. He pulled his dad aside for a long conversation. I don't know what he said, but he eventually came back to me and said, "We're goin' with things as planned."

So on January 23, 1984, I climbed into the ring at Madison

Square Garden, turned on all the Hulk Hogan charm, and whipped the audience into a frenzy as I won the belt from the Iron Sheik. My very first championship belt.

Verne Gagne, the guys down in Florida, and the wrestlers in Memphis and Alabama might not have agreed with it, but at that moment I became the biggest and best in the world. And it didn't matter what any of the old-school wrestling guys thought, because audiences were ready to embrace Hulk Hogan like they'd never embraced any other wrestler in the history of the business.

Out with the old. In with the new.

Hulkamania had officially exploded.

VINCE-A-MANIA

A few weeks after winning the belt, I went down to Allentown to tape my first TV match as the champion. I was back in the dressing room getting ready and decided I needed to go to the bathroom. Now, the bathroom in the dressing room of that facility was built real strange. You had to open a door and go up some stairs to get to this platform where the toilet was.

The door was closed, and I didn't knock. I didn't think anyone else was around. I just opened it. As I looked up those stairs, I caught a glimpse of Vince Sr. standing over the toilet—I didn't mean to look, but I didn't think anyone was in there—and I couldn't believe what I saw. His legs were spread, and all I could see was this bright red piss shooting down into the bowl. It looked like pure blood.

Holy shit. I closed the door and walked away.

I ran to Pat Patterson, who'd become a close friend of mine by then, and told him what I'd seen. He served as a close confidant of both McMahons—their voice of reason as far as business savvy. Pat went and gently told Vince Jr. about what I had seen.

Shortly thereafter we got the news that Vince Sr. had cancer.

And within a matter of weeks, he was gone. It was shocking, and so sad.

Vince Jr. stepped into his father's shoes and took the reins of the business, exactly like he told me he would. It just happened in a way that I never saw coming.

Vince was based in Stamford, and we needed to be close to each other to keep working on all of our big plans. So Linda and I moved up there and bought a house just a few weeks after Vince's father passed. From that point on, Vince and I were inseparable.

We spent hours and hours talking this thing through from every angle possible. The thing was, for as much as Vince had been around the wrestling business and thought he knew the business inside and out, he really needed to see it through my eyes—the eyes of someone who had lived it in the ring. At that point, Vince had never entered the ring himself. So in a way I became his teacher. I walked him through Wrestling 101: the wrestling psychology, the theory. Both of us were in sync about the fact that this business could be much bigger than the way Vince Sr. saw it. Beyond that, just like Tony Altomare had shown me the ropes and the back doors of the business side a few years earlier, I showed Vince my personal vision for how to raise the bar on everything that happened in the ring.

My view of this was different than any wrestler that came before me, and I wanted him to see that the little things I did in the ring to make the fans feel like they were a part of the match could be done on a much grander scale across the whole spectrum of the WWF. If we sucked these fans in on a personal level, they would live it and breathe it and be fans forever.

Vince knew wrestling was an art form, but I wanted to bring it to life for him. "Yes, you paint a picture," I explained, "and there's an arc to the story lines." He knew that—but there was a bigger way, a more emotional way, to paint those arcs and reach the fans so that the experience would last much longer than a three-hour show at Madison Square Garden. There was a way to make people believe that Hulk Hogan was a real hero, and that if you train and take your vitamins and say your prayers you, too, can be a hero. I wanted people to be absolutely hooked on this stuff so it entered their lives on a daily basis—not just once a month or a few times a year.

I explained how we could get more heat, and how to make the fans go crazy, and how to really make a comeback like no one had ever seen. It was like he needed to hear that from my point of view to awaken the full fire of his grand plan.

And man, were his plans grand. Vince was like the P. T. Barnum of wrestling promoters. He was aggressive—never afraid to make moves. He would rent buildings and put his ass on the line, leverage his house if he had to, in order to make something happen. He was fearless. And by that time, so was I.

The thing about Vince is he could match me toe-to-toe in the obsession department. If I was in 150 percent, so was he. We could put blinders on and just block out the whole world, the naysayers, the old-time wrestlers who thought the business should stay just the way it was. We'd power our way through any obstacle that hit us, and we pushed each other.

With his aggressiveness and my focus, we were a match made in heaven. Even though we were totally different types of people, our work ethic was hardcore. I used to call him the Terminator. I swear I've never met anybody else that can roll with me and keep up with me neck and neck when I get on something.

One example: A few years into the Hulkamania madness, Linda and I relocated to Florida, to a townhouse down on Redington Beach. One time Vince came down and we locked ourselves in a hotel room nearby. For forty-eight hours straight we sat at a table with a pencil and paper and wrote the movie *No Holds Barred* from beginning to end. It was a ridiculous movie, but we wrote it from beginning to end without stopping, without sleeping, for forty-eight hours. It was like three hundred pages before we handed it to a writer to polish up. I'd never met anyone who could hang with me like that.

We were a great team. There's no other way to put it. I wasn't his "employee." He wasn't my "boss." He needed me as much as I needed him. Hulkamania got started when I was working in Minnesota, but it never would have blown up the way it did without Vince and the WWF. Likewise, there's no way the WWF would have broken down all the old territorial boundaries and taken over the world if Vince didn't have Hulk Hogan.

From the moment this whole thing took off in '84, we were partners in the best sense of the word. We both had this vision and this manic drive. Nothing was gonna stop us.

CHAPTER 9

Livin' the High Life

Remember how I missed out on that whole sex, drugs, and rock 'n' roll vibe when I was playing in bands down in Tampa? Let's just say I was a late bloomer.

The thing is, when wrestling took off in this unstoppable international explosion in the 1980s, Hulk Hogan was as big as any rock band going. The first WrestleMania had a million viewers on closed-circuit TV. A million viewers all paying to watch! We even slammed this thing directly into the music world with the whole MTV/*Rock 'n' Wrestling* phenomenon. Before I knew it, I was acting as a personal bodyguard to Cyndi Lauper one night and taking her to the Grammy Awards in my sleeveless tux.

That excitement from the audience fed me in the ring and made the whole thing even bigger and better. I'd keep mixing up the moves and mugging to the crowd, making sure every fan got involved in the show so they felt like they were a part of the match.

It was such a trip, too, because when I'd hit Joe Louis Arena in Detroit, the heads of GM and Ford and Chrysler—the most powerful businessmen in the whole wide world at that time—would jockey to see who got the best seats. Vince used to laugh about that all the time. Or I'd be in L.A. coming out of the ring and I'd

see John Travolta and Gene Hackman and Suzanne Somers—
some of the biggest stars of the '70s and '80s—sittin' right along
the aisle. Going to see Hulk Hogan was like the hot thing to do for
a while, you know?

My T-shirts and merchandise were flying off the shelves. We
were traveling from town to town, selling out arenas. And forget
about the tiny MSG Network—we knocked ourselves onto NBC
on Saturday nights. Major network television! Dick Ebersol, who
was producing *Saturday Night Live* at the time, had us filling in
on weeks when SNL was off the air, and that opened doors to every party in town.

Hell, going all the way back to my days running in and out of
L.A. between trips to Japan there were a bunch of times when a
few other guys and I put John Belushi's ass to bed. That's the kind
of crowd we were running with—sliding right into the craziness
of Studio 54 before that wild New York party finally came to a
halt in March of 1986.

Linda was right beside me for the ride and loving every minute
of it. If she had been an actress or something, maybe playing second fiddle to Hulk Hogan would have been too much to take. As
it was, being in that number-two position worked just fine for her.
She had a certain respect everywhere she'd go, just because she
was my wife, you know? People would want to talk to her and ask
her all about what it was like to live with the Hulkster, and the red
velvet ropes would part for her at any party. She loved that.

When we hit the road, the party was on. I was the world's
champion and had more money rolling in than I knew what to do
with. And Linda was always in charge of that money. For as long
as I can remember, whenever I'd get a check, I'd stuff it in my
wrestling bag and hand it over to Linda when I saw her. With all
the running around I was doing, it was just easier for her to deal
with going to the bank. Plus, can you imagine Hulk Hogan walking into a local bank? It would be chaos.

We were never ones to waste money. Especially on the road.
Instead of blowing our dough at the Peninsula or the Beverly
Hills Hotel, Linda and I would always stay at the Marriotts or

Ramadas with all of the other wrestlers. We didn't want to be separated from the pack. That just wasn't our mindset back then. It was much more fun to be around everyone.

I was drinkin' a lot of beer, and Linda would always drink her wine, and all the wrestlers smoked pot, so I would smoke pot, too. But the thing that's most memorable about partying in the late '70s and early '80s was the cocaine.

It first showed up in my personal circles about halfway through my run in Minnesota—right around when Linda and I started dating. I'd go to wrestle in Denver or someplace, and when we'd hit the hotel afterward to drink a few beers, somebody'd break a little gram out.

At first I didn't know what the fuck it was, but everybody tried it, so I tried it, too. I didn't know what it was supposed to do. It didn't seem to have that big an effect on me. I mean, if it wired me up where I could drink an extra beer or five, I don't remember that, and I don't remember it like some kind of "Oh my God" epiphany. But it was there, and I did it.

Before long, it was showing up in the locker rooms at the arenas. Then it started showing up in every hotel room, every night. Those hotel rooms would just get wild—and that became the standard routine, almost every night. "Let's go up to the hotel and do a couple lines and have some drinks."

I never did large amounts of the stuff, and the most I probably hit it was four days a week. If it was there, it was there; if it wasn't, I didn't care.

When it got real heavy I couldn't handle it. If I bought a gram of cocaine it would last me a whole week. You could buy it anywhere, of course—from other wrestlers, from fans. Or you wouldn't even have to buy it, you know? It was just there. But if I would hand a gram to Linda and she would get with other wives or girlfriends, it'd be gone instantly.

I'd always ask her, "How can a gram disappear in one night? Where did it all go?!" But she certainly wasn't alone. It seemed like everybody was doing that. More, more, more. Man, if I did too much coke, though, it made me chew my fingernails.

Sure it made you feel good, like, "Hey, man, I'm awake, and I feel like a genius, and I feel young!" But when it came to functionality? I didn't want to eat, I couldn't sleep at all, and I definitely couldn't get a hard-on. Still, it's so addictive that you keep doin' it anyway. It's like a rat to poison. You just can't stop.

Almost all the wrestlers loved it, and it was just part of the culture back then. It seems like every big star had a run with cocaine at one point or another. The *Saturday Night Live* gang was running wild. You'd walk into Studio 54 and shit was everywhere, you know? Right out in the open!

It's kind of embarrassing to talk about it now, thinking about my kids and what a bad example that is, but that's just the way it was. It was a different era.

It doesn't mean my kids should follow my example. Just the opposite. We're all smarter than we were then. We know more about what drugs can do to you, and how dangerous they can be. I want my kids to learn from my mistakes so they don't make the same mistakes I made, you know? And I'm certainly not gonna lie about it.

It's also weird to think about the fact that I was doing all of this—and the steroids—while telling all of my young fans week after week, "Train, say your prayers, and take your vitamins." That line was like my own Bob Barker catchphrase. I threw that sentiment out into the world day after day after day. Not that there's anything wrong with that message. It's a great message. It was just a little bit hypocritical that my activities behind the scenes didn't match the role-model persona I was putting out there.

I'm glad I did it, though. Putting that kind of positive message out there to millions of kids is one of the least self-centered things I did in all those years. I put it right up there with visiting kids for the Make-A-Wish Foundation and other charity work I did. Throwing that kind of positive vibe out into the universe can only bring positive things in return.

Plus, there was almost no chance that any kid would find out about what I was doing late at night. There weren't packs of paparazzi everywhere like there are today. There weren't all these celebrity magazines and entertainment-show videographers stalking you everywhere you went, either. If you partied with fans, they certainly weren't forwarding embarrassing photos to some Internet blog—that whole culture just didn't exist. Instead the fans would just brag to their friends about whatever happened that night. Unlike today, it was actually fun for everyone involved—on both sides of the equation.

I can't even describe to you how much fun it was to wrestle Madison Square Garden and hear that crowd, with those twenty-two thousand people making my jaws water, and to come off of that high and head over to the Ramada on 48th Street with all the other wrestlers and drink in that bar with all these fans going nuts and then head up to a hotel room for more drinks and a couple of lines.

But the side effects and the whole crash of that next day just wasn't worth it. By late '85, I threw more coke away than I snorted. It got to the point where I'd buy an eight ball, which is three grams, and I'd do a little bit of it and have a few drinks, and get so wired I'd start grinding my teeth, so I'd drink a little more to take the edge off and then go to bed and wake up feeling like shit. So I'd get up before Linda and I'd flush the rest of that eight ball down the toilet.

Next thing I know I'd have one of the other wrestlers callin' me up, "Hey, man, you still got that eight ball?"

I'd tell 'em what I did.

"How the fuck could you flush that down the toilet?!"

It was easy. I didn't care. I didn't want to keep having that feeling. But flushing it wasn't enough. There was always more of it around the next night. And even though I never did more than a line or two at a time, and I never did it on a daily basis, I'd find that I kept going back for more.

Like I said, a rat to poison. Until I finally had a wake-up call in '86.

ALAN'S END

Was it fate or a big coincidence that Studio 54 got shut down for good in the spring of 1986? I think the collective party in this country had just gone on for far too long and got far too crazy. I mean, life has a way of slapping you in the face when things go too far, and I think that can happen on a grand scale as easily as it can happen in any one man's life. We had all been on this party train since the '70s, and all of a sudden it was running out of track.

Early that year, something terrible happened to my brother Alan's ex-wife, Martha Alfonso. While he had gone on his odyssey—through Texas, and riding with the Hell's Angels up in Frisco—and had remarried this lady named Marsha and started a new life in L.A., Martha stayed back in Tampa and raised their three kids on her own.

Martha was making a decent living managing a hotel by the Tampa airport. For a while she was dating a guy who had a whole lot of money, yet who never seemed to have a real job. Read into that what you will, knowing what kind of characters and families were running in and out of Tampa in those days. The kind that would be played by Pacinos and De Niros in the movies.

Well, one day Martha and her boyfriend got in a real big fight, and after work she went into the hotel bar and wound up dancing with one of the employees there. Her boyfriend walked in and shot her twice—killed her right there on the dance floor.

So all of a sudden I have two nieces and a nephew who lost their mom. (My nephew is Michael Bollea, who would eventually wrestle as Horace Hogan in the National Wrestling Alliance and over in Japan. He grew up thick and strong, like Alan.)

So these three kids started bouncing around between Martha's side of the family, the Cuban side, and my parents. I did whatever I could to send money back to try to help them out. But just a few months later we were knocked out by another wave of bad news.

Alan started showing up to my matches in L.A., the same way he used to show up in San Francisco and Oakland a year or two earlier. Only now, instead of having the Hell's Angels in tow, he'd bring his new wife, Marsha.

I remember one time after I wrestled at the Olympic Auditorium, I went to meet the two of them outside of the building and Alan and I couldn't find her. She'd disappeared. We looked around for a really long time, and we were starting to freak out a little bit when one of the maintenance guys came out of the building and told us he found her—passed out in one of the bathrooms.

So I knew that drugs were still a big part of Alan's life. He hadn't turned his life around as much as I thought.

It wasn't long before my brother came right out in the open with it. "I need pain pills, man. Can you help me out?" He knew that I knew a doctor named George Zahorian back in Harrisburg, Pennsylvania—this doc that would hook me and all the other wrestlers up with steroids and just about anything else we ever wanted or needed. It wasn't like I was giving him LSD, so I probably didn't think much about sharing a few pain pills with my brother.

This one day in 1986, though, I went back to L.A. and met up with Alan and Marsha, and something had shifted—like someone had pulled the rug out from under their whole world. The two of them started giving me this crazy fuckin' story. "We can't pay the rent on the house. We're behind on the van payment. Our carpet company's goin' under." They were late on Alan's motorcycle payment, they were out of groceries, they were desperate and needed my help. It was this, that, and the other, nonstop.

So I wrote 'em a check. I can't remember if it was for five grand or ten grand. I was making enough money that it didn't make a difference at that point. Anyway, as soon as I wrote that check, the two of them just started arguing like hell in this restaurant we were in.

I finally pulled my brother aside and said, "Alan, look. Why don't you just come with me to San Francisco tonight?" He looked real stressed out, and I told him it was only an hour flight up there. I was scheduled to wrestle at the Cow Palace. "We can just hang out and talk and, you know, maybe we can see some of your old friends. Then we'll just fly back. We'll be back by midnight tonight." The last flight out of San Francisco airport's an eleven o'clock. I was happy to pay for it. It was no big deal.

"No," he said. "I can't, I can't. I gotta stay here. I wanna do this, I wanna do that."

I really thought he should get away from the craziness. Catch a break for a night. But he needed to go pay those bills right away and get everything taken care of, he said. So I gave up. "Okay. I'll call you when I get back."

That night I flew up to San Francisco and wrestled as the main event at the Cow Palace as planned. As I came out of the ring, Blackjack Lanza, this old-time wrestler who worked as the on-site agent, who always stayed in back and dictated who would win or lose the matches, came up to me looking real serious and handed me a note. "It's an emergency," he said.

I open the note to see what the hell he's talking about, and all it says is "Call Marsha, it's an emergency."

Fuck, I remember thinking. *What now?* Who knew what Marsha's idea of an emergency was? I mean, I don't know what I expected other than another crazy sob story about how the money I gave them wasn't enough and how they were in even more trouble or whatever. But she's my brother's wife. So I called her.

"They found your brother dead in a hotel room."

Apparently Alan took all of that money I gave him and rather than paying off bills or getting a handle on all the shit in his life, he went out and bought a boatload of whatever his drug of choice was. Then he overdosed and died.

I guess I'll never know if it was on purpose or not. Whatever it was, he did it with my money. The bread that I gave him. My big-time wrestling career and big fat wallet made it possible for my brother Alan to die that night.

That's not what I thought about when I first heard the news. That sorry fact would hit me in the middle of the night sometime later. No. When I hung up with Marsha, all I could think about was my mom and dad. I was so worried about how they would react. I knew they were going to get that phone call, and I knew how crushed they would be.

"One day, we're gonna get a phone call about your brother," my mom had been saying for years. Her nightmare had finally come true.

Even with all the problems, all the hell he put them through, Alan was still their favorite son. That's just my opinion, of course. My mom will totally disagree. Every time I see her she says, "Terry, you're my number-one son." I don't want to seem mean or anything, but there are times when I'll be sitting there with my mom for an hour, watching TV, and she'll want some water and she'll still say, "Alan, get me some water." She doesn't even know she does it, and I don't ever feel the need to correct her.

"Okay, Mom."

My dad was the same way. It was always "Alan this, and Alan that." I never had anything against it. I just knew that Alan was his favorite, too. As a younger brother you can just tell.

Even right before my dad passed away, whenever he would talk to me he would always start with "Alan—I mean, Terry." So I knew this news was gonna crush them. Not to mention those three kids who now had lost both of their parents in the course of six months. Even though they hadn't lived with Alan since they were little, can you imagine the pain they must've gone through, knowing that the possibility of ever seeing their father again was gone?

I quit using cocaine right then and there. After seeing what drugs could do to a person, and do to an entire family like that? I was done. Smoking pot was one thing, and drinking beer was another, but I was done with any kind of hard-core drugs. There was no way I would ever meet an end like Alan's.

As for how his death made me feel? My emotions? I guess I didn't really have any.

Emotions were one of the things I didn't have time for back then.

COMFORTABLY NUMB

I don't know how to explain this really, 'cause I've never really talked about it before, but the weirdest thing about wrestling was how numb it kept me.

I worked so much, and worked so hard, there just wasn't any time for personal feelings.

In those days, there was no Rock. There was no Stone Cold Steve Austin. When this thing took off, I was the main event seven days a week—twice on Saturdays and twice on Wednesdays—and never at the same venue. Even on those double-match days, I would hit the Philadelphia Spectrum for a 1:00 P.M. match and then wrestle up at the Boston Garden that very same night, or wherever.

And it never stopped.

I got on planes an average of three hundred days a year.

I'd hear flight attendants on the old Eastern Airlines complaining endlessly, "Oh, they've kept me running for nine days straight." And I'm sittin' there thinking, *I've been going for ninety-one days and I haven't had a day off yet!*

To really blow your mind, think about this: If I say I wrestled four hundred days a year, it's no exaggeration. My years were actually longer than 365 days.

The American audience had no idea that I was wrestling in Japan during the whole Hulkamania thing. There were times when I'd fly back and forth to Japan twice in a week just to wrestle. I used to complain about driving nine hours between matches in the Memphis territory. Now it was nothing to wrestle in Madison Square Garden one day, then fly all the way to the Egg Dome in Tokyo on the same day, 'cause you'd gain fourteen hours, and then fly back to the West Coast and hit San Francisco or L.A. before getting right back on a plane to fly to Narita International Airport before jumping on another plane to fly back to Boston.

So I could wrestle in Japan today and then fly back across the international date line and land in another town *yesterday*. I was constantly adding days to my years!

The thing was, in my mind, I couldn't slow down. Just like when I was working for peanuts back in Memphis, this job still had no security. There was no retirement plan or medical benefits. More than that, I was the top of the food chain, and every wrestler coming up wanted to dethrone the king. If I broke my leg tonight in Madison Square Garden, not only would I be left to tend to it at my own expense—and simply be out of a job until I could get myself back in the ring—but someone would try to replace me as America's big hero the next day.

But the biggest obligation that pushed me forward was the expectation of the fans. I mean, when this Hulkamania thing really took off, I don't mean to brag and say every night was sold out, but it was! It was like the Beatles or something. Which is crazy to say, but these giant stadiums were just packed every night of the week. There were screaming mobs wherever I went. And when you're six foot seven, there's nowhere to hide.

So when Marsha told me that Alan died, there was simply no time to react. *Okay, your brother died. Tomorrow you gotta be in Tokyo 'cause it's sold out, and the next day you gotta be in Osaka and then Boston Garden and then back in Kumamoto—they're all sold out.*

Instead of taking a month, or a week, or even a couple of days off to mourn and be with my family, I kept wrestling. Nonstop. It was like a fear that they were going to replace me. A blind instinct to just keep going.

Part of that instinct was driven by the fact that I couldn't believe none of the other wrestlers had caught on to what I was doing. *How come nobody else has figured it out yet?* Junkyard Dog couldn't figure it out. Rowdy Roddy Piper couldn't figure it out. Ultimate Warrior couldn't figure it out. Even André didn't quite get it—this whole thing of just getting the crowd involved and getting thousands of people to eat out of the palm of your hand. You didn't have to be a great wrestler. You just had to draw the crowd into the match. You just had to be totally aware, and really in the moment, and paying attention to the mood of the crowd.

For some reason I couldn't allow myself to be in the moment and totally aware when it came to paying attention to my personal life or my feelings and emotions. In the ring, though, that sense of control and presence came easy to me.

Looking back, I realize that it was much more than just my ability to work a crowd that kept me on top. It was the whole package: the blond hair, the tan body, the red and yellow. Even the fact that I claimed I came from Venice Beach, California—that was all just part of working the show, you know? I'd never even been to Venice Beach when I started using that line on the New York circuit, but I knew that image of California had an effect on people. It represented something. The American dream. Hollywood. All of it. So the whole idea that this bronzed god had emerged from Venice Beach, where all the musclemen lifted weights outdoors by the golden sand and the glistening ocean—it just made sense that crowds would get into that whole thing.

Of course, none of it was rocket science. Back then I was convinced that at any minute some other wrestler would emerge with an even better plan, an even better story, an even better gimmick that would win over the audience and make Hulk Hogan yesterday's news.

So I just kept going. I kept looking ahead to the next venue, the next match, the next TV spot or interview. I didn't live life for the present. I just kept living for the future. I stayed numb to my immediate surroundings. I stayed numb to what was happening in the here-and-now of my life.

As a result, it's not a stretch to say that I don't really remember half of my career.

People always come up to me with questions about the places I've been. Local journalists are notorious for that. "You've wrestled in St. Louis every couple of months for the last twenty-five years. Where are your favorite places to go?"

"Well, I've been to the Marriott and the arena and the airport." That was my answer.

People ask me about Paris or London, and it's the same thing: the airport, the hotel, and the arena.

I barely even stopped to marry my wife. Think about that. Think about how disconnected I was to not even bother slowing down to get married—to treat that commitment, that unbreakable bond, like a blip in an otherwise busy schedule.

That's what I did. In fact, I'm pretty sure I was married for about ten years before I ever took three days off in a row. It took that much dedication and drive to stay on top.

I just didn't think about the consequences that might have on my relationship with Linda.

CHAPTER 10

The Perfect Family

In the early days of Hulkamania, the thought of having kids didn't really cross our minds. Linda and I were newlyweds, and we were riding high.

Plus, for me, I knew we didn't have enough money saved. I still felt wrestling didn't bring any security. Even at the peak of this I was still scared that it was all gonna disappear at any moment.

So we just kept partying and reveling in all the fame and fortune we could. We were constantly getting on planes, going to the next photo shoot, hitting the next party or awards show or premiere. In fact, the first three years of our marriage we were hardly ever alone.

I remember one time I wrestled in Hawaii, and Linda and I decided to stay on and take a mini vacation at the hotel afterward. It was only a two-day break—but by the second day, Linda was so bored she was crawling out of her skin.

Times like those were when the early cracks in our marriage started to emerge. Especially that third year in.

There were times when Linda would start yelling at me for what seemed like no reason at all. She'd just suddenly start cussing up a storm and freaking out on me over the littlest things—like not being able to find her shoes, or if we forgot to pack something.

When it started happening frequently, I went to Linda's mother and asked her if she'd ever witnessed any of these anger issues in Linda before—and she acted like it was an everyday occurrence. "*You're* the one who married her," she said. She was practically laughing at me.

Thanks a lot, lady.

Those were my first glimpses of the mean streak Linda had in her—this thing that I think she inherited from her father, Joe, an ex-cop.

It was just one of many little secrets I learned about Linda and the Claridge family in the months and years after we married. Little bits of information kept trickling out—all of which were distressing to me, but none of which seemed too big to overcome when I took them on one at a time.

Remember the Corvette that Linda was driving when I met her? Right after we married I learned that she didn't own it outright. In fact, she was barely making the payments and needed my help. And that nail salon she supposedly owned? She was just a part owner, and the whole place was deep, deep in debt.

Linda didn't just have minor problems with her father, either—she had tremendous problems. They fought like cats and dogs when she was young. It got so bad, Linda left home when she was just a teenager and led a wild, rebellious life. One day she told me that she had sex with her PE teacher in high school. I'm not sure it was true, but I think she thought it was funny, or cool or something.

I didn't learn any of this crazy stuff until after she had that ring on her finger. By then, of course, I thought it was too late to do anything about it. So I figured I'd just have to live with it.

It got so bad, I remember having conversations with buddies of mine—like maybe it was time to leave her. Maybe this married life wasn't for me. My pal Ed Leslie (Brutus Beefcake) was in the middle of divorcing his first wife around the same time. He had joined the WWF, and we were even tag-team partners again at this point, and I remember wondering out loud with him if getting married was the wrong thing to do. "Linda and I always had so much fun just hanging out on the road together," I remember saying. "Maybe it should have stayed that way. Maybe getting married put a damper on things." All I knew was that she kept showing this angry side, and I couldn't figure out what on earth was making her so unhappy.

As the anger progressed over the years, there would be a few times when I wished I had done with Linda what I did with Donna—just taken the ring off her finger and told her she was free—but I always stopped myself. The thing is, if that had happened, then I wouldn't have Brooke and Nick in my life, and those kids are my whole world. So you can't second-guess these things. Everything happens for a reason, right?

It's funny, though—and I never really put this together until recently—those cracks in the marriage first started to show the same year that I lost my brother Alan.

More precisely, they started the same year that I stepped back from the fast lane—and Linda didn't.

It's more dramatic in retrospect than it was at that time in some ways. I mean, whenever we had a fight I would just get over it and move on. In my mind I'd always tell myself that it wasn't that bad. The fact is, I was proud to be married. I was proud to have my wife with me out on the road instead of a different girl-friend at every port or a bed full of floozy groupies after every match. And as long as we were rolling with it, Linda would con-stantly rise to the moment—climbing on that next airplane, driv-ing in a hot car, walking into the stadium to the cheers of fans who had lined up for hours to catch a glimpse of me. We still had lots of fun in those moments. The high of that would get her—and me—through most of the next couple of years.

But that was it. Once we were five years into this marriage, I noticed a real change in Linda. Traveling with Hulk Hogan was a blast for a while. I guess it got old.

I don't know. I've never been Hulk Hogan's wife. I've tried to put myself in Linda's shoes, though. When the arena's emptying out at eleven at night, and your husband's still in the shower 'cause he wrestled the very last match, and you're the last one there waiting, all by yourself? That shit *has* to get old after a while.

I understand why someone would get sick of seeing me tear my shirt off for the thousandth time, and there are only so many nights you can watch your husband drop a leg drop on an opponent and still get a kick out of it.

So we fought about it for a little bit, and we talked about it like two reasonable adults. Linda finally decided she just didn't want to be on the road anymore.

It made sense. We had some money in the bank. We had bought that nice townhouse down on Redington Beach and had relocated to Florida. We both agreed that not only was it the perfect time for Linda to stop following me around, it was time for us to start a family.

It felt good to be in sync about something like that. It's kind of how I always envisioned a marriage should work, you know? You go through changes in your life together, and adjust to new situations together, and make decisions together as a unit—and there were a lot of decisions to be made.

When Linda decided to stop taking birth control, I decided to stop taking steroids. I didn't know for sure if that would have any effect on a child or a pregnancy, but I didn't want to take that risk. With the whole thought of bringing a child into the world, I just wanted my body to be clean, you know? It just made common sense to me. Linda wanted the same thing. I quit smoking pot for a while. I had already quit the cocaine a couple of years earlier. Linda even quit drinking in order to start a family. We just wanted our bodies to be the best they could be, to give every chance to our child to be as healthy as he or she could be.

I guess it worked. Almost as soon as we started trying, we got very fortunate and Linda got pregnant with Brooke. We were both so excited. We felt so blessed, you know?

On May 5, 1988, on one of my rare days off, I was getting ready to go out for a ride in my boat when I got the call from Linda that she was on her way to the hospital. For Christmas Linda had bought me a phone for the boat—one of these big clunky cellular phones that you had to hang up on the wall of the boat like you'd hang a regular phone in your house. So right as I'm getting ready to put the boat in the water at the marina I get this call, and I rush back and meet her at the hospital.

It was seven, eight hours later when she delivered Brooke, who popped into the world weighing ten pounds. She was a big healthy baby. And when I held her for the first time, I found myself counting her fingers and toes. I just couldn't believe how perfect she was. She was our little girl.

Right then and there, life as I knew it ceased to exist.

All my priorities switched in an instant. Yes, I had to keep the Hulk Hogan persona happening, but now my number-one priority was to spend as much time with Brooke as I could. It's all I wanted to do. Somehow having a daughter made everything make sense.

When I say that I was running so hard I can't remember half of my career, I think part of the reason was that I didn't have a child in my life. Sometimes I sit back and wonder, *What the hell was I doing before Brooke came along?* It's like none of it meant anything, you know? All of a sudden, in 1988, my career actually *meant* something.

Handing Linda those checks every week meant more than just me and Linda saving money. Now it was me and Linda saving money for our kids, and me and Linda working hard for our kids. Whereas before it was more a self-satisfying type of thing, now we were doing this for someone other than ourselves.

It didn't make me any more aware as I was out on the road. I didn't suddenly slow down and take time to smell the roses. In fact, it actually made things worse because all I wanted to do was get home between matches and TV appearances. So that added even more flights to my already crazy schedule.

If I was wrestling in Louisiana one day and had a day off before wrestling at Madison Square Garden, instead of flying in a day early and actually getting a good night's sleep, maybe catching a workout and regrouping, I'd fly to Florida to spend half a day with Linda and baby Brooke before flying back up to New York.

Vince and the other wrestlers would freak out. "Why are you flying all the way to Florida for a couple of hours?" Sometimes that's truly all it would be. I'd land in the morning and get home by noon even if I had a flight to the West Coast that left that same night at five or six. Those two or three hours with Brooke and Linda in between trips to and from the airport meant the world to me. I'd do whatever it took to get home to them.

Honestly, those were some of the happiest times I can remember. Having a new baby just seemed to refocus everything in my life. Even as hard as it was to be traveling back and forth all the time, it didn't bother me. I was just so grateful to have Brooke that I would have done anything to keep our family happy.

After Brooke was born I went right back on the steroids. It was just a part of what I did. It's how I kept that big Hulk Hogan look. I smoked a joint now and then, too, and drank a few beers after coming out of the ring. I pretty much got back to the normal routine—as did Linda, who always favored her wine over any other kind of booze.

Linda went back on birth control, but it wasn't long before we started talking about wanting another child. We wanted Brooke to have a friend—to see her grow up with a little brother or sister.

It was all just talk, of course. We weren't going to rush into it. It wasn't a serious plan, and parenting is serious business. If we were gonna try again, I'd go off the steroids, quit smoking pot, quit drinking, the whole nine yards, and I expected Linda would stop drinking. We were both so happy that Brooke was born healthy and that Linda's pregnancy had gone so smoothly, it only made sense that we would take the same approach when it was time for baby number two.

Shortly after Brooke was born we bought a beautiful house on

Belleview Island, just west of Tampa on an actual island in the middle of the Intracoastal Waterway. We were basically pioneers out there and had almost the whole island to ourselves. Over time they'd put in a resort and like thirty other houses—all the construction noise would be one of the reasons we'd eventually move out—but we had one of the first properties there in this stunning location in the middle of the bay.

I loved coming home to that beautiful house, to my beautiful family. Until one day the weirdest thing happened.

I came back from wrestling one day toward the end of 1989 and walked into the house to find Linda's grandmother Nini was in for a visit.

"Did you hear the news?" Nini asked me.

"No, what news?" I said.

That's when she hit with me words I never expected to hear. "Linda's pregnant."

I laughed and said, "What do you mean Linda's pregnant?"

"Oh, yeah, Linda didn't tell you? She's pregnant."

I thought she was kidding around or something. "No, no, Linda didn't tell me she's pregnant," I said.

It wasn't a joke.

"Oh, yeah," Nini said. "Linda quit taking her birth control pills about six months ago. So she's pregnant!"

Can you imagine hearing something that important from your wife's grandmother? Can you imagine how it felt to have your wife just nonchalantly forget to tell you that she'd gone off the pill and was pregnant?

Dude, we had one of the biggest fights that night.

"Linda, why wouldn't you tell me? We were gonna plan this so I wouldn't take a shot of steroids. So I wouldn't smoke a joint. So I could get my system totally cleaned out. Why wouldn't you tell me?"

Linda started in with this "Oh, well, I thought we agreed."

"No!" I said. "The word 'thought'? You *thought*? We didn't agree. You just *thought* we did, Linda, because you know if you'd told me you were gonna quit taking your pills I wouldn't have had any alcohol or smoked a joint."

I mean, me doing something to *me* is one thing, but me doing something to my kid is another deal. Maybe I was just paranoid. Maybe steroids don't make any difference. Even if that were the case, and even if a little pot and a few beers wouldn't hurt the health of the baby at all, it doesn't matter. The fact is, it made a difference to me. Linda knew that. I guess she just didn't care.

For the first time, I felt like Linda had totally betrayed my trust. She had been having those outbursts, getting angry at me for seemingly no reason, but she had never broken my trust before. It took me a long time to get over that.

Nick came into the world on July 27, 1990, and when I held him for the first time I counted all ten of his fingers and all ten of his toes, just like I had done with baby Brooke. He was perfect. He was a perfectly healthy baby, despite my fears.

That pregnancy was definitely a struggle for Linda, though. There was something about how Nick was sitting in her stomach that cut off a lot of the feelings and nerves in Linda's legs. She had these big blue veins all through her inner thighs that she didn't have with Brooke, and she always complained that one leg hurt all the time.

She had a real hard go of it during the delivery, too. Nick wound up being delivered by C-section, and the doctors told us we almost lost Linda in the delivery room. It was a real close call.

Did the drugs and alcohol and steroids have anything to do with that? I can't really say. Either way that pregnancy took a major toll on Linda, and when it was all over she said, "That's it. No more kids."

I felt the same way. My God, we had two beautiful children. We had our dream family, you know? A beautiful boy and a beautiful girl. I was so thankful and we felt so blessed. And there's no way I would want to risk losing my wife in the delivery room.

So that was it. My family was complete. The four of us would go through this crazy adventure together.

The way I remember it, for years and years and *years* we were happy. Whenever I came home, it was all about those kids. We took vacations and headed over to Disney World and did all that stuff families are supposed to do together.

It's the little stuff that really sticks with me. Like with Nick, I'll always remember sitting there playing games with him while trying to feed him his eggs in the morning—putting them on the fork and doing the airplane noise. "Open the hangar!"

He was a real skinny kid, and he never wanted to eat anything. So when he'd eat dinner I'd put his green peas in rows and make smiley faces with them. I would just play games for hours trying to get that kid to eat.

Nick didn't have a growth spurt until he was eleven or twelve years old. I guess I shouldn't have worried. There was no need to rush it. Everything happens in its own time, and Nick's about two hundred pounds now and solid as can be.

I always worried, though. I guess that's just what fathers do. I worried for my kids. I worried for my family. All I wanted was the best for them, all the time. To make sure they had a life that was better than anything I was even capable of imagining when I was a kid.

And that meant more money.

When I wasn't home—which was most of the time—I was out chasing every angle I could to bring home more dough so that Linda and the kids could have everything they ever wanted.

But there was something I failed to understand at that point in my life. Something I failed to understand until all these years later: Putting all of your focus on "more, more, more" can wind up costing you, big-time, in the end.

PART III

TRIALS AND TRIBULATIONS

CHAPTER 11

Pain

Wrestling isn't fake. It's predetermined. **So what?**

We live in an era now where that grand revelation doesn't make any difference to the fans. Is there anyone who goes to a movie today who doesn't realize there were lots of digital special effects that went into making it? Look at so-called reality TV: It's still exploding in popularity even though most of the audiences are tuned in to the fact that a lot of what they're seeing isn't really "real." People love the drama and the characters, so they suspend their disbelief and enjoy it.

Some people get real mad at me for pointing out the obvious when it comes to this stuff. The fact is, professional wrestling is called "sports entertainment" for a reason, and at its best, it's some of the greatest entertainment in the world.

But let's be real clear about something: The matches may be predetermined; we may not be in there trying to kill each other for real—in fact, the main goal is to come out of that arena just as good as when you went in because you have to wrestle again the next night, and the next—but the blood, the broken bones, the brutal injuries that happen in that ring? Those, my brother, are as real as real gets.

I don't care how perfectly straight I lay you out, or how perfectly you've practiced landing in a way that breaks your fall, if I pick you up and body-slam you to the canvas, I guarantee you it's gonna hurt like hell.

From the day Matsuda broke my leg until now, not a day's gone by when I haven't been in some kind of pain.

I've torn through both of my biceps. My triceps are torn in three places. My back is uneven because the muscles never healed properly after I body-slammed André the Giant at WrestleMania III back in 1987. You can see ridges and divots all through my shoulders. I've even torn muscles in my butt.

I've had other nasty injuries, too. I got a trophy stuck through my chest out in Minnesota—there's an obvious scar from the hole it punched. I've even got bite marks on my thumbs from some of the old-school barbaric guys I faced on the road in the early days.

Yet for some reason people get all squeamish when they hear wrestlers talk about "blade jobs."

When that Mickey Rourke movie *The Wrestler* came out in 2008, everyone talked about that first scene in the ring where he pulled a razor blade from the tape on his wrist and made a little cut on his forehead for dramatic effect. Mickey really cut himself for that scene. There were no special effects at all. He totally over-dramatized the moment, though. He made such a big deal of it—cutting real slow, and wincing as he pressed the corner of the blade into his skin and the blood started to flow.

I couldn't help but laugh a little. In reality, a blade job is probably the least painful part of any match, and if anyone did it as slow as he did, the whole audience would spot it.

Remember Dusty Rhodes and how he rose up from the canvas in that very first match I saw with his whole white afro just a crimson mess? That guy was running a blade all over his head—not just a one-inch spot on his forehead. So how could I do anything less in my own career? Steal from the best, right?

For my own personal blade jobs, I always used an old-fashioned Blue Blade. I'd take time in the locker room to prepare it just right—cutting off a little corner of that blade, taping it up so just the very point was sticking above the tape. The whole thing was just a couple of centimeters wide. Rather than tape it to my wrist,

I'd usually hide the blade in my mouth. I can keep it right between my gum and my bottom lip, no problem. It got so comfortable over the years that sometimes I'd be out to dinner after a match before I realized I still had that blade in my mouth.

When it came time to use it, I'd wait for a moment when my opponent hit me in the face and I'd spit the razor blade into my hand. Then in one quick swipe, *zip!* I'd run it across my forehead. I challenge anyone to go back and catch me doing it on camera. I got real good at hitting the same spot, too—in this crease I have just below my hairline. I'd hit that river in the blink of an eye.

I actually had a problem sometimes because my forehead healed so easily. I'd be walking in the airport the next day and fans would see me and go, "See? He's not cut. They just use fake blood in the ring!" So I started wearing Band-Aids just for show, even though I didn't need them.

Blade jobs don't hurt. It's like getting a little cut when you're shaving. It bleeds like crazy, but it's not painful. If I really wanted to get the blood flowing, I'd press a little harder and zip it all the way across my forehead, from coast to coast. I'd go up in my hair and get the blood dripping down over my ears. Whatever it took to amp up the drama and get the crowd going.

To me, doing a blade job is like lacing up a boot. Easy. The hard stuff was when André would throw me over the top rope. I was never real good at going over the top rope. Way back in '78, I managed to hook my arm on the rope and swing my body in so my leg crashed right into the metal on the side of the ring. I had a blood clot like a baseball just sticking out of my leg for what seemed like forever.

That was nothing compared to the beating my knees took. The old wrestlers always told me to wear knee pads, but I just refused for the longest time. I thought it looked stupid to be wearing knee pads in the ring. When you lay a knee on an opponent with a knee pad on, how is that gonna look real to the fans? I should have listened, because it only took a couple of years before my knees starting giving me problems, and by 1988 I needed regular surgeries just to keep me walking.

Dropping down on an opponent to land my right knee to his chest or his neck or his head meant catching all of my body weight on my left knee. *Bang!* I had to support my weight so the knee that was hitting him wouldn't actually kill the guy, you know? So I blew that left knee out all the time.

Eventually I smartened up and put the knee pads on, but the closest I came to a career-ender was right when Hulkamania first blew up—on the night I won the belt from the Iron Sheik in 1984.

The stakes were so high that night, every move I made was over the top. Halfway through the match I jumped up in the air real high and dropped a knee in the Iron Sheik's chest. Even when the mat is perfectly flat it hurts, but that night there was a board in the ring that was out of place—the edge of that board was sticking up into the canvas—and that's exactly where my left knee landed.

I exploded my kneecap.

Here I was at Madison Square Garden, knowing I was going to win the world title. There's no way I wasn't going to finish that match. It was the ultimate high being in that ring, so I just pushed through the pain. A few minutes later when I couldn't take any more, I started Hulking Up—I hadn't really perfected that whole thing yet, but I had to do something to end that match quick. So I rallied my strength for everyone to see, and got ready for the finish, and I pulled the crowd right with me. With that kneecap totally blown, I laid the leg drop on the Sheik, and "One . . . Two . . . Three!" I won the title.

If all my teeth were knocked out—hell, if the Sheik had broken my leg like he was gonna get paid to do—I still would have found a way to finish that match somehow. Even when it was over, there was no way I could let anyone find out what happened. Showing weakness at that point could have meant the end of my career. There's no way Vince would have let me keep that belt if he knew I was lame. He would have switched up all of our plans and found another way to dominate the wrestling world. I have no doubt about that.

I remember going back to the hotel that night and telling Linda about it. We had only been married a little over a month at that point, but I needed her support. "You're not gonna believe this. My knee is totally blown." I'm sure she was scared to death. We'd just left Minnesota and started this whole new life. But I told her, "I'm not telling Vince," and she was 100 percent behind my decision.

So Vince never knew. I never let on that I was hurt, and I never let it slow me down for a moment.

Today's wrestlers, the new generation, if they tear a bicep it's "Whoa!" They go and get cut on (that's the phrase I use for surgery) immediately and sit out of commission for three, four months. Me? Like I said, I was the main event seven nights a week. There was no one else. So when I got hurt, I just iced it up, took some Motrin or an anti-inflammatory, wrapped it, and kept fighting.

Of course, if I wore a wrap into the ring, my opponent would go straight for that spot—knowing it was a point of weakness that could be easily attacked. The audience would eat that up. How could he not try to exploit it?

It was all a "work"—that term we use for making it look like you're killing a guy when you're really not hurting him much at all—but a work can still hurt, especially if it's not executed correctly. And if you're working a spot on the body that's already been hurt, chances are it's gonna get hurt worse.

After tearing all the muscles in my back at WrestleMania III, I wrestled the very next night in Tokyo. In fact, I wrestled for twenty-nine straight days after that match. No surgery. No therapy. Nothing.

I wasn't immune to pain. I could feel it as much as the next guy as far as I could tell. So I think my ability to put up with pain and push through it goes right back to that obsessive penchant I have for completing just about anything I set my mind to. Even if I'm dead wrong, once the switch flips and I've made up my mind about something, I won't deviate.

To put it another way: If I say "I'm gonna knock down that lamppost," I don't care if I have to keep hitting that pole till I knock it down with my head, that pole will come down.

Oddly enough, the wrestler who nearly put me in the grave was the Undertaker—and it wasn't even his fault.

In November of 1991, at the Joe Louis Arena in Detroit, we stepped into the ring for the championship title. It was a brilliant matchup. Good vs. evil. The red-and-yellow hero vs. this dark figure who rolled his eyes into the back of his head and looked like he'd walked straight out of the underworld.

The Undertaker has a big finish he calls the Tombstone—it's essentially a pile driver where he picks you up and flips you so your face is right in his crotch. He bear-hugs you in that position and then drops to his knees. It looks like your neck snaps. Up until that point, no wrestler had ever stood up after facing the Tombstone.

Well, in the middle of this match, the Undertaker laid that Tombstone on me, but I popped right up from the canvas while his back was turned. The audience went nuts. If you look at the tape, there were little kids in the arena dressed in red and yellow—I still had so much support. The fans desperately wanted to see me win, like always.

But I wasn't destined to win that night. We went in there knowing the Undertaker would walk away with the belt, and that he'd finish me off with yet another Tombstone—this time with a dirty twist.

The thing that made the Tombstone work was that the Undertaker stopped your head about a half inch above the canvas. There wasn't much room for error, but that was true of a lot of the moves we performed in the ring.

As the match progressed, suddenly Ric Flair walked down to ringside. I saw him out there and I taunted him, and when I wasn't looking—and the ref wasn't looking—Ric pushed a folding metal chair out onto the canvas.

The Undertaker grabbed me again, and flipped me over, and dropped my head on the metal chair in the nastiest Tombstone of all Tombstones.

That was all part of the plan.

What wasn't part of the plan was how hot it was in the arena that night. By that point, I was sweating like a pig. So whether my body was too slippery to hold, or I didn't hang on tight enough, or we both just miscalculated, I'm not sure, but when he dropped that Tombstone on me, my skull made contact with the chair. The jolt of the whole move threw my neck out.

My neck, calves, shoulders, biceps, triceps, forearms—everything went numb. Instantly. My trap muscles went up around my ears. It's like my body knew I was getting hurt, and responded to protect me.

It took a few minutes of lying there before I could even get my wits about me. Then, with help from some of the officials, I stood up and walked out of the arena—don't ask me how. It was probably an extremely dangerous thing to do. I wound up in the hospital for days, pressing the morphine button as many times as I could once the numbness subsided and the pain set in. It just ate away at me.

A series of medical consultants came in from the Mayo Clinic on down, and every doctor thought the danger of further paralysis was severe. They wanted to slice me open, but I wouldn't let them.

I still had that old mentality that getting cut on was the absolute last resort. So Linda finally helped get me out of there and down to see the head of the Florida Chiropractic Association, Doug Price, back in Tampa. Doug set me up with a deep-tissue massage therapist, and even then my shoulders stayed pressed up toward my neck for nearly three months. After about six months of hard work, I finally got back to some sense of normalcy.

The repercussions of that move have never gone away. The backs of my triceps are still a little numb, and I still can't feel anything in the tips of my fingers. I have trouble tying my bandanas on every day. I have trouble buttoning shirts.

Whenever I have X-rays taken, the doctors recommend that I get my neck fused. The wrestler John Cena had two fingers go numb after an injury and immediately went under the knife to get his neck fused. He's recommended it to me wholeheartedly. But to me, it's like, "My fingers are numb. Why on earth would I now want to go and willingly get my neck cut open?" Maybe it's a generational thing. I'm just one step closer to the old barbaric style of wrestling than all of these guys who've become superstars in recent years.

Or maybe I'm just too stubborn to listen. After all, I had a family to support, and any significant break from wrestling meant a significant break from the steady stream of income my wife had become accustomed to.

'ROID RAGE

You always hear the term "'roid rage"—referring to a supposedly unstoppable anger and fury that steroids bring out in their muscle-bound users. It's something people who've never used steroids tend to talk about and laugh about, as if it's a real phenomenon. The media make it out to be no laughing matter at all. They try to pin it on wrestlers who've taken their own lives—and in some cases taken their families' lives with them—when in fact, I can't think of one of those cases where the suicide victim didn't have lots and lots of other drugs in his system as well.

The fact is, I've been around more steroid users than the average person in my lifetime, and 'roid rage is something I have never, ever seen. It's certainly nothing I've ever felt.

I almost think it's some sort of an urban myth.

Anecdotally, all I can think about when I hear people use that term is this one particular wrestler who was 320 pounds of pure pumped-up muscle. Not an ounce of fat on him. He was just ripped. Every day in the locker room, he would pull out three rigs (that's the slang for needles), at 3 cc's apiece, and just pull 'em so full that the needles were wobbling. If ever there was a guy that was going to suffer some crazy side effects from steroids, he was that guy. Yet he was the sweetest, most soft-spoken, calm man I have ever met. I ran into him just a couple of years ago. He's working security now, since he hurt his back and had to leave the ring. He was still the same way. "Oh, hi, Mr. Bollea. Nice to see you."

The only aggressiveness those shots and pills ever laid on me was a powerful desire to lift weights and eat. Maybe it gave me a sort of "mat mania," where I was more pumped up than the next guy about getting back into the ring to wrestle. I'll certainly admit I was addicted to that high of being in the ring. But that's about it.

Taking testosterone made a lot of guys super horny, where they were chasing girls every night of the week. Not me. Others were rendered completely useless in the bedroom, and that wasn't me, either.

The worst thing I can say about steroids is they made me sweat a lot, which could be kind of embarrassing. They would occasionally give me killer acne—like I'd get a monster zit on my ass, the kind that's so tight you felt like you could bend over and shoot it across the room: "Hey, catch this!"

I always developed these ingrown hairs on my neck, too—these crazy welts that you can see in old pictures. It felt like if you squeezed one a whole palm tree would pop out. Even when they weren't ingrown, sometimes I'd grow hairs that were as thick as ten normal hairs put together. I'd pluck one out with a pair of tweezers and this giant round ball of a root would come out with it. *What the hell is that!?* I'd look in the mirror and there'd be a gaping bloody hole in my neck.

The worst side effect of steroids for me, though, wasn't anything physiological at all.

In 1988, the laws changed. Whether it was some twist in the never-ending War on Drugs or some other agenda, the federal government decided it was time to crack down on the use and distribution of steroids. They went after football players and weightlifters with the same kind of forcefulness the media has laid on professional baseball players in recent years. But that was nothing compared to the target the Feds tacked on professional wrestling.

Their Enemy No. 1 was Vince McMahon Jr.

I'm not sure why they had their sights set on Vince. Maybe it was his cocky attitude they didn't like. Maybe it's the way he muscled the WWF over every territory in the country like he was running some old-fashioned monopoly you'd read about from the Industrial Age. There's no faster way to draw jealousy and rage than to go out and be successful.

Or maybe they just thought Vince and the rest of us were a bunch of marks—that wrestlers were the low-class hicks of the sporting world who'd be too dumb to know how to fight back.

Whatever it was, they seemed intent on bringing Vince and his whole empire down. To do that, they needed Vince's number-one wrestler: me.

I first caught wind of what was happening in 1989 or 1990. I called up Dr. Zahorian one day—the wrestling world's go-to doc in Harrisville—and as soon as I said hello he said, "I can't talk to you," and he hung up the phone. I called back again, and no one answered.

Dr. Zahorian was a real nice guy. We actually became friends, and used to talk on the phone now and then about things that had nothing to do with what drugs I needed. Just a couple of weeks before this he had been asking my recommendation for the best video camera to buy because his three little girls had a ballet recital coming up.

He was the man who had whatever we needed. He'd show up in the locker rooms with his two little black briefcases full of testosterone, Anavar, growth hormone, pain pills. He'd give us a hundred Valium in a little unmarked matchbox-type container if we needed them. You could always call ahead so he'd have what you needed whenever you blew through town.

A couple of days later I mentioned the hangup to Pat Patterson, who had become Vince McMahon's agent by then, and he told me, "Don't talk to Zahorian anymore. He's in a lot of trouble. There's an investigation . . ."

I knew right then this gravy train had come to an end.

We had all been real careful. We kept using steroids after the 1988 laws were passed, but strictly under doctor's orders. Zahorian examined us and kept track of everything for us. There was no more going out with a prescription for one bottle and buying ten more off the street. But even that wouldn't last for long.

What I couldn't understand at all was that the Feds wound up going after Vince for something that wasn't even true: They claimed that he was distributing steroids and forcing every wrestler in the WWF to take them or be fired.

I was Vince's best friend, his partner in crime. There was no way they could nail him without my help. Vince was freaking out. "You have to disappear, Terry. Now!" So I actually hid out upstairs at Vince's house for a couple of months while this whole controversy swirled around. I left Linda alone at our house in Stamford, until finally I said, "This is ridiculous," and I came out and got sucked into the whole tornado.

All of a sudden, the press started calling me a suspected steroid addict. So much for my "prayers and vitamins" reputation.

Trials take a long time. Zahorian's trial didn't happen until 1991. So for two years I watched as the Hulk Hogan name was dragged through the mud.

Finally, I couldn't take it anymore. I felt the need to defend my name, and I thought the best way to do that would be to go on TV. Arsenio Hall had the hottest TV show at the time. It's the show Bill Clinton went on to show off his saxophone playing—a move that many consider crucial to his winning broad support from a younger generation of voters. So there was no doubt *Arsenio* was the place to go when you wanted to be heard in those days.

Vince didn't want me to do it. My lawyers didn't want me to do it. I guess maybe I should have listened. I didn't have a publicist in those days. I don't even think I knew what a publicist was. So I did what I thought was best.

That summer of 1991, in front of millions of viewers—not to mention the millions more who would read about it in the papers the next day—Arsenio asked me if I was using anabolic steroids.

I said, "No, I'm not."

I told the truth—but I wasn't being honest. I told the truth in so far as I wasn't using anabolic steroids right at that moment. I might have been using them three weeks ago, but I wasn't using them right then.

I was playing with words.

I talked about how big I'd always been. I held up a photo of me from my Little League days. I went on and on about how long and hard I'd worked out to gain this physique. All of that was true! But it wasn't honest. There's a big difference.

And it only made my problems worse.

I should have told the whole story. I should have apologized for making a mistake. Instead, I was calculated and deceptive, and it came back to bite me.

In 1992 I quit using steroids entirely. It just wasn't worth it anymore. The public humiliation, the cover-up—I'd just have to work out hard like I always did and hope that the edge I always felt in the ring didn't shrink away like my muscle mass.

If I had just owned up to it, I could have moved on.

Instead, the humiliation of being called a steroid addict would follow me through most of the decade.

THUNDER

The federal investigation got so heavy between 1991 and Vince's indictment in 1993, it tore Vince and me apart. It tore the entire WWF apart. Nobody has enough money to fight the federal government.

It felt like everything I knew about the business was crumbling at my feet as this investigation kept getting bigger. Everyone was so nervous and scared, it started to feel dangerous. Vince was distancing himself from me, which I understood—he didn't need any additional heat from the Feds because of the heat I had taken in the press after my *Arsenio* lies—but I had this real weird feeling that Vince might do more than that. I felt like I was a lamb being led to slaughter.

My fear seemed almost irrational at first. I just had this instinct that Vince might try to deflect the charges and flip the whole focus of the investigation on me. As if I were the one distributing steroids to everyone in the WWF.

At the same time, the pain I was in from all those injuries had really started to catch up to me. I was hobbling more and more on my left knee, and my hip was hurting. It reached a point where I had no choice but to get cut on, and once you start down that road, it seems like one surgery just leads to another, and another.

I had some additional pain from outside the ring, too—like when I was out Jet-Skiing with some buddies and I fell in the water and got slammed by one of those massive machines right in the face. The impact broke both of my eye sockets, but I was out there wrestling just a few days later with a hundred stitches and my face all swollen up.

How long can a guy do that?

Combine all that fear and instinct and pain with my damaged reputation, and it just seemed to me like the universe was telling me it was time to stop wrestling and try something new.

I bowed out of the WWF as gracefully as I could in 1993. At that point, I didn't think I ever wanted to come back. I wanted to find a way to stay in one place. I wanted to spend more time at home with my wife and kids. And the perfect opportunity to do that landed right in my lap.

The creators of *Baywatch*, which was a huge franchise at the time, had asked me to coproduce and star in a new TV show called *Thunder in Paradise*, to be shot at the Disney Studios in Orlando. I had a bit more acting experience under my belt by then—starring in *No Holds Barred*, *Suburban Commando*, and *Mr. Nanny*—and I enjoyed the process of movie-making. So I figured I'd enjoy making a weekly one-hour drama.

Brother, I could not have been more wrong. Filming one of those shows is just a nonstop series of eighteen-hour days. That's no exaggeration. It was compounded by the fact that I was an active executive producer on this thing, so I had to deal with key grips coming in from L.A. and problems with the catering and every little thing under the sun. All of that was in addition to trying to memorize ten to fifteen pages of dialogue per day. My brain couldn't take it. My head was spinning. I had to put cheat sheets all over the set.

In the meantime, something really fascinating was happening in the wrestling world: Vince McMahon's WWF was facing its first major competitor.

Media mogul Ted Turner and a real smart guy named Eric Bischoff had launched a televised wrestling program called the WCW—World Championship Wrestling—and with Vince mixed up in a federal investigation, they exploited the whole fiasco. They stole some of the WWF's best wrestlers—and they stole some of the WWF's big audience.

All they needed was a Hulk Hogan, and there was no doubt they could knock McMahon's socks off.

Strangely enough, the WCW filmed their matches on the very same Disney lot as *Thunder in Paradise*. I was in Studio A. They were in Studio B. Small world, right? It wasn't long before Eric Bischoff and his buddy, former WWF superstar Ric Flair, started paying me visits.

"Hey, Hulk, we have all these tourists coming through on the Disney tours, and they see the wrestling ring, and the first thing they ask is if they might get a glimpse of Hulk Hogan!" they said.

They started giving me the sales pitch, about how big the WCW was getting, and how we could walk right over Vince McMahon if we all worked together.

The thing was, I really thought I was done with wrestling. My reputation was so damaged, and I was just so hurt and tired. I basically ignored them and kept plugging away at this TV show—until a little situation with Linda forced me to rethink my current career choices entirely.

HOME SWEET HOMES

As if my career meltdown and the stress of working on *Thunder in Paradise* weren't enough, it was right in the middle of those years when Linda first started complaining about living in Florida. I'm not sure if she was suddenly homesick in her mid-thirties or if she thought she'd get more help raising the kids being close to her mom in L.A., but she kept insisting that we needed to move to California.

It's a theme that Linda would never let go of for the rest of our marriage.

We had this beautiful home on Belleview Island, but Linda insisted we needed to at least give it a try. Her mother was always dabbling in real estate and actually had a house not far from her own that she offered to rent to us. I wanted Linda to be happy, so I said yes, and we wound up bouncing the whole family back and forth between these houses in Florida and L.A. (The kids weren't in school yet, which made it easy to do.)

I wound up paying like eight or nine grand a month for this house we rented from Linda's mom in this gated community called Ridgegate—only to find out later that her mother's mortgage payment was less than half of what we were being charged for rent.

Her mom also asked me if I could front her the money to put a pool in back of that house. She said she would pay me back after we moved out and she sold the place. So I forked over about fifty to sixty thousand dollars to build this unbelievable pool, with hot and cold running waterfalls. Just gorgeous. Of course, I never got anything in return.

Money matters aside, the fact was, my wrestling business— and even *Thunder in Paradise*—was based on the East Coast. Linda knew that. Living in California only meant more traveling and longer plane rides than I had already endured all those years trying to get back to be with her and the kids. She didn't care. And her mother was there backing her up all the time. "I don't understand why you don't sell that place in Florida and just move here?"

Whenever we were in that rented house in L.A., the moment I would come downstairs I'd be hit with Linda's mother or grand-mother or someone telling me about all these things I should be doing. All I'd want to do was get to the gym and have some sort of a normal routine, but Linda's family was always in the house.

The bickering with Linda and her sudden tantrums turned a corner in those years for some reason, too. Even way back then she started throwing out the word "divorce" when she was yelling at me about something. "Well, why don't we get divorced and then you can stay in Florida all you want!"

There were times when it seemed like nothing I did would make her happy. She seemed to complain all the time, about ev-erything. I remember one day we went to the beach and it was a little bit windy, and she said, "I hate the fucking wind."

How does somebody hate the wind?

I was a complainer, too, don't get me wrong. I was complaining about wrestling, complaining about money, complaining about the Feds, complaining about the rift with Vince, complaining about the eighteen-hour days on the TV show, complaining about how the fans had turned on me. It's real easy when two people are in a marriage to start bolstering the worst aspects of each other's personalities instead of fostering the best part of the two people who got into this bond in the first place. Before you know it, you're complaining about your significant other and all of their faults to your friends and family and anyone who'll listen.

That is not a good way to live.

Marriage for me was a lifelong bond, though. Even though I barely took a day off from wrestling to get married to Linda, I loved her. In fact, I was crazy about her. And despite all the prob-lems I just wanted to do whatever I could to make her happy. I wanted to find some way to bring back that old bubbly, shiny per-sonality that had blown me away the first time we spoke at the Red Onion.

Right after I left the WWF, just as I was getting ready to start *Thunder in Paradise*, the thing that Linda said would make her more happy than anything else—the thing that would allow her to live in Florida, which would allow me to spend more time at home, which is what I really wanted more than anything else in the world—was if she could have the money to build her dream house.

Fine. Done. If it would make Linda happy, that sounded like a great deal to me.

So we bought a piece of property on Willadel Drive, in the Belleair neighborhood of Clearwater—the town's poshest spot. It's a neighborhood where Lisa Marie Presley had lived, and where Kirstie Alley had a place, and where John Travolta and Kelly Preston lived before they moved to that spot in Ocala where he lands jumbo jets in his own front yard. (On a side note: Yes, those names are all associated with Scientology. Clearwater's the big center for the Church of Scientology. I've never been pulled in that direction at all. They've tried. Representatives of that church have been after me for years, but I just never went down that road. There were no other reasons behind our selection of that neighborhood than the fact that it was absolutely beautiful.)

In the end, we spent $2 million on a house just to tear it down. It was a stunning location, right on the corner of this cove with a private boat dock exclusively for the neighborhood's residents. The plan was to build Linda's seven-thousand-foot dream on the footprint of that big old house.

One contractor started the job but was on the job for only six months before another contractor took over. And the contractor who took over? Linda's brother.

I would wind up putting millions and millions into the Claridge family's pockets before I was through with this marriage.

Just before construction was set to start, I paced the footers and did the math in my head, and I couldn't figure out what had gone awry. The way I figured it, this house that was laid out in the dirt there wasn't seven or eight thousand square feet—it was more like twenty thousand!

I asked Linda what was up, and she said, "Oh, I talked to my mom, and my mom said, well, if we're building a house and making all the rooms, why not make each room four, five feet longer. It won't make a difference anyway."

Well, it did make a difference. The next time I showed up at the work site, instead of seeing a wooden frame going up, I saw I-beams—the same steel beams that you'd use to build a skyscraper.

The whole look of the home was like a Tudor style, French country house kind of a look. Which is interesting, since Linda's parents' house was a Tudor-style home. Linda decided she needed to go 100 percent authentic, so she started flying in these four-hundred-year-old roof tiles from France.

She tore down three French châlets to get this authentic French farmhouse-style roof, when at the end of the day you could've bought a tile roof here that looked exactly the same for a quarter of the price. Not good enough. This was Linda's dream. She even flew over extra tiles, so we have crates and crates of them in storage just in case, God forbid, a hurricane ever blows that roof off.

All the doors are thick and hand-carved. Everything is custom. The pool is gorgeous. My gym was perfect. Don't get me wrong, I love that house, and I miss it every single day. But we were about midway through construction with bills mounting up to our ears when Eric Bischoff and Ric Flair came poking around the *Thunder* set.

The thing is, once I left the WWF I really thought I was through with wrestling. Even though the one-hour TV drama was too grueling a schedule for me to take, I would have found some other way to make a living had we just kept the home on Belleview Island.

I knew that nothing could bring me income the way wrestling did. Movies, TV shows, endorsements, none of them were nearly as lucrative as selling out Madison Square Garden in a pay-per-view special. Not even close.

So I took a look around at this massive house, and I remember saying to myself, "You know what? I better go back to work."

TOP LEFT: Who could have imagined that this little guy would grow up to be the Hulkster? *(Courtesy of the author)*

TOP RIGHT: Not only was I taller than all the other kids in Little League, I was taller than the coach! My size helped me hit, but I couldn't run, and my head was too big for most of the helmets. *(Courtesy of the author)*

Look at the size of those guns! This was 1980, at
the peak of my juiced-up, bronzed-god look.
(*Courtesy of* Pro Wrestling Illustrated)

January 23, 1984. Madison Square Garden. The
first time I took home the championship belt,
defeating the Iron Sheik. You can see the uneven
floorboards in the ring where I shattered my
kneecap. *(Courtesy of World Wrestling Entertainment)*

I'm still the only professional wrestler to ever appear on the cover of *Sports Illustrated. (Courtesy of* Sports Illustrated/*Getty Images)*

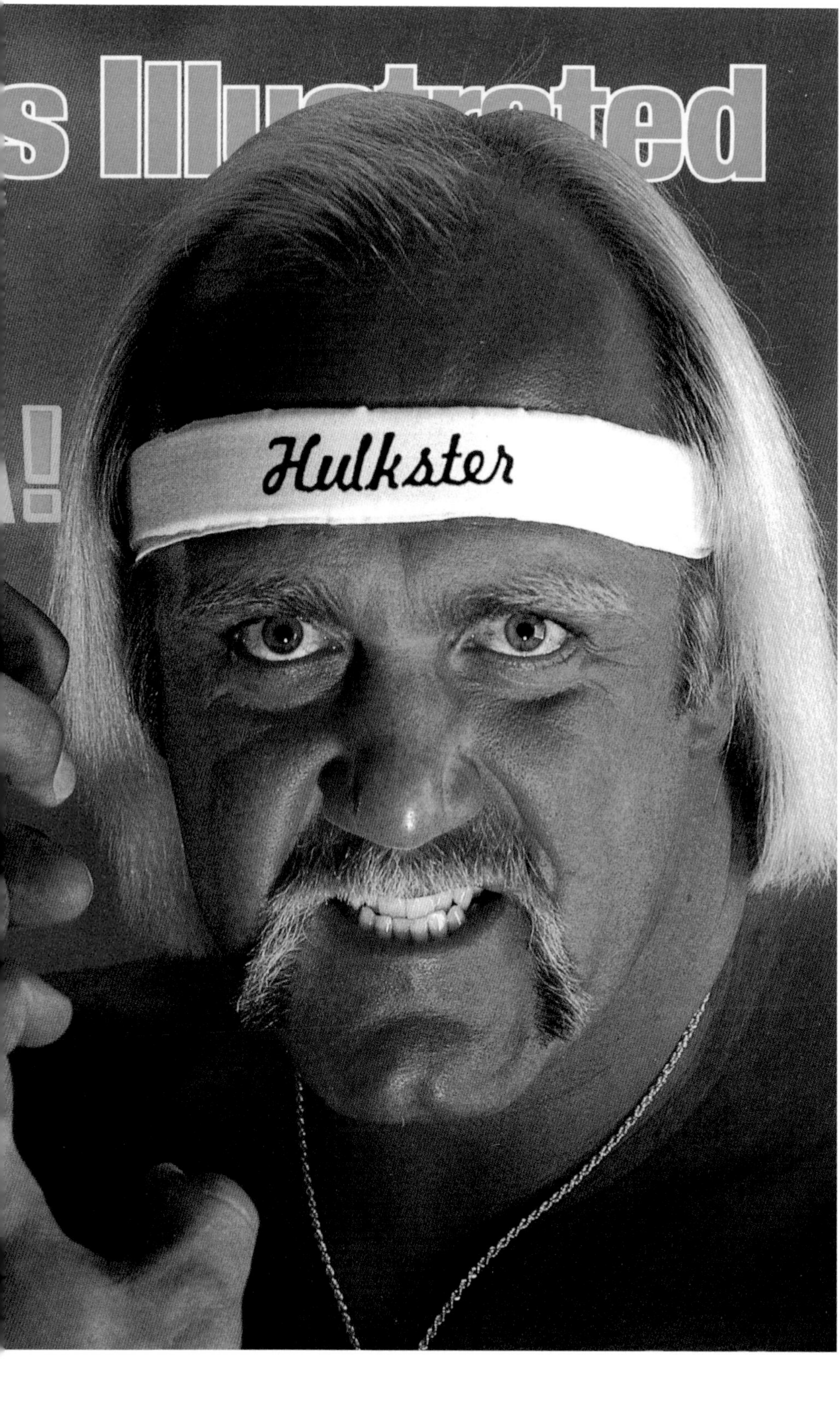
Hulkster

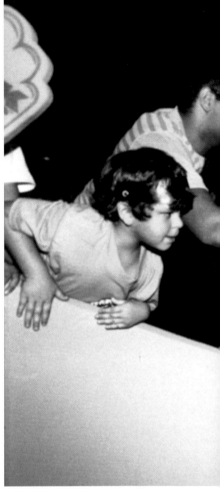

"Bigger! Better! Badder!" was the theme when I took on André the Giant for the World Heavy-weight Championship at WrestleMania III in 1987. Look at the size of that guy! No wonder I tore my back to shreds when I bodyslammed him. *(Courtesy of World Wrestling Entertainment)*

Even with the shadow of the steroid scandal growing, fans went nuts when I won the Royal Rumble at the Miami Arena in 1991. *(Courtesy of Acey Harper/Time Life Pictures/Getty Images)*

Nick was just a year old and Brooke was three when this photo was taken at our home on Belleview Island in 1991. Those were pretty happy times for all of us. *(Courtesy of Acey Harper/Time Life Pictures/Getty Images)*

I truly thought my marriage to Linda would last forever. *(Courtesy of Acey Harper/Time Life Pictures/Getty Images)*

WrestleMania IX in 1993 marked my brief return to the WWF, alongside my tag-team partner and longtime pal Brutus Beefcake. And that's Mouth of the South Jimmy Hart in the flashy jacket. They're two of my absolute closest friends to this day. *(Courtesy of World Wrestling Entertainment)*

The ultimate heel! Hollywood Hulk Hogan. This was WrestleMania XVIII, March 17, 2002, at the SkyDome in Toronto—the night I battled the Rock. *(Courtesy of George Pimentel/WireImage)*

On April 2, 2005, Sly Stallone himself inducted me into the WWE Hall of Fame—and Vince McMahon Jr. was right there by my side. That's a lot of history in one photo! *(Courtesy of Frazer Harrison/Getty Images)*

"The Legend vs. The Icon." I was a bloody mess by the time I laid the leg drop on Shawn Michaels to win SummerSlam 2005. The bad news? All those leg drops over the years hurt my spine far worse than they ever hurt my opponents. *(Courtesy of World Wrestling Entertainment)*

TOP: We all had fun enjoying the sudden success of *Hogan Knows Best*. But in private, by the time we arrived at the Teen Choice Awards in 2005 I was already struggling to keep my family together. *(Courtesy of Frazer Harrison/Getty Images)*

BOTTOM: The fiberglass shell of Nick's Toyota Supra crumpled when it hit that palm tree. But all the pictures in the media, like this one, were taken after rescue crews tore the car apart with the Jaws of Life. So it looks worse than it actually was. *(Courtesy of Tim Boyles/Getty Images)*

With Jennifer I've found a whole new happiness.
She's been my light going on two years now.
(Courtesy of the author)

If it hadn't been for that house, I honestly believe I would've retired from wrestling completely.

In the end, I forked over somewhere around $14 million to get that house completed, the vast majority of which went to Linda's brother.

Fast-forwarding a bit, a few years later Linda still insisted that she needed a home in California. She wanted to live there in the summers, and go back and forth whenever she had time. So I forked over another $4.5 million for a gorgeous place in Thousand Oaks—right next to where Heather Locklear lives.

After that Linda wanted a little retreat on the sand, away from the big house, but somewhere nearby in Florida as well so she could try out a whole different decorating scheme. So we bought a house on Clearwater Beach with nothing but sand between us and the ocean, and she filled it with tartan-plaid carpet and paisley wallpaper on the ceilings.

Of course, Gail Claridge Interiors—the home furnishings and furniture store that's owned by none other than Linda's mother—furnished all of these homes. Guess who's always been her best customer? Moi.

From the early 1990s through the end of our marriage, Linda kept jonesing for real estate. It was just so weird. We'd stop in Vegas and she'd suddenly be out looking at properties to buy, saying how great it would be to own a home in that desert. We'd blow through Atlanta and she'd suddenly be out looking at properties in Atlanta's posh suburbs. I swear if we had gone to Alaska she would have spent a day driving around looking to buy a high-end igloo. It just never stopped.

Anyway, it was Linda's dream house that made me change my mind and start talking seriously with the WCW.

At a time in my career when even Ted Turner himself thought the Hulk Hogan name had been too tarnished by the steroid scandal to transfer over to his organization, Eric Bischoff, Ric Flair, and a guy named Bill Shaw stood up for me. As the dark cloud of Vince McMahon Jr.'s federal trial loomed in early 1994, they truly believed in me and fought for me. "We're fans," they said to the powers that be, "and we think the rest of Hulk Hogan's fans are more loyal than to let this controversy keep him from the ring."

I certainly hoped they were right.

Once Vince's trial finally began at the U.S. District Court in Uniondale, New York, in the summer of 1994, I was set to be called as the prosecution's star witness. When I found out what the charges against him were the year before, I told him, "We've got nothing to hide!" I honestly didn't think he had anything to be scared about. He just couldn't believe I would go up there as a witness for the prosecution, though. I had no choice! But he was so angry. I guess he thought I was gonna make up lies to hurt him, which wasn't the case at all. Vince was my hero. He's the guy who opened up this whole universe for me. Why would I do anything to hurt him?

I made sure I had full immunity in exchange for my testimony, of course. I wasn't a fool. Then all I did was tell the truth—a truth the federal prosecutors didn't want to hear.

The night before the trial I got a taste of why Vince was so nervous. I was sound asleep at the Marriott across from the Nassau Civic Center—right by the courthouse—when someone started pounding at my door. I woke up in a start and rolled over and looked at the clock. It was 2:00 A.M.

"Who's there?" I asked.

It was two of the federal prosecutors on the case. They seemed worried about how the case was going. They wanted to go over my testimony and were hoping to get some control over the situation, so they walked me through what they expected I would say: about buying steroids from Vince, and how he shot me up, and how he sold steroids to all the other wrestlers, and how steroids were a job requirement in the WWF. The gist of the conversation was that they had spent millions on this case, and they needed me to hit the ball out of the park for them. Maybe I was just nervous, or overthinking the situation, but the whole scene in the middle of the night seemed like something out of *The Godfather* to me. I was scared to death. So I yessed them as much as I could just to get them to leave, even though the things they seemed to be counting on me saying didn't match the whole truth that I knew and expected to share in that courtroom.

As they left, they said they would pick me up in the morning to make sure I got to the courtroom on time. The moment they were gone I called my entertainment attorney, Henry Holmes, and his response was simple, "Bullshit!" He came to my hotel before sunrise and made sure I was out of there before the prosecutors could come back.

Outside the courthouse that day, it looked like a scene from the O.J. trial. The parking lot was just a sea of satellite news trucks. I had never encountered anything like it.

I still had this instinct that Vince was somehow going to try to flip the whole case and blame it on me. I had no idea how he would do that, but I just thought it would be an easy way out if he pointed a finger at Hulk Hogan and let the media run wild.

My instinct was right. As I walked into that courtroom, I looked over and saw my mule—the guy who used to carry drugs and steroids for me on the road—sitting right next to Vince and Vince's attorney. *Why is* he *here?* I wondered. If my testimony hurt Vince, I have no doubt that they would have used my mule to tell every tall tale in the book about my steroid use and how I was running them all over the country, or selling them, or forcing them on my opponents. This mule must have been there as a backup to crush my credibility. That would have meant the end of my career. Forever.

Vince truly had nothing to worry about. On the witness stand the Feds asked me if Vince had ever sold me steroids. I answered, "No." They asked me if he had ever injected me with steroids. "No." I even explained to them how I wouldn't trust anyone else to stick a needle in me because I'd stuck myself a thousand times and knew how to do it without hitting any nerves. I would never trust Vince to stick a needle in me!

They asked me about every angle of their entire case, from Zahorian's role to Vince's secretary's role. I answered honestly about everything. The fact was, *I* had introduced Vince to steroids during the filming of *No Holds Barred,* the movie we wrote together in a forty-eight-hour run down in Florida, and I testified to that fact. I also spoke about how I shared steroids with Vince, and Vince shared steroids with me—the same way two buddies might share cigarettes. That's as far as it ever went.

Vince hadn't done anything differently than any of the rest of us. He wasn't distributing steroids. If they were gonna put him in jail, then they needed to put every single wrestler in jail along with him. I said that on the witness stand.

The prosecutors were dumbfounded. And dude, the moment the judge dismissed me I slipped out of that courtroom through a side door, hopped in a cab to Teterboro Airport, and chartered a plane down to Florida as fast as I possibly could. I didn't go back to New York for five years. I was scared to death that those Feds would find a way to arrest me or put a hit on me, or something. Even when I was with the WCW, no one in New York had a chance to see me wrestle in the flesh—I wouldn't show up at those New York arenas. I was just too scared.

It was worth it, though. There is no better feeling than telling the truth, no matter how much it hurts and what terrible repercussions it might bring.

The truth I told on that witness stand that day was the reason that Vince McMahon Jr. walked away a free man, and that's all I ever wanted to see.

How did Vince thank me in return? He stood on the steps of that courthouse, in front of all of those microphones and cameras and satellite trucks, and he buried me. "I'm happy with the verdict," he said, "but I wish Hulk Hogan had told the truth." What did he mean by that? I had told the truth.

It only further proved to me that my instincts were right: If it came down to it, Vince was willing to throw Hulk Hogan under a bus to clear his own name. When he didn't get a chance to do it in the courtroom, he did it in the court of public opinion.

By then, Vince knew I was going over to wrestle for his competition. "It was just business," Vince would say years later when I asked him why he did that to me.

Well, I guess my taking the Hulk Hogan phenomenon over to the WCW was just business, too, Vince.

Just business.

Three days after testifying in New York, I wrestled Ric Flair for the WCW championship belt. The Bash on the Beach was a massive success—even though fans held up signs saying HOGAN, DID YOU TAKE YOUR SHOTS TODAY? and DON'T LEAVE HOME WITHOUT YOUR STEROIDS!

Like I said, I had stopped using steroids by 1992—but that's the lesson I learned the hardest way possible about the media, and how a trickle of a lie can snowball into an avalanche. Once that trickle gets started, the way it did with my *Arsenio* comments, there's no way to stop it. All you can do is ride it out and hope you don't get buried so deep that you're lost forever.

Over time, the taunts from the fans went away. As my massive bulk from the steroids went away, too, something really strange happened: I actually started to look better on camera. I didn't know anything about how cameras and lighting work on a body when I set out to develop my twenty-four-inch guns back in 1976. Nearly twenty years later, I started to notice that it was all about proportions. As my steroid-free waist got a little bit thinner in proportion to my shoulders, I actually looked bigger on-screen. With the water weight gone, my muscles just had a more ripped and powerful-looking appearance than they ever did before. And I put that lean-mean power look to good use.

I blew the roof off of the WCW. The audience exploded. For a long time, we absolutely crushed Vince McMahon in the ratings.

Better still, with the help of Eric Bischoff I started to make far more money than I ever made with Vince and the WWF. I had a bigger cut of every T-shirt and piece of merchandise that was sold, I was sharing in revenues from broadcasts, I had a bigger cut of the gate at the arenas. For the first time in my whole career, I could finally look out at a stadium full of people who were there to see me and know that I was getting my fair share of that massive revenue that was walking in the door every night. That's a tremendous feeling.

Like I said before: All I wanted to do was to give my family every opportunity to have whatever they desired in life. Ever since that first moment when I held baby Brooke in my arms, this was all for them. To know that I was going to be able to give them more than ever? That was a rush.

CHAPTER 12

Behind Closed Doors

While the shadow of steroids hung over my public persona through the mid-1990s, a much darker cloud hung over my personal life.

On Christmas Day 1994, a process server handed me a letter from a woman named Kate Kennedy. In that letter she claimed that I had sexually assaulted her, and she demanded three things: that I write an apology and publish it in *USA Today*; that I complete some sort of sexual rehabilitation class; and that I pay her one million dollars.

Some of this hit the press. A lot of it became all too familiar to radio listeners in the Minneapolis area, where Jesse Ventura had a radio show back then and just beat this whole situation to death over the airwaves. The public humiliation of being charged with something like that wasn't the worst part, though.

The worst part was the thorn it drove into my marriage.

It went down like this: Kate Kennedy worked for and managed the merchandise at Hulk Hogan's Pastamania, a fast-food restaurant I had opened at the Mall of America. It was one of many ventures I lent my name to as a way to keep money flowing in without getting hit over the head with a chair. I knew a day would eventually come when I could no longer wrestle. I wanted to be prepared.

After one of the WCW's big *Monday Nitro* matches in Minneapolis, Kate Kennedy and her fiancé, a local police officer, came out partying with a bunch of us. We went to a bar, and I sat in with a local band and played a few tunes. (I still play guitar and bass now and then.) After a while we turned it into a typical wrestler's night—hitting the hotel for some beers.

Some time in the wee hours of the morning, Kate and her Minneapolis police officer fiancé called it a night and left. I said good-bye to both of them.

I remember noticing that we only had about three hours to sleep before we had to catch a flight that morning, so I went back to my hotel room to start packing.

That's when Kate showed up again.

Her lawsuit against me was eventually settled, and part of that settlement involved the signing of confidentiality agreements.

I can't get into the details of what happened.

All I can tell you about is the fallout.

When I first received that letter from Kate Kennedy's attorney, I was so scared about how Linda would react that I didn't tell her. I went for a whole year without telling her. Two Christmases passed. After I went through the second Christmas without smiling, Linda saw how down in the dumps I was and she started pressing me for answers.

A man can only keep something from his wife for so long. So I finally broke down and told her exactly what happened. I didn't hold anything back. I let her hear it all.

At first, Linda was really, really angry with Kate Kennedy. This was a woman Linda had befriended and personally approved to work for Pastamania. She couldn't believe she was about to put our family through this ordeal, and she encouraged me to fight back—which I did, with great success, in 1996.

Eventually, though, the inevitable happened, and Linda got really angry with me. She threw the word "divorce" around, loud and often, for months on end, and even though Linda didn't follow through with her threat, not a week went by for the whole rest of our marriage that she didn't bring up the Kate Kennedy fiasco at least once.

I don't blame Linda for being angry. There is no excuse for my getting into a situation like that—no matter what happened in that hotel room.

But the problem in Linda's eyes was much bigger than just that incident. When this happened, Linda finally had the proof she had been after for years: proof, at least in her eyes, that all of her long-standing suspicions about me cheating must be true.

Almost from the outset of our marriage Linda was sure that I was cheating with some girl or another. It never made any sense to me. I'm just not the cheating kind.

In the early days I met Drew Barrymore in passing at a party once—I think Drew was still a teenager at that point—and Linda accused me of having an affair with her. Can you imagine? Another time in the '80s, Vince threw a gigantic birthday party for Pat Patterson at the Twin Towers, and right in the middle of dinner someone came up and told me that Cher had sent a limo for me; she was throwing her own big party in Manhattan that night, and she wanted Hulk Hogan to join her. I had never even met Cher, but rather than laughing about how bizarre it was, Linda accused me right then and there of carrying on an affair with Cher. *Cher!*

The suspicion and jealousy even affected my career. She got so crazy over this stuff, I was actually afraid to leave home for four or five months to make a movie. I feared that Linda might be gone when I got back. So I turned down some major stuff: the lead in *Highlander*, the role of Little John in *Robin Hood: Men in Tights*, and through the *Baywatch* guys I had an offer to make a movie with Pamela Anderson, when she was just red-hot. I really messed that one up. I had gone out and bought a copy of the *Playboy* magazine she posed in. Before I even had a chance to look at it,

Linda saw that and said, "That's it! There's no way you're goin' to make that movie!" And she threw the *Playboy* in the trash.

Of course, I really blew it when I took it out of the trash when Linda wasn't looking. I hid it in my closet like a teenager—and when I finally pulled it out for a look, Linda just happened to walk in. We fought about that forever.

It wasn't just a celebrity thing, either. Whenever a girl was nice to me Linda would get suspicious. Like with Cory Everson, the professional bodybuilder. Cory is one of those real outgoing, touchy, kissy kinds of people, and I was friendly with her husband, Jeff, the editor in chief of *Muscle & Fitness* magazine. There was absolutely nothing between Cory and me other than friendship—in fact, Cory was friends with Linda, too—but every time we'd see them Linda would go off on me. "You're screwing her. I know it. You're having an affair."

She did the same thing with the wife of one of our neighbors on Willadel Drive—a woman I rarely even spoke to.

And get this: Linda even accused me of carrying on an affair with my pal Brutus Beefcake. I swear to God! From the outset of our marriage she insisted that he and I were lovers. She insists the same thing about me and my friend Bubba the Love Sponge, the radio DJ here in Tampa, too.

I know it sounds funny. It's completely ridiculous. Not to mention it's not true! There were plenty of times I tried to brush it off as part of Linda's weird sense of humor or something. But it wasn't a joke. None of this was a joke. She thought all of these affairs were real. So I don't want to make light of it at all.

Linda's suspicion—scratch that—her *belief* that I was cheating was like a hole way down in the hull of a ship. No matter what I did or said to try to patch that hole, the water would keep breaking through.

As far as I am concerned, until our marriage was almost completely over, I never cheated on Linda. Not once. That's the God's honest truth. Unfortunately, the truth was never enough for her.

As for the question of whether Linda cheated on me? I have

more suspicions now than I ever did back then. Especially when I think about her behavior in the last few years of our marriage.

One of the great lessons I've learned in life is to listen to where people are speaking from. A person's perception is often born of their perspective, so if someone is accusing people of stealing all the time, it could be that they're guilty of stealing something themselves.

The past is the past. I can't change what happened. Still, it's hard not to second-guess the way we handled our relationship after 1996.

There are times when I think, *If Linda had divorced me right then and there, it could have saved our children so much pain and anguish.* No one should have to live under the stress of their parents' unhappy marriage.

That's me talking *now*, of course. Back then I didn't really think it was all that bad. As far as I was concerned, my family had lots of happy times. We were living a dream life, in Linda's dream house, with boats and cars and all the toys that money can buy.

So we had a few problems. So what? I loved Linda, and I thought she loved me. Why else would Linda stay if not for love?

PLAYING THE BAD GUY

In the aftermath of the steroid trial, I decided to use the negative sentiment some of the fans felt toward Hulk Hogan to my advantage in the ring. It was time for a New World Order—to flip this whole game on its head. To shed the red and yellow for nothing but black.

Playing the heel was easy. I'd spent the whole first part of my career in the bad-guy role. Only now, just like I took this Hulk Hogan character to a whole new level of heroism, painting broader pictures and wilder story arcs than anyone had ever seen in this business, I decided to make Hollywood Hogan the most powerful antihero to ever step foot in an arena.

It worked. The fans exploded.

When I made that turn in the summer of '96, determined to take over the WCW with my nWo partners, Scott Hall and Kevin Nash—two top-notch wrestlers who left the WWF at the beginning of that year—the fans in Daytona started throwing shit into the ring. Just picking up and throwing whatever they could find. They were incensed!

I had 'em in the palm of my hand. I knew it would go down as one of the greatest story lines in wrestling history, and that's exactly what's happened.

I can't tell you what a high that is. After all the lows I'd been suffering, that high was addictive. And getting back in that ring week after week was all I wanted to do.

From that point forward, the WCW's *Monday Nitro* beat out the WWF's *Monday Night Raw* in the ratings—for eighty-four weeks in a row. I was beating Vince at his own game.

Refocusing the crowds on this new dark character seemed to almost erase the negative publicity I'd suffered. Too bad it couldn't erase the physical pain I was suffering every time I came out of an arena.

Maybe it's just what happens when you hit your forties. Or maybe that Tombstone that the Undertaker laid on me was the straw that slaughtered the camel's back. Either way, the old days of going six, seven years at a time without getting hurt enough to require surgery were completely gone. Now, every time I wrestled I'd wind up getting cut on. At the very least I'd have to get my back shot up with steroids—not the muscle-building kind, but the medical kind.

The pain was so bad in my lower back, I actually had the nerves there burned just to quiet the agony. Doctors would scorch them from about five inches above my belt line all the way down to the crack of my butt—so that whole region would go completely numb. I used to tell people they could hit me with a shovel right there and I wouldn't feel it.

I had my knees scoped so many times I accumulated a massive collection of crutches that lined the wall of my gym at the big house—right near the high-tech water-massage table that I'd lie in constantly just to get some relief.

Wrestling became a part-time deal for me not because I wanted it to, but because my body couldn't take it.

After all those years of being on the road 24/7, the best part about all that pain was the fact that I got to stay home. I was glad to spend some real quality time with my kids as they started to grow up. I loved watching them develop their own personalities, and knowing I wasn't missing all the milestones like I had been those first few years.

Before long, I got the sense that Linda didn't know what to do with me hanging around the house all the time. It's like we never quite figured out how to live together in the same space. We had twenty thousand square feet to work with, so it wasn't so bad to move around each other and just come together over the kids, but there was part of me that really thought she'd be excited to finally have her husband at home. That didn't happen. Ever.

It seemed like I was cramping her style and impinging on her days, even though I was happy to be a good house-husband and chip in and help around the house, especially with the kids. I installed a washer and dryer in the gym so I could take care of my own gym clothes, and I would always be the one to get up and make breakfast for Brooke and Nick before school when I could—so Linda could sleep in if she wanted.

For some reason that became a big deal for me. I'd always cook this massive breakfast with eggs and bacon and pancakes and cereal and fruit, and serve it up to Brooke and Nick in the mornings. It was real important to me that they always had a home-cooked breakfast. Even that seemed to annoy Linda.

"Just let 'em pour themselves a bowl of cereal in the morning," she'd complain.

I couldn't do that. It was just one of my quirks. Like if someone doesn't close the microwave door all the way, I have to go over and close it. I just can't stand that microwave door being left open, you know? I always had to cook that big breakfast for the kids.

As annoyed as Linda would get at having me hang around the house all the time, though, she wouldn't want me to leave. "You've gotta leave for a whole week to go shoot a commercial? Why can't they shoot it in two days?" There was always something.

She even started complaining about how much money I was making. I'd book a commercial or an appearance or an event, and she'd ask about it, and no matter how much it was paying she would say, "That's it? You should be making a million bucks for doing something like that. Can't you get more money?"

"Well, I don't know, Linda. You're welcome to get a job anytime. I'll help you launch whatever career you want!"

Of course, that never happened.

Her complaining all the time made me real nervous—I was almost always scared that she was going to up and leave me. When I say I was crazy for her, I really think I was a little bit *crazy* for her. There were so many times when I'd be in the wrestling ring, going through the motions, playing to the crowd, creating this frenzy, doing all the things I know how to do, when really, on the inside, all I'd be thinking about was getting out of that ring so I could call Linda. Just to check in with her. To make sure she was still there. If she didn't pick up the phone? Then I'd really go nuts. I'd be dialing and dialing nonstop until I got ahold of her.

It's hard to explain all of this. Things happen on a daily basis that might not seem like any big deal at all, but somehow when you add them up over time, they grow into this eight-hundred-pound boulder that's up on your shoulder and suddenly too heavy to carry around.

That's how it was in our marriage.

By the turn of the millennium, I was a little bit lost again. I had announced my retirement from wrestling on Jay Leno's show in 1998, but I never really planned on retiring. It was just time to change things up. In fact, I wound up wrestling Leno in a tag-team match, and found myself in a bunch of other celebrity exhibition matches with people like Dennis Rodman. It all devolved into fun and games as my run with the WCW came to an end.

I don't know much about the mergers and acquisitions games that go on in corporate America, but as AOL merged with Time Warner in 2001, Ted Turner wound up selling the WCW. Guess who he sold it to? The WWF. So suddenly, me and Vince McMahon were playing on the very same playground once again.

Time heals a lot of wounds, and the idea of Hulk Hogan making a return to the WWF was almost too hard to resist. Audiences love a comeback. But I was in so much pain my wrestling was strictly part-time anyway. I wasn't sure if my body could continue to handle it.

I was also in a lot of emotional pain—my father started to get real sick in 2000. It just seemed like one illness after another. Time was catching up with him. In those later days, that old-school Italian lack of outward affection I had known from him as a kid seemed to vanish. When I saw him now, he openly told me that he loved me and how proud he was of me. Somehow, that newfound affection made it all the more difficult for me to take when he passed away in 2001.

I took my dad's death real hard. I wasn't the same person I was back when Alan died. I took time off to grieve, to be with my family, to take care of my mother. In my late forties, there was just no running away from pain anymore. Pain of any kind.

When it came to climbing back in the ring, I had to come to grips with the fact that wrestling had changed, too. Everything was ten times more scripted than when I got into the game. The new crop of wrestlers would spend hours going over every move, coordinating every punch, blocking the whole match like a dance. They would write out and memorize what they were going to say. They even had professional writers! It just never made sense to me, and it usually came off as stale and rehearsed—which is exactly what it was.

The fact is, if you've written this whole story line and then you get out there and the crowd isn't buying it, what are you gonna do? You have to be ready and willing to go with the flow and change the direction of the match on the fly. It's like improvisational comedy or playing jazz. It needs to be fluid and free or it just falls flat.

I faced this head-on when I went in to get ready for Wrestle-Mania XVIII.

Dwayne "the Rock" Johnson was the big hero at that point. His movie *The Scorpion King* was about to come out, and I had no problem riding that wave—keeping him the hero while I played the ultimate heel, carrying over what I'd built as Hollywood Hogan at the WCW. To make the fans salivate, we set up a match in Chicago to generate heat for this new rivalry: I hit the Rock with a metal hammer in the ring, and my cohorts carried him outside and put him in an ambulance. I tied the ambulance shut with a bunch of chains so the Rock couldn't get out, and then I crashed a semi into the ambulance. Of course, it was all just on film. So we said "cut," then the Rock got out, and *then* I ran over that ambulance with that truck. Things were a lot more elaborate than they were in the old days of choosing whether or not to pull a blade job in the ring. The story arcs were cinematic now, and I can't imagine an arc that could have painted me as more of a heel than that one.

Even with all that setup, the Rock still wanted to meet me face-to-face to talk about what would happen at WrestleMania. He started in with the scripting. "I'm gonna jump off the top rope and then I want you to kick me right here, and then ram my head . . ." I stopped him. "Whoa, whoa, whoa. First of all, I'm not gonna remember all of this. Second, we need to just go with the flow. We need to let the audience decide what they want to see happen in that ring, and then improvise. Trust me on this one."

I knew Dwayne's father, Rocky Johnson, from way back. He happened to be at the meeting that day, and he actually spoke up about it. "Dwayne, just listen to Hogan."

Sure enough, when we got in that ring at the SkyDome, in front of nearly seventy thousand fans, the first time I blocked a punch and hit the Rock back, the crowd cheered! It didn't matter that I was considered the bad guy. It didn't matter that we had filmed that crazy ambulance-crushing scene to make them hate me for attacking the big hero. The fans are so loyal to the Hulk Hogan persona, they saw through all of the setup and started to root for my return to the center of the WWF universe. It's like they were cheering and screaming to bring the red and yellow back to life.

The Rock was freaking out that the audience wasn't cheering for him and booing me. "Oh my God. Oh my God!" he said. I told him right there in the middle of that arena, "Just go with it, bro. I'll fix it!" So we did. I played everything just right so the Rock came out looking like the hero in the end. He won the match. Then the two of us teamed up as partners to defeat some other bad guys in a last-minute twist that made the fans just go crazy wanting to see more.

It wasn't long after that triumphant moment when the red and yellow came back full strength. It had taken an entire decade— and let me tell you, bro, that's a really long gestation period when you're living it minute by minute—but Hulk Hogan the hero finally came back to life in all his glory.

It wouldn't be full-time. Not even close. But the power of my character was strong enough that I could make an appearance in the ring every six months, or even once a year, and still have a massive impact on professional wrestling.

Those appearances would also send sales of my merchandise through the roof, and keep my name out there in a positive way that could help sell everything from grills to energy drinks with my image on them.

My image, once again, was good.

CHAPTER 13

Something New

Balancing my career with the duties I felt as a father was always a challenge. As my kids got older, I thought a lot more about how my own parents raised me. Especially about the way my parents supported my various interests. From bowling and baseball to music and wrestling, they gave me whatever I needed. And my dad—it brings tears to my eyes to think how hard he worked and how much he sacrificed for his family. To drop two weeks' salary on a guitar for your junior-high-age son?

Maybe he didn't hug me as much as I hug my kids. Maybe he didn't say "I love you" every time I saw him the way I do with Brooke and Nick. But he had no other motivation to make the sacrifices he did for me beyond the unconditional love that a father feels for his children. By this point in my life, I completely understood that kind of love. Looking to my dad as a role model, I had a lot to live up to.

I was blessed with two smart, healthy, really talented kids. The way I saw it, it was up to Linda and me to nurture whatever interests they had.

With Brooke, right from the outset, it was music. Linda and I used to sit there and watch her perform *The Little Mermaid* in our living room, from start to finish. She was just a little girl, but she knew every word and had dance moves to go with every song.

That girl can sing. As she grew older, she developed the kind of spot-on pitch that producers dream of finding to put in the studio. She also took to the piano real quick from lesson number one.

More than that, she had an innate sense of songwriting. When it came to putting words and melodies together, she just knew how to do it—the same way I innately knew how to move through chord progressions on the guitar. I got such a kick out of seeing her play and sing. It brought me right back to my early days of playing music myself.

Nick went in an entirely different direction than anything I had ever shown an affinity for: He fell in love with cars. And I'm not talking down the line when he was ready to get his license. Even when he was really young and we'd all go to Celebration Station, this amusement-park-type place where you'd spend fifty bucks playing games to win enough tickets to get you a one-dollar toy, Nick would spend all his time there riding the go-karts. But he really started to get fascinated with cars by the time he was ten or eleven. That fascination turned into an obsession once he discovered the Toyota Supra.

The Supra was only sold in the States until about 1999, but it was quickly developing this whole subculture with a certain breed of young car enthusiasts. Nick got totally caught up in the movement.

In 2002 I came home from a trip to Germany to find a black Toyota Supra parked in my driveway.

I walked in the house and didn't see anyone visiting, so I dropped my bag and said, "Whose car is that out there?"

"Oh, it's Nick's," Linda said to me.

"What?"

"Yeah. I bought Nick a car."

"Linda," I said, "Nick's twelve years old!"

I supported my kids' interests, but this was crazy! Who buys their twelve-year-old a car?

Well, it turns out Linda's decision wasn't off base at all. Nick was real serious about his passion for Supras, even at that age. He spent all kinds of time reading about them and learning about them, and now he wanted to mess around with the engine and learn how to take it apart and put it back together.

The thing with these Supras, and Honda Civics, and some of these other little Japanese four-cylinder cars, is that just by switching a couple of hoses on the turbo you can get a big boost in horsepower out of them. With a fifteen-hundred-dollar conversion the thing can really put out some speed. With a few more modifications, like four or five grand, these vehicles can become full-on race cars.

That's why there's a whole cult following for these things. It even crossed over into Hollywood with those Fast and the Furious films. Nick was right in the thick of it from when he was twelve years old—begging me to take him up to Gainesville and all of these other towns for Supra meets on the weekends.

So all of a sudden, Hulk Hogan is standing in the parking lot of a Wal-Mart with all these car buffs coming up to me going, "What are you doing here?" For a while, that's how I spent almost every weekend with my son. Heck, even Linda and Brooke got into it.

Before long, Nick knew the names of all the drivers and who owned what car. His enthusiasm was so great that he got the attention of some of those drivers, and started befriending some of the people he would eventually team up with when he got into racing. At fourteen he was becoming friends with guys who were nineteen and twenty. Their mutual love for these cars seemed to erase the age difference, and some of these guys saw a real promise in Nick as a potential driver someday.

As for Brooke, I was able to get her some big-time meetings in her early teens. As soon as it looked like she was serious about pursuing a career in music, I used the leverage of the Hulk Hogan name to get her off on the right foot.

When she was just fourteen, I managed to get her an audition with Lou Pearlman, the guy who had managed the Backstreet Boys and 'N Sync. She was really excited. Who wouldn't be? He didn't hire her at first, though. In fact, he told her to go and work on her dance moves and learn to sing from her diaphragm—a term that refers to the breathing methods real singers use to sup-port the notes rather than pushing all the sound through their throats the way your average karaoke singer might.

Brooke took it hard. No one ever wants to hear that they're not good enough. Then she got to work. She was determined to win this guy over, and Brooke—like Nick—definitely has some of that drive to succeed like I did.

Almost a year later, I rented out a club at the Universal City-Walk in Orlando and brought Lou back to see Brooke perform. She won him over that time, and he signed her up.

Brooke was elated. She was living her dream by the age of fif-teen. She went into a recording studio to produce her first single, a song called "Everything to Me." Lou and I were set to become fifty-fifty partners supporting Brooke's career—we'd both put up half the money to record her first album.

The one thing Lou suggested was that Brooke should look for a TV or film platform that would put her on an even playing field with the hot young female performers of the day. This was right around when Lindsay Lohan was trying to bridge the gap be-tween film and music. Hilary Duff had become a major phenom-enon through her tween-oriented TV show. Jessica Simpson, whose career was floundering (at best), found massive success in 2003 after shooting a reality TV show called *Newlyweds* with her husband, Nick Lachey. And by 2004, even Jessica's little sister Ashlee was getting her own show and a record deal thanks to re-ality TV. So it definitely seemed the way to go.

Ever since rocker Ozzy Osbourne put his family on display for the world to see on MTV, and *The Osbournes* blew up into a mas-sive overnight hit, a whole slew of producers kept approaching me to do a reality TV show myself. Most of them were pretty obvious ideas: "Let's see Hulk Hogan make a huge comeback to wrestling, and film all the behind-the-scenes drama!" No thanks. I'd been there and done that with the comeback routine, and I didn't want to do that again—especially with cameras in my face.

But right as we were trying to launch Brooke, VH1 came around with a different idea: They wanted to film a one-hour special called

(Inside)Out: Hulk Hogan, Stage Dad. They had done a series of these specials, taking a different look at various celebrities' lives, and this one would concentrate on my trying to help my daughter break into music. *Perfect,* I thought.

The VH1 crew was only scheduled to come out and follow the family around for three days, but on the second day of filming they asked if they could keep shooting for the next month. Right then and there I had my suspicions that they might offer us our own series. There's no way they would have spent the money grabbing six hundred hours of footage if they didn't really like what they saw.

What they wound up capturing on film that month was a side of Hulk Hogan that had never been seen before. They showed me as a dad, as a human being. This was around the time that I was getting my hip surgery, so rather than standing up as the ultimate "strong man," I was down for the count. Linda was left in charge of everything that happened with Brooke's career as I lay helpless— but supportive—in bed. All of it was captured for the audience to see.

Linda jumped at the chance to manage her daughter's career. I think she really enjoyed calling the shots. Suddenly she was the big man in charge, so to speak.

Rather than commute to the recording studio in Orlando, Linda decided to temporarily relocate there with Brooke. She rented a townhouse and filled it up with new furniture. It was only about forty-five minutes away from the big house, but she was so excited about it. Even though Brooke only recorded two or three days a week, Linda would stay there, live there and not bother coming home. Looking back, it was really the first time that Linda took a step toward distancing herself from the life we'd built together.

I'm not sure if the new living arrangement and sense of power went to her head or what, but as Brooke's single was about to be released, I got a call from Lou Pearlman.

Apparently Linda had been badgering Lou so much that he couldn't take it anymore. Linda had been calling him and yelling at him about every little snag in Brooke's routine: "Her room wasn't ready when she got to town, and why were the travel arrangements messed up, and why isn't there any security at her appearances?!"

"I'm not a whole record label," Lou said. "I'm just a manager trying to help your daughter. I'm being tortured here and I can't take it anymore."

He pulled out of our deal. "I love your daughter to death and I wish her the best, but I cannot take your wife anymore," Lou told me.

That was it. I couldn't convince him to stay.

Lou went on to get in a whole lot of trouble through a Ponzi scheme he was running—things I knew absolutely nothing about. So maybe it was a blessing in disguise. Still, Brooke was crushed.

Her single came out and went straight to number one on the Billboard Singles chart. It stayed number one for eight weeks! It even broke into the Billboard Hot 100. I was so proud of her. Without Lou on board, though, the plans to finish an album by fall went right out the window. It was a major setback in her brand-new career.

As for the *(Inside)Out* special? It was the most successful *(Inside)Out* special VH1 had ever seen. Just as I predicted, the powers that be came and asked me if I'd be interested in turning this into a reality show. Not a reality show about Hulk Hogan, the wrestler, but a reality show about my whole family. I knew this could be a huge boost to Brooke's career. I also knew it could be a huge boost to Nick as he got into racing.

But I had massive trepidations.

By the time VH1 offered us this reality show, I already felt like the glue that held my family together had started to erode. Even though she moved back after a few months, this thing with Linda moving to Orlando with Brooke freaked me out. The arguing and cussing had gotten much worse in recent years, and it just seemed like Linda was headed in a whole different direction.

For one thing, to me it seemed like she was just tired of being a mom. It wasn't just the breakfast thing, and sometimes leaving, letting the kids take care of themselves. It's that she was actually talking to the kids about quitting school.

"Aw, school's ridiculous," she would say to them. "You don't need to go to school today."

There were lots of days when she'd keep Brooke home just to go shopping. Wow, great life lesson there. In a two-week period she would go to Wal-Mart eight or ten different times, and spend two or three grand each visit!

I guess it was fine. We had the money. But to take your daughter out of school to go with you? Or to go get her nails done? That's not what a good parent does, is it?

Now, I realize she had to handle all the parenting duties by herself when I was on the road, and I know that parenting is a really, really difficult job. There's never a day off. I get that. But was it really so bad that she had to try to weasel out of it at this important stage of our children's lives? It would only be a few more years before the kids moved out, and then she could do whatever she wanted. Unfortunately, Linda hit a point where she no longer wanted to wait. For anything.

Around the time that Brooke's record deal was heating up, Brooke was suffering some taunting from other girls at her Catholic high school. So Linda took that as a cue to finally convince Brooke to be home-schooled. Of course, once that happened, Nick was asking, "Why can't I be home-schooled?" Eventually, we pulled him out of regular school, too.

The craziest thing of all started happening in 2004: Linda started disappearing. Just plain disappearing. We'd get in a fight over something, or she'd just blow up and I'd have no idea what set her off, then all of a sudden she'd get in her car and go. Gone. No one had any idea where she was. Not me. Not Brooke. Not Nick.

Sometimes she'd disappear for days.

So all of that was going on as we got offered this show. Plus, beyond all the behind-the-scenes strife, it just made me nervous that my wife and kids might not fully understand what kind of a commitment they were making.

One night, I sat them all down at the dinner table at the big house and I laid it all out for them. "It's a ton of work," I warned them, "and there'll be no more privacy." I tried to explain the depths of what that could mean, based on some of the bad press and negative things I'd been through in my own life and career—most of which happened when the kids were too young to remember.

"In some ways, doing this show might make you feel like you're in prison. It might be a nice day outside and you just want to go hit the beach, but you can't, because you're stuck in the house filming from sunup till sundown, or later. You might want to run off to the mall, but you can't, because you're filming."

At the end of my speech, I asked who wanted to do it—and everyone in the family raised their hands, enthusiastically.

As for me? I raised my hand, too. The fact that my wife and kids were all sitting there on the same page about something gave me hope. The idea that we would all be working together was heartwarming to me.

I actually remember thinking to myself, *Maybe this show will be the glue that puts my family back together.*

WHO KNOWS BEST?

I remember when I first watched *The Osbournes*, I assumed that they must've had cameras in their house 24/7 and camera people following them everywhere they went just waiting for that magic to happen. How else could they have captured all that crazy material?

Of course, that isn't the case with reality TV at all. Just like anything else in Hollywood, there are unions and crews and budgets to deal with. A production company (in our case an organization that called itself Pink Sneakers) isn't going to pay the crew overtime and double time just to sit around when nothing's hap-pening. That's why reality TV shows are soft-scripted.

In other words, they give you a scenario—hopefully some-thing close to what you might encounter in your real life, or at least a pumped-up version of your real life—and they tell you the potential outcome, and some possible beats in between, and then you improvise and see what happens.

Sound familiar?

I'd been doing versions of this in the ring my whole career. Now I just had to do it with my Hulk Hogan personality toned down to somewhere just above the real Terry Bollea—so the fa-miliar elements of Hulk Hogan would be there for the viewers, but the "reality" of my off-screen self would shine through.

A lot of people have a hard time with this stuff. It is a form of acting, in a way. As we started the first season, we all had to find our footing.

Brooke was no problem. She was the extrovert, the actress, the singer, from the moment she popped out of the womb. She'd go with the flow and always looked great on camera. The only thing the producers forced on her was to act all boy crazy. Brooke was more of a slow starter, like me, and she wasn't boy crazy at sixteen at all. They needed that to make the show more interesting, though, and she went along with it.

It all came natural to Nick. He was quiet on camera but had a real natural instinct when it came to the "acting" part of reality TV. It got to the point where the producers knew they could rely on him to do things that were way outside of his character just to try to make some magic happen on screen. Like when he was up in his room one day, just sitting at his computer while Linda and I filmed a scene downstairs in the kitchen. The producers asked him to go to the window and toss water balloons at the neighbors. They wanted to show him exhibiting that typical rich, spoiled-brat, obnoxious-little-brother behavior. Nick would never do that in real life. He was actually a much more serious and focused kid than anyone ever saw on TV. But it created scenes that the pro-ducers could work with in the editing room.

As for Linda? This was her moment to shine. It's like she had been waiting twenty years for the cameras to be pointed her way instead of mine. She only wanted to be seen with full-blown makeup and perfect hair—and she put some of that attitude on Brooke as well. "Put on a different dress. Make sure your hair's blown out!" She was right, in a way. We were trying to build Brooke's career, and you wanted her to be as appealing as possible. But Linda just went over the top when it came to herself.

There were times when I'd give the producers the keys to the house, so they could come in super early in the morning and shoot us in bed while we were still sleeping. I didn't care if my butt was hanging out or I had drool on my pillow. That was part of the appeal of the show—to let people into the Hogans' "real life." Linda wouldn't have it. On those days, she would set her alarm really early and get up and brush her hair and her teeth and get some basic makeup on before the camera people ever arrived.

In fact, on the very first day, the very first scene we shot in the kitchen, the cameras rolled and Linda caught a glimpse of her reflection in the window—and noticed that her hair was messed up.

"Turn the camera off," she said. The director, Scott Bennett, who liked to keep the cameras rolling so he wouldn't risk missing any great moments, didn't turn off the camera right away. Linda just tore his head off. "I told you to turn that fucking camera off!" she yelled. She started cussing him like a dog. The poor guy went scrambling out of the house with his tail between his legs trying to find some support from the producers. He thought he blew the whole show in the very first setup.

But that was just Linda. The whole crew would get to know that over the coming weeks.

Just as I suspected might happen, Linda got bored and fed up with the whole process real quick. She wanted the fame and the glamour of being on TV. She just didn't want to put in the hard work and long hours that go along with it. Before long, I was spending my entire morning trying to get her to come downstairs so we could start filming. "I don't want to come down today," she'd complain. "Just tell them to shoot something else!"

"Linda, I can't tell them that. We all signed contracts. We have to do this according to their schedule."

There really were schedules, too. They would need to shoot a scene with me from 8:30 till 9:30 A.M., and then they'd need the whole family from 10:00 to 12:45. Then there's a lunch break. It was pretty regimented. Even if you weren't filming you couldn't go running off to the mall or something. If I was cooking break-fast for the kids and happened to cut my thumb off, they'd want to be sure Linda was close by so they could get her reaction and not miss the magic, you know?

But for all the headaches, the show itself worked. When it launched in July 2005, *Hogan Knows Best* had the biggest debut of any show in VH1 history.

Suddenly, my whole family was living a red-carpet life. They were invited to all the big parties: MTV Awards, the Grammys, not to mention the after-parties. They were getting that big-star treatment. Even Linda seemed really happy for a while. We were all riding high. I loved watching my family get a chance to bask in the glory of that spotlight.

I started working with a top-notch publicist in New York City named Elizabeth Rosenthal, who landed us stories in *People* mag-azine and booked the whole family on *Larry King Live*. We did CNN, MSNBC, and Fox News. I appeared on Jay Leno, and we all went on Jimmy Kimmel's show. It was wild!

We had money flowing in. We had offers flowing in. This red-hot record producer, Scott Storch, suddenly showed interest in working to get Brooke's recording career back on track. VH1 upped us for a second season.

It was all rolling out just the way we'd hoped it would.

In public, we were all having the time of our lives, but that pub-lic image only further masked the problems that were growing behind the scenes.

Most of the cracks in my marriage didn't show up in the first three seasons of that TV show. There were moments where Linda or I rolled our eyes at each other's behavior, but that was just about the extent of it. There were plenty of times when Linda would lose it and start cussing me out in front of the crew, but no one wanted to see that kind of ugliness on TV. So the producers never aired it. They aired the footage where we hid our true feelings and just pretended to get along like a normal—if somewhat eccentric—couple.

Off-camera, an entirely different story kept unfolding. Linda's complaining about how miserable she was reached epic proportions. Every day she talked about how much she hated Florida. Every day she talked about how much she hated our neighbors and never wanted to see them. Anything you can think of, she'd find a reason to hate it.

Her drinking also started to affect the family. It seemed like every night she would get into the wine, and before long she'd start cussing everybody out—including Brooke and Nick.

I can't tell you how many nights I went to bed and the last words I heard before my head hit the pillow were "Fuck you, Terry." It got so bad, she wouldn't touch me. We'd go to bed and roll over, and there was no physical contact whatsoever. Just the "Fuck you" ringing in my ears.

At her worst, she said those same words to the kids. If I ever said F-you to one of my kids, I wouldn't be the same person. It would shake me to my bones. But when she was drunk, she didn't hesitate to use foul language in front of the kids. I even heard her use the C-word on Brooke.

The next morning we'd wake up, and everything would be fine. She'd act as if nothing happened. I'd try to talk to her about it, the kids would try to talk to her about it, but she just wouldn't hear us out.

She blamed me for everything. I kept blaming myself, too, thinking I had let her down, thinking I had somehow caused her to be this miserable.

The drinking reached a point where it seemed to affect our social life. After Linda got her second glass of wine in her, people would start to leave. They probably didn't want to be present for the Jekyll and Hyde act that I had witnessed one time too many.

The night we wrapped filming on the very first season, we held a wrap party at this bar called Shephard's on Clearwater Beach— the in spot where all the twentysomethings love to party.

Linda was drinking and she refused to leave. When I tried to pull her off the dance floor we got into a huge fight, right in front of everybody. "It's only three thirty in the morning!" she screamed. "I'll stay out as late as I fucking want!"

The next morning, Linda got on a plane to California. I called her parents and told them how bad things had become, and even Linda's mother, Gail, told me she thought Linda needed help. She had received so many phone calls from Linda just complaining and moaning about everything in her life. It was clear to me that she'd crossed the line with her drinking.

So Gail and Joe picked Linda up at the airport that day and drove her straight to the Betty Ford Clinic.

A few days into her stay, Linda started calling me, begging me to let her come home. I didn't know how to handle it, so I actually called Gail for advice. "No, don't let her out. Don't let her out," Gail begged me. "It's too soon."

But Linda begged. "I'm in here with AIDS victims and heroin addicts. I don't deserve to be in here." Publicly, Linda's attorney would later say she was only in there for evaluation.

The thing is, Linda had the right to leave whenever she wanted. It wasn't jail. I think she was too afraid to walk out of there without having one of us give her the okay.

I'm the one with the soft heart. She knows that, and she played me like a fiddle.

After just ten days, I let her come home, and she swore up and down that she would never drink again. The kids begged her to stay true to her word: "Please, Mom. For us." She swore to it. "I'll quit for the kids. I promise."

Her promise only lasted about three days.

I was so afraid of setting her off, I soon found myself tiptoeing into the house each night. If I had been out wrestling and came home at two in the morning, I would walk in to the stench of alcohol in our bedroom. She reeked of it—that nasty, fermenting smell that oozes from your pores and floats out on your breath.

Her anger came roaring back. And the blame for everything.

And the disappearing. When Brooke went through some surgery in 2005, I coincidentally had to get knee surgery at the exact same time. Neither of us were supposed to get out of bed for a few days. If I ever wanted to wrestle again, it was real important that I let that knee heal. Of course, that was just one of the more memorable times that Linda decided to disappear and let us fend for ourselves.

Not knowing where she was or when she'd be back, I wound up hobbling around trying to take care of Brooke and get Nick everywhere he needed to go. My doctors freaked out when they heard I was walking, but what was I supposed to do? Linda left me with no choice.

MISS MIAMI

It's hard to comprehend when I look at it in retrospect, with a clear head, but Linda's rage and fury was so frequent it just became expected. It was almost routine. Her cussing and swearing and disappearing felt like the new "normal" in our household. In fact, we were bombarded by so many moments of misery that anytime she said something positive it was shocking. And in 2006, she started saying all these really great things—about Miami.

As we filmed the second season of the show, we spent more and more time in that city, where Brooke was recording some new music. I'm not sure what it was about that town, but Linda suddenly became intoxicated with Miami's "ambiance." She raved about the restaurants, and the people, and the excitement. She loved that she could actually get a "decent glass of wine." She loved the celebrity culture there, and the money culture there. I think it reminded her a little bit of what she thought she was missing in Beverly Hills.

Suddenly she started talking about wanting to move to Miami full-time.

With the properties we owned already, we were stretching ourselves thin. The thing about multimillion-dollar mansions is the maintenance and upkeep can be tens if not hundreds of thousands of dollars a month. The gardeners and maintenance crews, cleaning crews, electric costs. Our caretaker, George, worked full-time just for us, and he barely had time to get everything done. It's an overwhelming amount of money and effort just to keep those places operating. So buying another home in Miami scared me. I was hardly wrestling at all—which meant I was hardly bringing in the millions I once made.

But I was desperate. I was desperate to make Linda happy. So we sold a home we owned in California and started seriously shopping in Miami. We wound up buying a spectacular $12 million property on North Bay Road—right next to the owners of Market America, whose guesthouse regularly played host to people like Jennifer Lopez and Eva Longoria. It was a road where members of the Bee Gees lived. Where Shaq had a home. Just a spectacular spot.

Linda was flying high for a while. She loved it. She felt like we were suddenly living where the action was. It was go, go, go.

There were plenty of problems when we moved in, of course, that were all played out on season three of *Hogan Knows Best*. The place had some issues, including a lack of garage space for all of our various vehicles, and a lack of space for all of Linda's dogs. Well, that was the price of living in the big city, right? We'd make the best of it and make it work because Linda was where she wanted to be.

Wouldn't you know it? Linda's high wore off after just a few months. Little things set her off like crazy. Her car kept getting towed, and rather than finding a solution to the parking situation, she just kept parking on the street and blaming everyone else for the lousy parking laws in Miami.

She started flipping out and cussing and swearing again. She also started crying for what seemed like no reason at all. Nick and Brooke and I would all try to help. We all asked what was wrong and what we could do to fix it. But she never had any kind of answer.

Then she started disappearing again.

In November of 2006, we were barely settled into this new $12 million house when Linda flew off the handle and took off.

It was the day before Thanksgiving. Linda's hairdresser, Tracy (and her assistant), came down that morning to do Linda's hair. According to Tracy, Linda had some wine as she sat in the chair. She always liked to do that. It was relaxing for her. But on this day, for some reason, Linda worked herself into a tizzy about how unhappy she was and she got up and walked out the door. Tracy wasn't sure what set her off, but at that point in our marriage it could have been anything. And I mean *anything*. The wind would blow a door shut and she'd yell, "Who slammed the fucking door! I'm sick and tired of doors slamming! I'm *leaving*!"

Whatever it was, by the time I came home she was gone. I tried calling her, but she never picked up. I went driving all over South Beach that afternoon trying to find my wife, but I never tracked her down. That night I told the kids not to worry. "I'm sure she'll be back. She's never missed a holiday," I assured them.

Linda and I had a triple-king-sized bed in our bedroom, and the kids wound up sleeping in that giant bed with me that night. It didn't matter what I said. They were worried sick. Their mom was missing. For all we knew, she had crashed her car somewhere and was lying in a ditch on the side of the road.

Thanksgiving morning came, and no Linda. I walked all over the house, opening and closing doors, hoping that she had come home late and just slept in another room. She wasn't there. I kept thinking that she'd show up by dinnertime, so the kids and I started cooking. I've never cooked a turkey in my life, but I put it in the oven and did my best. A few hours later, the three of us sat down and ate Thanksgiving dinner in that house alone. The kids without their mom. Me without my wife.

In my mind, on that Thanksgiving Day, I didn't have anything left to be thankful for at all.

Two days later, Linda called. She was in California, happy as could be, acting as if nothing was wrong. I tried to get an explanation, and she just said she needed to go to California. "Why?" she asked—as if my asking for an explanation was the most ridiculous thing she had ever heard. As if her behavior was normal.

I loved her so much and I wanted to help her. I wanted to get to the bottom of why she was acting this way. But I couldn't. I felt helpless. I felt lost.

CHAPTER 14

Season of Change

By the time season four of *Hogan Knows Best* came around, Brooke's music career was really heating up. It should have been a really happy time, but Brooke had so many problems with her mom that she kept breaking down and crying at the recording studio and before her performances out on the road.

The fact is, Linda's rage and fury kept crossing into her managerial role. When Brooke was hired to sing the national anthem at the Daytona 500, in front of 125,000 people, Linda made Brooke so upset she barely got through the performance. When she opened for this real hot group, My Chemical Romance, same thing. She would get on her about her clothes and her outfits and how fat she looked, her hairstyle. She'd yell at her for missing notes, not sounding good. It was affecting Brooke's ability to get the job done, in a real big way.

So the record company tried to keep friends and handlers around Brooke all the time—just to take care of her and make sure she was all right.

One of those handlers the record company brought in was a woman named Christiane Plante. Christiane was so great with Brooke. She did everything she could to look after her, and I loved seeing someone take care of my daughter that way. She was just so positive and caring. She was thirty-four, but she and Brooke became really close. Almost like best friends, in a way.

Linda was disappearing on a regular basis by January and February of 2007. If she wasn't flying out to California, she was driving all the way back to Tampa. I never knew why, and half the time I didn't know where she was. The F-yous were just out of control, and now always coupled with her threatening to move to California and file for divorce. It's like she was taunting me, trying to get me to pull the trigger and leave her first. There was no back and forth anymore. No give and take. I don't think you can even call it a marriage. It wasn't a partnership, either. It wasn't a friendship. It was nothing but awful.

On the first day of filming for season four, Linda just didn't show up. The production crew was all set up, and the whole staff was there and ready to go, and no Linda. We missed the whole first day. We missed the whole second day. Suddenly the producers and the VH1 guys are threatening to sue me. "Don't sue me! I'm here! It's Linda," I kept telling them.

At first I didn't know where she was. I was just worried sick. I got real depressed about it. I was worried something had happened to her. When she finally called from California she didn't even have an excuse. She just kept telling me to have them start without her. I told her she needed to get on a plane, and she refused. It was awful. It took almost two weeks before we got Linda back and actually started shooting. I was just a wreck. The fact that our personal problems were spilling over into Brooke's career, and now this show? I was embarrassed, and I didn't know what to do.

None of this is an excuse for what happened next. I just want you to understand the state of my relationship, and how fragile my emotions were.

One day in the middle of all of that, Christiane Plante called. Brooke had broken down again, and she wanted to ask me what I thought she should do to help her, but as soon as she heard the sound of my voice she said, "Oh my God. What's wrong?"

She turned that caring attention she had given Brooke on me. So I told her. "I'm just real worried about Linda," I replied.

Christiane knew what Linda had been pulling. She heard about it all from Brooke, and witnessed plenty of Linda's behavior firsthand. She knew how much trouble Brooke had been having, and she sympathized with my situation. "I don't know why she's doing this to you and Brooke."

Over the phone that day, Christiane gave me a shoulder to lean on, at least verbally. I can't tell you how much I needed that.

Maybe a month or so later, Brooke made an appearance up in New York City, and I went along to introduce her from the stage. Christiane was along for that trip, and the three of us—she, Brooke, and I—went out to dinner afterward. Back at the hotel that night, Christiane and I both stopped by Brooke's room to check on her at the same time. I eventually left the two of them there and went downstairs to my room. A half hour or so later, because I'm always over the top and have to check one more time, I called Brooke's room again just to make sure she was okay.

Christiane answered the phone. She said Brooke was going to bed and she was just leaving. Then she asked me what I was doing.

"I'm probably gonna drink a glass of wine and just hang out," I said. Then words came from my mouth that I didn't expect. "Why don't you come down and join me?"

It felt like two seconds later we were in a room together. We were both drinking a glass of wine, just talking, but I felt like she wanted to do more than that, you know? I was real attracted to her, for so many reasons—and my wife and I hadn't been intimate in so long that I can't even tell you how long it had been.

All of a sudden, Christiane reached her arm over to put her hand on my back—and I ducked. It was a weird instinct. I ducked the way a dog that's been hit too many times would cower when someone raises a hand.

"Are you okay?" Christiane asked. Apparently it surprised her, too.

"Yeah, yeah. You just caught me off guard there," I said.

Next thing I know, the two of us started kissing. Not to sound perverted or anything, but it was fantastic. Here I am in my fifties now, and this was a really attractive thirty-four-year-old woman, with dark hair and a curvaceous body. And just to have some affection and genuine caring mixed in with that kind of physical attraction? It felt good. It was such an emotional and physical release.

We didn't have sex that night, but it opened the door. Over the course of the next two months we did have sex, maybe five different times. That was it.

Linda had no idea. For a while it had that sort of naughty appeal, like a kid sneaking some chocolate that he's not supposed to have. Just seeing Christiane during the course of a normal business day with Brooke became this real exciting thing. It was an entirely new experience for me. Like I said, I had never done anything like this in twenty-two years of marriage.

In a way, that Christiane excitement kept me going for a couple of months. It helped me just to get through the days.

It was no coincidence that the very first episode of the final season of our reality show was called "Wedlock Headlock." I think the crew filming our visit to a marriage counselor was as much for their benefit as it was ours.

Yes, Linda and I kissed and made up on TV, but things went right back to the way they'd been whenever the cameras stopped rolling. Heck, even when the cameras *were* rolling. We couldn't hide it anymore. But the really bad stuff hit the editing room floor.

They call it "reality," but I guess the real inner workings of the Hogan family's married life didn't make for good TV.

To get away from all of the headaches, the scripts seemed to go further out on a limb to put us in funny situations. They sent us to a dude ranch in Wyoming for vacation. We went up to Universal Studios in Orlando, where we figured the only way we could ever have a normal day of family fun without being mobbed by fans was to wear all this prosthetic makeup and go into that park in disguise.

The weird thing was, it actually worked for a while. They put a big nose and a big belly on me and made me look like a real old man. They put a big butt on Linda and warts on her face and made her look like some redneck chick. Brooke wore a black wig, and Nick looked like a mudwhomper. As we walked through the park, and genuinely started having fun, it made me realize that things had to be fake in order for this family to have fun and be happy anymore.

I looked around and saw, once and for all, that for our family to be happy we either had to pretend to be something we're not, or keep moving so fast that we wouldn't have time to fall prey to our normal routines.

Which basically meant that my family wasn't functioning at all.

GOING HOME

That spring of 2007, in the last days of filming our final season, the whole family made a trip back to the big house in Clearwater. Almost as soon as we arrived, the production company insisted that we take a ride over to visit the house that I grew up in. I guess they had already cleared it with the guy who owns the place now, 'cause he was waiting on us when we pulled into the driveway.

It was so strange to drive into Port Tampa and see those old brick roads; to drive past the houses of old friends, and enemies, and girls I wished I'd had the nerve to kiss. It was the first time I had been back since right after my dad died in 2001, and my perspective on the whole place was just so different now.

Some of the houses looked exactly the same, even after all those years. Not mine. That little square house I grew up in had a big extension off the back, which at least doubled its size, but you could see the shape of what the house used to be when you looked at it straight on from the front. Honestly, it seemed smaller than ever to me that day.

When I walked into the kitchen, it looked like some kind of fancy bistro. The new owner had installed a stainless steel stove with one of those fancy air vents, and had a plate on the counter filled with corks from all the red wine he liked to drink. There were beautiful hardwood floors. Nothing about the place was the same. It was shocking that a place that small could turn out so beautifully.

The owner, this real nice guy who was probably about forty, said he had something for me. All of a sudden he pulled out this little die-cast truck—a toy tanker. I recognized that truck. It was mine.

It was a real weird feeling, and it hit me so off center.

I had driven over that day with Linda and my mom and the kids in the car. My mom didn't want to go in the house. She's mostly blind now and couldn't really see it anyway, but she didn't want to come in for some reason. I think it made her sad. And all I was thinking about as I walked into that house was how fed up I was with Linda's complaining.

Then all of a sudden this guy handed me this little truck. He said he was doing some gardening and he found it buried in the dirt. I remembered that dirt. It was black, and hot. I used to play in that dirt all the time—with my big yellow Tonka truck and this little blue tanker. And here it was.

After all the thirty or forty years it'd been buried, the paint had faded almost entirely, and it was all pinkish-white underneath. I thought about being a kid in that house; how I'd play in the back and stuff rocks up my nose. I remembered how awesome it was just to sit in that dirt without a care in the world, and how happy I was back then.

I was happy in that moment, too: to be out of that car and in a situation where Linda was forced to stop her complaining. "Do we have to do this? Oh, Jesus Christ. What the hell are they gonna do with *this* story line?"

Holding that little truck just switched gears on me, emotionally.

Half of my father's ashes were spread in the backyard there, under the grapefruit and tangelo trees that he loved so much. My dad hated staying indoors almost as much as my mom hated the Florida heat; so she'd stay indoors and run the air conditioner all day while my dad stayed out in that backyard from sunup till sundown. They found a way to make their marriage work in that tiny house, with no money at all. Now part of him was there forever, under those trees that made him so proud, while the rest of him I'd scattered out in the Gulf of Mexico, knowing how much he always loved the water.

I found myself wishing that Linda and I could be happy again, praying almost—even though I hadn't gone to church or spent any time praying for years.

I thought about how crazy my life had become. *What am I doing in a twenty-thousand-square-foot house?* I think I was happier when I was living out of a van by the beach in Pensacola, just waking up and feeling the wind on my skin.

How can Linda say that she hates the wind?

I felt sick to my stomach as I got back in the car. I wanted to stay lost in happy childhood memories forever.

There had to be some way that we could be happy again. There just had to be.

FATHER OF THE YEAR

The very next day, Linda, Brooke, Nick, and I all flew up to New York City, where I was set to accept the national Father of the Year Award from the Father's Day/Mother's Day Council. It was a huge honor.But all I can remember about that night is how unhappy and miserable my wife was, and how much she had been drinking.

She drank so much wine in the hotel room as we were getting ready, even Brooke was afraid what might happen once she got into the ballroom. "Oh my God, Dad," Brooke whispered as we looked at Linda putting her lipstick on crooked in the hotel mirror.

Up at the podium when I accepted the award, I told the audience that Linda deserved to be sharing it. She was the one who taught me how to be a parent first and not just a friend to my kids. I wouldn't be the father I was without everything Linda had taught me. All of that was true.

In my mind, though, I just couldn't figure out where it all turned, and how she had gone down such a different path in the last few years.

I tried my best to enjoy that moment. Despite what my critics might say, I think I deserved that Father of the Year Award. A good father is one thing I feel like I can say with 100 percent certainty that I am. Even though the rug had been pulled out from beneath everything else in my life, I can't think of how a father could be any more present than I'd been for my kids—especially as we'd gone through all these difficult changes in the last three years. The only part I felt horrible about was that Nick and Brooke had been forced to witness so much fighting between Linda and me. I told them that in the hotel room after the ceremony—as Linda looked on with her half-cocked smile.

It all wound up captured on film in the final moments of the finale episode of *Hogan Knows Best*—including my hope that by next year I might be eligible to win a Husband of the Year award, too.

That was more of a stretch than anyone could have imagined.

Linda had already started packing up her things at the house in Miami. She had a big 18-wheeler in the driveway filled with boxes before the cameras even wrapped for the season.

Without my knowledge she had gone and rented a house in Brentwood, California. We had just sold our house in California a few months earlier, right? That didn't matter. Part of Linda's frequent disappearing act had been making trips to L.A. to get this new home all furnished. And as soon as the season wrapped toward the end of spring 2007, she headed out there to live for God knows how long. She told me flat out that I wasn't allowed to come visit her. I just plain wasn't welcome.

But Linda wasn't the only one who had been keeping a secret.

It was right around this time that my affair with Christiane Plante ended.

I was still married. Even though Linda was in the process of moving three thousand miles across the country just to get away from me at that point, I still had a wife. I had a family. I had every intention of making my marriage work. When I prayed to find happiness again, in my mind I was praying for Linda and me to get back to the way we once were.

So divorce was not an option for me.

But that night, as I sat there in that tuxedo and that black bandanna making proclamations in front of the TV cameras about wanting to become Husband of the Year, I knew in my heart that I had failed.

PART IV

THE UNRAVELING

CHAPTER 15

Cruel Summer

By the summer of 2007, the rug had been pulled out so hard from under me that the floorboards and support beams and foundation went with it. I felt like I had nothing to stand on.

I moved back into the big house on Willadel Drive up in Clearwater and put the Miami house on the market. So at least I was home—but even my home didn't seem the same.

My body wasn't the same, either. I was just too old. I was just too tired. I was just in too much pain. I felt like I was dragging myself out of bed every morning. The pain in my lower back was so bad I had to sit in a chair to just brush my teeth. I knew it was all just downhill from there. Some days I wondered why I even bothered getting out of bed in the first place.

After the mess of the last season, and the mess that my family was in, there wasn't a chance in hell that we'd land a fifth season of *Hogan Knows Best*. So for the first time in my life I felt unemployed. At the age of fifty-three to suddenly not have a job to look forward to left me wondering, just a little bit, what on earth I was good for anymore.

I tried not to focus on that. I tried to spend my days focused on my kids' careers instead. Even that wasn't easy. Brooke was spending more and more time with her mother in L.A. and was looking for an apartment in Miami. The one good upshot of the *Hogan*

Knows Best fiasco season was that Brooke was in the process of getting her own spin-off show, but it kept her so busy she just wasn't around very much.

Even Nick seemed to be a little bit tired of having his old man around all the time, which I thought was just typical sixteen-year-old behavior. He was seriously into motor sports now, and spending lots of time with the buddies who made up his racing team: John Graziano, Barry Lawrence, and Danny Jacobs.

One of the best things about that was they were all spending lots of time at the big house. John, who grew up just north of Clearwater, in Dunedin, Florida, was pretty much living with us that whole summer. I loved having all of that young energy around. It wasn't what I so desperately wanted—the sound of a home filled up by my happy family—but at least I wasn't alone.

I just don't do well alone.

JOHN

John Graziano first came into Nick's life because of their mutual fascination with Toyota Supras. They actually met at one of those Supra meets that Nick and I went to before he got his license— one of those events where enthusiasts get together in a parking lot to talk about the cars, and look at the cars, and show off their cars.

John was about five years older than Nick, but that common bond seemed to erase the years, and it wasn't long before they became best friends.

When Nick finally got his license, he was constantly at the track. He was out there before the track even opened and would stay until they kicked him off at night. He was changing his own tires and getting behind the wheel taking turn after turn to get the feel of it down. He loved drifting—the form of precision racing in which drivers slide their cars sideways around the corners—and I would be there as much as I could to help Nick push the cars on and off the track. John was usually right there with us.

When they showed Nick racing on *Hogan Knows Best*, they made it seem like a celebrity thing—like he got a couple of quick lessons and was racing all of a sudden. It wasn't like that. He was as dedicated as any professional athlete to becoming a driver. He took it real seriously. John was like his right-hand man, pushing him and supporting him when he needed it. I loved the fact that my son had a friend like John to bond with, given everything else that was happening in our lives. In some ways it was like watching me and Brutus in the early days—just bonding over mutual interests, and knowing someone's got your back, is so important in life.

John started sleeping over at the house a lot so he'd be there first thing in the morning to head to the track—or to catch a workout with me. He seemed to get a kick out of working out with Hulk Hogan in the morning, and unlike my own kids, who liked to sleep in, he was right there pushing me at like 7:00 A.M.

So John became a real fixture in our house. Even in Miami. He was around so much, the editors had a tough time cutting around him on *Hogan Knows Best*—because he'd always wind up in the shots and was never miked.

Nick really looked up to John. He viewed him almost like an older brother. Because of that bond, Brooke sort of treated him like a brother, too. Things were real bad in the Graziano household. Real bad. His father, Ed, allegedly tried to beat John with a baseball bat one time. Another time John told the police that his father came after him with a screwdriver. John's mother, Debbie, even got a protective order against Ed after he allegedly beat her up. It's all in the police reports and court documents. "Domestic" reports were the norm in that family.

I'll tell you more about that whole situation a little bit later, but the gist of it was that John was absolutely convinced Ed was going to kill him. That's one of the main reasons he found peace hanging out at our house. He felt safe with us.

It's hard to explain, but John seemed real lost at times. He wasn't sure what he wanted to do with his life. When he joined the marines in 2005, I got real scared for him. While he was over in Iraq in 2006, he would always manage to get to a phone somehow. I thought it was amazing that he would trek out to make a call under those awful conditions, and when he did, he would call us. We loved hearing from him. He said his own parents wouldn't accept collect calls, so he just called us instead.

We were so happy when he got back safe and sound in the spring of 2007, we took him into our home pretty much full-time. He really was a part of our family.

But John was real uneasy when he got back. He seemed more lost than ever in some ways. He had seen some pretty rough stuff in Iraq. He was in a transportation unit and in charge of driving vehicles over there, and at one point a roadside bomb had gone off right in front of the vehicle he was driving. Members of his company died. I can't imagine going through something like that, and how much that must mess with your head. Especially at twenty-one years old.

From the moment he returned, John kept talking about death. He kept saying he was sure he was gonna die. It freaked me out. The rest of the family, too. Even with all the chaos we had with Linda, we all tried to support him and be there for him. He jumped right back into Nick's racing team, and I just thought he'd work through whatever issues he had right there in Florida.

Then he did something unexpected. Just a month or so after he got back, John reenlisted with the marines. That summer, we got word that he would ship out to Iraq again that December.

Part of me wanted to find a way to stop him from doing it. I was just so scared about what might happen to him if he went back over there. But there was no stopping John. He was an adult. He made his own decisions. For some reason, he had made up his mind that going back to a war zone would be better than the situation he faced at home.

AUGUST 26, 2007

August 26 started out like a typical Sunday. I went out to the gym that morning, came back, and decided I wanted to go out on the boat—this offshore cigarette boat we kept docked right off the backyard. Any day on the water was a good day as far as I was concerned. I really needed a good day, too.

I thought I'd take that boat out for a good run, maybe thirty miles, head down the beach, stop by and see who was around, maybe pick up some of my buddies and just cruise. Your basic Florida Sunday. I figured I'd bring a few six-packs with me for anyone who came along to enjoy, but we were completely out of beer, which was really strange, because there are like ten refrigerators in the big house: Sub-Zeros in the kitchen and the pantry off to the side of the kitchen; a smaller refrigerator in the wine room; a refrigerator up in our bedroom; a refrigerator in my gym, in the guesthouse, in the boathouse. All those refrigerators and no beer. Once every couple of months our caretaker, George, would do a run and stock all the refrigerators. I guess he forgot.

I was hungry, and so were Nick and his pals. So we all piled into my four-door yellow pickup that morning, and we grabbed breakfast at the little restaurant we always went to. As we were leaving, I said, "Guys, I gotta pick up some beer." So we stopped by the Albertson's liquor store.

While Nick and Barry waited in the truck, I went in with John and Danny—who were both of legal drinking age. I was buying, of course, and I knew I'd be buying a lot, because John drank like a fish. I mean, when we were on the road with Nick's team, one of the things John would brag about was "I can't get drunk."

I remember one night I went out to a bar with John and Danny, and John must have bought eight, nine, ten shots in a row. I drank one or two of them before saying, "That's it for me, man. I'm not really good with drinking shots." He wouldn't have it: "No, no, man!" In the gym, John was always giving me shit—he loved that back-and-forth of trying to push each other to the next level—and this was that same sort of thing. John was bragging that night, "I can't get drunk." You could see he was drunk off his ass!

He just wouldn't admit it. He had that mentality. He was a hard-core, hard-living marine. I don't mean anything bad by it, but at that point in his life, that's just the way he was.

So I go into Albertson's liquor store that day and buy four or five cases of Miller Light, which is just about the only beer I ever drink, and some wine just to keep in the house. Then John said, "Hey, look at this Miller beer with lime in it!" and I told him to throw it in the cart. Danny picked something out, too—so we probably walked out of there with ten, twelve cases of beer. As soon as I got back, I started stocking all the refrigerators.

Finally I was ready to head out on the boat, and I threw two or three six-packs in a cooler. By that point Nick and his buddies had all decided they wanted to go out on the boat with me, so John and Danny each threw a six-pack into the cooler on top of mine.

All of a sudden Nick came to me and said, "Oh, Dad, there's these people from L.A. that want to do a reality show on drifting, and they were planning to meet with me today. Can they just go on the boat with us, too?"

"Sure." So now we've got this big group going on the boat, including these two reality TV execs whom I've never met.

It seems like right after we all got on the boat these huge thunderheads started rolling in. "Shit." I ran south about four or five miles to avoid the rain, and all of a sudden another thunderhead moves in.

John insisted he knew this island where we could hang out, so we ran really hard to escape the rain, like seventy, eighty miles an hour, and we pulled up to this island. It was deserted, and it would have been a nice place to hang out, but the rain clouds started pushing in again. So we went running back and decided to pull into Shephard's.

Shephard's is where I had that problem with Linda during the wrap party for the first season of *Hogan Knows Best*. It's kind of the hot place to be in Clearwater, although Linda never wanted to hang out there any other time. At least not with me.

So I backed the boat in and anchored, and we all slid off the back. For some reason, that spot stayed sunny. So I just stood in the shallow water there talking to these TV guys for over an hour while Nick, John, and Danny went up on the docks.

They're real strict at Shephard's, and I knew the security guards wouldn't let Nick inside. Even so, I kept checking up on where Nick was, and it turned out he was further down the dock with his boys, talking to some girls. Of course.

When the rain clouds started moving over Shephard's, I decided to reel it in. We gathered everyone up and zipped across the Intracoastal Waterway to the big house, which you can actually see from those docks.

Once we were there, the TV guys decided to head back to their hotel and everybody else decided to catch a shower. That's when Nick said, "Let's go out for dinner."

"What do we want?"

Someone suggested Arigato.

Decision made, we all headed for different bathrooms in the house to get ready.

As usual, I'm a little slower than everyone else. So just as I was getting out of the shower, Nick yelled to me. "Dad, we're gonna go ahead and get a table."

"All right. I'll be right behind you."

Three or four minutes later, I was dressed and in my Mercedes—never imagining for a moment that my whole world was about to change.

REALITY CHECK

There's been a lot of talk about what happened that day. You have to understand that when you live under the microscope of media attention like I do, you get used to people talking trash about you. You live with the fact that half of everything that's out there is wrong, and there are days when the tabloids or some radio show will go wild and almost everything that's said about you is just plain false. It's no big deal. Most of it's laughable. Most of it has no impact on your life. But when this car accident happened, it was like somebody lifted the floodgates. Suddenly everybody was out to take potshots at me and my family. Especially here in Tampa.

In many ways, Tampa's just a small town with big buildings. It's got that small-town mentality, where everybody seems to know everybody's business, and because I grew up here and made it big, Linda and I were kind of like local royalty. The problem is, when something goes wrong in the royal family, the wolves outside the castle start salivating.

I don't want to recount everything that's been said, but let's just say that a lot of people wanted to blame me for what happened to Nick and John that night. Those that didn't want to blame me directly wanted to blame me and Linda for letting our son pursue an interest in racing cars.

Forgive me if I wanted to help my kids pursue their dreams, whatever those dreams were. Just because Nick wanted to race cars doesn't mean that I let him off the hook when it came to being a responsible driver. Whenever Nick tried to take his need for speed off the track, he was punished. Big-time. After his second speeding ticket, I took away every electronic he had: computer, cell phone, iPods, the works. You know how big a deal that is to a kid in today's world. I even took his keys and grounded him. What else can a parent do?

Nick knew I wouldn't tolerate reckless driving, and in fact

it was just the opposite of the discipline he was learning in the precision-driving world.

Based on everything I know, Nick wasn't driving recklessly that night. Was he revving the engine? Was he making jackrabbit starts when the light turned green? Maybe, but that typical teen-driver stuff is a long way from driving dangerously. Remember, this accident happened less than two miles from our house. It's not like Nick and his pals were out carousing and driving wild all over town. They had just left!

Besides, none of the rumors and false reports out there even matter, because I've done the research. I've hired forensic experts. I had my lawyers subpoena the security tapes from businesses up and down Court Street that show Nick driving that yellow Supra, and his pal Danny driving my silver Viper. Those tapes show clearly that they were not drag racing or driving wild that night the way some people have reported.

It's not that I didn't believe my son when he told me he wasn't racing or being crazy that night. I did believe him, but if it ever came down to going to criminal court, or even for the civil suit from John Graziano's family, I had to assume that no one would take our word for it. That's just one of the many costs of celebrity, and I accept that.

But when someone out there started telling the media that I'd walked into a store with Nick at my side that Sunday in August and bought beer for him? Come on. I even had my lawyers subpoena the security tapes from Albertson's, just to prove a point, and they clearly show that Nick waited in my truck. So the supposed "eyewitnesses" to Nick's liquor-store run are just plain wrong—just like the supposed eyewitnesses who claimed that the boys were street racing that night. Ask any lawyer or police officer in any town or city in America and they'll tell you: Eyewitnesses are notoriously unreliable. Why someone would talk about things they don't know, or just plain lie to add insult to an already painful situation, is beyond me.

There would be plenty more lies to come.

On August 26, I didn't know what had happened. All I knew was I had to deal with the second-by-second unfolding of the events at hand. The horror of driving up on that mangled yellow wreck. The pain of seeing John's bleeding head and motionless body. The chaos of saws and helicopters. The phone calls to Linda and Brooke. It all unfolded so fast that night. In the back of that police car on the way to the hospital, as I prayed for John and Nick, everything else that was happening in my life just seemed to drift into the background somewhere.

Suddenly my mind started to focus in on John and Nick. John and Nick. They were all I wanted to think about. All I *could* think about.

When I arrived at the hospital that night, the scene was almost as chaotic as the accident scene. That police officer drove so fast, we actually beat the helicopters, so I was there when Nick and John arrived.

Doctors and nurses were buzzing everywhere. So were the cops. This one particular Pinellas County sheriff's officer clearly had orders to get a blood test on Nick, and he would not let it go. He was arguing with the nurses who were trying to get Nick into X-ray to make sure there was no internal bleeding, but this cop would not let up. For some reason he kept screwing up and having a hard time finding a good vein in Nick's arm.

The fact is, there was no legal indication whatsoever that Nick might have been drinking. My attorneys have showed me the police and EMS reports. The first thing they do at any car accident is look for signs of intoxication, and in the report, the cops said Nick's eyes were clear. They got really close to Nick's face when they talked to him. They couldn't smell any alcohol on him. His speech wasn't slurred; he looked alert and fine. That was in the police report. The EMS report? Same thing: no signs of alcohol, no signs of intoxication.

Now, I don't know if it's standard procedure when there's that type of accident or if it's because Nick happens to be my son, but why was that sheriff's officer so hell-bent on getting blood from Nick before they even set his broken wrist?

They had already taken John in a whole different direction, since he had the more serious injuries. They were treating him. They wouldn't let me see him, but that's certainly what I was being told—'cause I kept asking about him, over and over. It was making me crazy that I couldn't see him.

Instead of the doctors getting to fix my son, though, he had to sit around and wait for this cop to administer this blood-alcohol test. I heard later that the way this test was issued was not proper procedure at all. The guy had to order a second kit because he screwed the first one up entirely.

From what I understand, the nurses had wiped down the area on Nick's arm where the needle goes in with alcohol. Their concern was his health. They were testing him for drugs or conditions that could have interfered with medications or anesthetics if he wound up needing them. Alcohol was not their concern. I've since learned that you're not supposed to wipe the area with alcohol when you're testing someone for a blood-alcohol level. That spot's supposed to be wiped with Betadine so you don't get a false reading. Yet that's the same spot where this cop was drawing Nick's blood.

Was it an honest mistake? Maybe so. Like I said, it was pretty chaotic in there. But there's a real possibility that an improper procedure could have shown a false positive on my son. Heck, messing up the procedure would show a false positive on someone who'd never swallowed a drop of alcohol in their whole life, the way I understand it.

Of course, we'd never have a chance to refute that blood test in court, and when the cops released their findings, showing Nick had a .055 blood alcohol level, everyone just assumed the worst despite all the evidence to the contrary. "Guilty until proven innocent" seemed to be the way this whole thing would go down for my son. The fact is, this wasn't a DUI case at all. The legal limit in Florida is .08. So impairment wasn't the issue. All the release of that finding did, in my opinion, was give the prosecutors extra support as they went after Nick with a reckless driving charge. Because all the media reports saying it was a "high-speed crash" were wrong, too. Speed wasn't much of a factor at all. Like I said, I've hired forensic experts to go back and figure out what happened. So have the police. All of those reports, including the police reports, show that Nick was driving somewhere between 40 and 60 mph—at the most—on a stretch of road where the speed limit is 40.

If you saw the photos from the scene, I know what you're thinking—because it's the same thing I was thinking when I drove up on that crash: It looked like that car hit the palm tree going 300 mph. But you have to remember, this wasn't a normal car. It was a wide-body Supra with a fiberglass shell and the widest tires you can buy. It was a street-legal version of a precision racing vehicle. It was lightweight and built for speed and handling, not durability. So when Nick changed lanes, from the left lane to the right—again, this is what forensic experts have told me—he hit a deep puddle, hydroplaned and completely spun around. By the time the rear end of the Supra hit that palm tree, it was only doing about 30 mph.

Thirty. It seems crazy, right? The car looked mangled. But you also have to remember that the photos that showed up all over the news and the Internet were taken *after* the rescue workers hit that car with a saw and the Jaws of Life to make sure they had a clear path to get John out of his seat.

Even then, if you look at the cockpit of the car, the driver and passenger seats are intact. The rest of the car looks like an aluminum soda can that I just laid a leg drop on, but I know in my heart that if John had been wearing a seat belt, he might have walked away just like Nick.

I just wish I could go back and find out *why*. What was John thinking? Why *wasn't* he thinking? The sad thing is, until a miracle happens and John's completely healed, that's a question I'll never get answered.

It's these kinds of questions that have rattled around in my brain every day since that horrible day. Every day. Nonstop. I can't stop thinking about it.

CHAPTER 16

The Vigil

We never left the hospital that night. Once Nick's wrist was set and they'd checked him to make sure there wasn't any internal bleeding—which there wasn't, thank God—we camped out and waited for news about John.

At some point, John's family started to arrive, along with this girl Ashley who claimed to be John's fiancée. His brother Michael showed up, and his sister came. Seeing John's mother, Debbie, really choked me up. I just remember hugging her. I remember her hugging Nick. She was so glad Nick was okay. We were all just sitting there worried to death and praying together to hear some good news about John. Debbie's son. My son's best friend. The marine. The soldier. This kid whom I'd grown surprisingly close to in the past few years.

By the end of the first day, it was clear that John had suffered a real serious brain injury. He was unconscious. He was unresponsive. Doctors were using every drug in the book to try to reduce his brain's massive swelling. His condition was so serious, they kept him in the ICU, and for days and days no one was allowed to visit him for more than fifteen minutes at a time, once every few hours. Brooke and Linda were there by morning, and between our family and the Grazianos there were a lot of people trying to see him. So the hospital set aside a room where all of John's family and friends could gather.

When it comes to brain injuries, the first hours of treatment are critical. That's when most of the damage is done. I've learned a lot about this stuff since the accident happened, and in my opinion John was flown to the wrong hospital that night.

I wish he had gone to Tampa General, where they have an advanced brain trauma center, not to mention some of the best neurologists you can find anywhere in the United States. He didn't. Instead, the medevac helicopter had dropped him at Bayfront Medical Center in St. Petersburg, where doctors were giving a grim diagnosis from the start. They pumped him so full of drugs to try to reduce his brain swelling, they seemed fearful that the rest of his body just might shut down altogether.

By the second day, John's father, Ed Graziano, seemed to have given up on the idea that his son could recover. He got real mad and started pacing the halls making all kinds of noise—saying terrible things that I just couldn't believe could come out of a father's mouth.

Ed basically wasn't even a part of John's life in the last couple of years before the accident. John told me he wanted nothing to do with him. Like I mentioned ealier, John was convinced Ed was going to kill him someday and Debbie had already gotten an order of protection against him. Anyway, by the time the accident rolled around, they had separated.

The whole world would learn just what a hothead whack job this Ed Graziano was later on. Truth always has a way of rising to the surface. Right after the accident happened, though, Ed tried to make it seem to the courts and the media like he and John were as close as a father and son could be. I would learn pretty quickly why he was spinning those lies: In Ed's mind, I'm pretty sure, he thought of his son's crippling condition as winning the lottery. I know that's harsh, but that's just the way it seemed.

On the second day after the accident, Ed started talking about pulling the plug. I just couldn't believe a father could talk about his son that way. He wasn't dead! In fact, there was a lot of hope about what might happen when the swelling in John's brain went down. So for Ed to talk like that was just sick and disgusting to me.

After a few days of monitoring John's condition, I didn't feel that he was getting the best treatment. So I took the advice of one of my neighbors on Willadel, Steve Chapman, and called Dr. Fernando Vale (pronounced like "valet")—one of the top neurosurgeons at Tampa General. He took a look at John and convinced the doctors there to remove a large portion of John's skull to allow the brain to swell naturally, and then retreat when it was ready—so they wouldn't have to keep pumping him full of drugs.

I truly believe that if they had taken that action and removed the pressure on his brain immediately when John was brought in on the night of the accident, John would have been well on his way to recovery.

From the moment that accident happened, I pretty much stayed at the hospital every afternoon and every evening. Nick, Brooke, and Linda were there a lot, too, in the first few weeks. I was there all the time.

Ed would hardly ever show up. He'd come for a couple of hours at most and then leave. But John's mom, Debbie, was there and never left. Truly never: She slept right there in that hospital.

I guess we were a little over a week into this vigil when I finally said to Debbie, "You know, there's a beautiful Hilton hotel a block away from the hospital, or if you don't like the Hilton, there's a Holiday Inn right here." I told her I'd be happy to pay for it. I just thought that she should get a good night's sleep. As concerned as she was, she wouldn't be any good to John if she got sick herself from lack of rest.

I was finally getting Debbie to come around to thinking maybe it was a good idea when Ed chimed in. "Well," he said. "I always stay at the Vinoy." The Vinoy is kind of like the Peninsula Hotel in Beverly Hills. I thought it was a little much, and thought it was probably pretty unlikely that he'd ever stayed at that hotel—they weren't wealthy, as far as I knew, and they really didn't live all that far from St. Petersburg—but I didn't want to argue over something so trivial when we had all been through so much. I cared about John, and by default I cared about his family.

So I got three rooms at the Vinoy: one for Debbie, one for Ed—because they were separated—and one for Ed's parents, who had flown down from New York.

I realized pretty quickly that I'd made a mistake. Debbie was so unhappy with Ed's behavior that she asked me if she could change hotels. Police were even called in because Ed was brawling with family members at the hospital one day.

So of course I let Debbie change hotels. And once Ed started threatening me, I canceled his room and stopped talking to the guy.

Because of all the trouble he was causing, Debbie filed an injunction against him. Finally, Ed was only legally allowed to visit the hospital for an hour a day. I don't think he even bothered doing that.

MY HAPPY HOME

The Grazianos weren't the only ones who had trouble in their home life, of course. As much as I didn't want to think about it or focus on it, the trouble with Linda was still unfolding even in the aftermath of this accident.

It was real strange having Linda back home. I was hardly there. I stayed at the hospital as much as I could. Linda, Brooke, and Nick were sometimes with me, but when we crossed paths at the big house, it was tense.

Linda was drinking pretty much every night, and it seemed that her behavior after the accident was more more volatile than ever.

Three or four days after Nick's crash, I came home and heard Linda screaming upstairs. She was up in Nick's room, and the door was closed. When I realized she was yelling at my son, I opened the door—and found Linda standing over Nick with a wine bottle in her hand and screaming like a madwoman, "You're going to fucking jail! You're finished!"

I pulled Nick out of there as quickly as I could, and she flailed off screaming unrepeatable obscenities as she stumbled toward our bedroom.

Nick was a wreck. He was so fragile already. This accident had put him in a terrible place that he'd never been in before. He felt deeply responsible for what happened to John. He felt guilty. He didn't need this. No one needed this.

As much as she was on Nick, she was on me and Brooke, too. For a long time I had been wishing for my family to come together again. Now I wished that Linda would just leave.

Every night she was threatening divorce. She meant it this time—I saw how she had changed—but how could she be thinking of divorce right now? It just seemed so selfish to me.

I practically begged her, "Please, don't file. Our son's just had this accident. If we do this now, it'll make us look like the Britney Spears family. Please, don't file for divorce!"

I thought the idea that we would be publicly humiliated and raked through the tabloids might have some effect on her. Linda enjoyed her newfound fame, so obviously she wouldn't want this in the papers, right? I went so far as to tell her that if she was really hell-bent on ending this thing, I'd be willing to go ahead and get a mid-nuptial agreement. I said we could go to our financial attorney, Les Barnett, and draw up some papers and separate—but we wouldn't have to tell anybody. We could keep it private, and try it for a while; she could have all the money she wanted and everything she needed to live on her own in California, and then we could see if things got better.

Linda wouldn't hear it. I couldn't talk any sense into her. It's almost as if she wanted things to stay as awful and miserable as they were.

Linda was often perfectly normal by day, just like before she split for California. Once the wine wore off, we'd get along and get through this, and communicate as best we could. I even saw glimpses of the old Linda I fell in love with.

As we went into the second week of the hospital vigil, waiting and waiting for even the slightest improvement in John's condition, Debbie still looked real tired to me. I finally said, "Debbie, you know, this hotel thing is just too much. For John's sake, you need to go home and get some rest."

That's when she hit me with something I never expected to hear. "Well, I don't have a home," she said.

"What do you mean you don't have a home?"

She stated it more clearly. "I'm homeless."

In the middle of all of this, Debbie told me, Ed had kicked her out of their house.

At that point, John still wasn't showing signs of making a rapid recovery. None of us knew how long this might go on. I really felt bad for her. I wanted to help her. And Linda felt the exact same way when I told her Debbie's story.

So we rented Debbie a beautiful townhouse on Island Estates. Linda went out and bought her tons of furniture, just to make her feel at home. Comfy beds, and sofas, and flat-screen TVs, and every appliance and utensil she'd ever need in the kitchen. Believe it or not, Linda did that out of the kindness of her heart. Linda's got two sides. When the chips are down she'll take her shirt off her back for you—and then if she doesn't like you, she'll stab you in the back. But I know that she would have gone out and spent that kind of money for anybody in Debbie's situation.

Months later, the Grazianos' lawyers would accuse us of making a hollow attempt to pay Debbie off and convince her not to sue us. That simply wasn't the case at all. I knew the Grazianos would likely have to sue in order to pay for John's medical care. I understood that. I even talked to Debbie about it. "Debbie, I know you're gonna have to sue me. I understand that eventually you'll need to find a way to help pay for John getting back on his feet. Let's not even worry about that."

In a time when it seemed like nothing could make the situation worse, Debbie's father died. She asked if we could help with the funeral expenses, and we did. We took her other son, Michael, and enrolled him back in college, simply because he hadn't been in college for a while and we were trying to get their life back to some type of normalcy.

Normalcy. It seemed like the thing she wanted most.

If John had been injured by somebody else, or in some other car accident, or if he had come back from fighting in the Middle East with some life-threatening injury, I think we would have done the exact same thing for his family. It wasn't unusual behavior. I mean, Linda used to buy our housekeepers new carpet when they needed it. I haven't had a housekeeper yet that I haven't bought a car. That's how Linda is. She's over the top. That's the Linda I fell in love with, who was always so positive and uplifting. I loved seeing glimmers of that. It actually gave me some hope for our marriage again.

Considering how much time John spent at our house, and how close he was to Nick? Doing everything within our means to help his family wasn't even a question.

DEAD OR ALIVE

It's hard to remember the time line of how things went down in that hospital. The days and nights seemed to blend together. I think it was right around the start of the third week when something terrible happened. Something that I still can't shake.

I came to the hospital that night, right around dinnertime, and no one was in John's room. Even though he couldn't respond, I rubbed his hand and talked to him like I always did—saying all these real positive things, trying to pump him up and challenge him to get better, telling him he could do anything he put his mind to. That same sort of push we would give each other in the gym. He always responded to that kind of motivation before the accident, so why wouldn't his mind respond to it now? That was my thinking, anyway.

By this time I'd started to learn what all the lights and beeps on the machines meant, and I noticed that his oxygen level was real low. I asked a nurse about it, and she said they had blood on order for him. His blood levels were down about four pints is what they told me, but the blood hadn't come up from downstairs yet. It's the kind of stuff that happens in hospitals that just makes you insane. Someone needs blood and they have it downstairs, but no one's brought it up yet? Excuse me? It's not a pizza delivery!

So anyway, I'm in there talking to John, spending some time with him, and Debbie and a friend of hers came in. As soon as they walked in they both commented that John's color didn't look so good. And not three seconds after I put John's hand in Debbie's hand, he flatlined.

Beeeeeeeeeep. It happened out of nowhere. Just like that. The alarms went off, and about ten nurses and other hospital personnel came rushing into the room while the three of us pushed back against the walls, worried to death.

I've never been around anything like that. This big, heavy lady started pushing on his chest. The others were all checking the tubes and wires. But nothing was happening.

Then out of nowhere this male nurse Jamie, this guy with a small frame on him but who's really well built and muscular, came rushing in and pushed that big nurse out of the way. He yelled at one of the other nurses to get him this box of some kind that was on the floor, and she grabbed it and put it down on the other side of the bed. "No!" he yelled. "On this side!" He wanted the box to stand on.

So Jamie climbed up on that box and started pumping on John's chest. It looked like he was completely crushing John's ribs. He pumped and pumped and pumped. This must've gone on for like two or three minutes. It was intense. Jamie just wouldn't stop.

He was soaking wet with sweat—and then all of a sudden, as quickly as this whole thing started, it stopped. The machines came back on. The beeping started. John's color came back. He was breathing again. Just like that. He's remained pretty stable ever since.

I honestly thought that was it for John. I was really shaken up by it. Nick was real upset when he heard about it, too—to think that his best friend had actually died and been brought back? In some ways I don't think Nick has ever been the same since that moment.

In some ways, neither have I.

TRIUMPHS AND SETBACKS

It was the first week of November when we finally got approval to move John out of that hospital and over to the VA Medical Center. I say "we" because I'd been working with Debbie Graziano the whole time to make that happen. She was still John's appointed guardian at that point. It had been a long process with all kinds of paperwork, but we just thought he'd get more individual care over there than he was getting at Bayfront. The two of us were so happy it was finally happening.

John was still nonresponsive, but doctors had started him on rehabilitation exercises to keep his muscles in shape. I was sure the new location would help him improve. Then, just as things started looking up a little bit, I got walloped.

After what they called an "extensive investigation," the Pinellas County Sheriff's Department issued an arrest warrant for my son—charging him with reckless driving and driving with alcohol in his system (despite what I said about how the blood test was issued). They even cited him for having dark tinting on the windows of the Supra.

On November 7, my now seventeen-year-old son turned himself in. I couldn't believe he would have to go through this, and go to court. It was a one-car accident. His best friend was crippled, and even the top doctors were saying he would likely require hospital care for the rest of his life. Isn't that punishment enough?

But Nick understood, and he faced it like a man. They booked him. We put up the ten-thousand-dollar bail so he could come home with us that same day, and we girded ourselves for what was to come, all the while hoping that this would play out in a court of law and not in the press like so much of this had already.

The very next day, November 8, we moved John over to the VA hospital. As I headed in the front door to visit him, just as I had every day since the accident, these police officers stopped me. They had received a call from Ed Graziano, they said, and they were told to stop me from going into John's room. I talked them through it, and talked to Debbie, and I managed to visit John one or two more times after that. But that was it.

The Grazianos forbid me to come see him anymore.

No one ever gave me a reason, but I knew it was because they were preparing to file suit against us. I knew it wasn't Debbie making that decision. No way. I guess I should have seen it coming. How could you sue a guy who was talking to your son in his hospital bed, trying everything he could to help motivate your son to get better? I wanted nothing more than to see him up walking again. But my whole thing was that I wouldn't take a lawsuit personally.

Of course it was my son behind the wheel. Of course it would take a lot of money to give John the best care possible. I *wanted* to make sure John got the best care possible, and I was more than willing to pay for that. If a lawsuit was what it took to make that happen, so be it.

What really bothers me is that because of all these ulterior motives they had, they actually removed Debbie as John's legal guardian and put some court-appointed guy in charge of John's care instead of his own mother. From what I could gather, the court did that because they felt Debbie had been swayed by the gifts and money that Linda and I gave her in the weeks right after the crash. What saddens me is that soon after this, Debbie started badmouthing Nick, and my whole family, in the press. I'm not sure what Ed Graziano did to make Debbie change her stripes. I don't even want to think about it. The fact is that he somehow convinced his whole family to make a united front against the Hogans.

Months later, after the Grazianos formally filed a civil suit and I learned how much money they were after, I became convinced that no one, even that court-appointed guardian whose sole purpose was to do what was best for John, truly had John's best interest in mind. It became brutally clear, in my opinion, that all anyone wanted to do—including and especially the lawyers on every side of this thing—was to get rich off of this tragedy and to do it at my expense.

At that time, my biggest challenge was learning to live with the fact that I wasn't allowed to see John anymore. They couldn't stop me from praying for him, which I did every day and still do, but not seeing him was tough on me. It had become a daily ritual. Going to see John was a part of my life now. I felt a responsibility and an overwhelming desire to be there as much as I could. It's all I would think about at times.

I was worried about what might happen to him if I wasn't there. I was worried that he'd lose motivation if he didn't hear my voice. Honestly, I was worried about what his father might do to him if no one was looking.

I was worried for my son, too. So worried I was sick. I felt tired and drained. Why was this all happening?

In the middle of all of that, Linda decided it was time for her to up and go back to California—and she wanted to take Nick with her, to get him away from all the local press. Not to mention that Brooke was barely speaking to me. She wouldn't tell me why she was angry, and I worried myself to death about that, too.

I suddenly opened my eyes to the fact that my whole life, which had been falling apart before this accident, had continued to fall apart while I was focusing all my attention on John.

About the only thing that kept me going was that I finally had something to look forward to at the end of November: a job. Not just a one-off wrestling gig, either. A new job that I hoped would help put everything in my life back on track.

A KICK TO THE CHEST

Three months had passed since Nick's accident. There I was, standing on the Los Angeles set of *American Gladiators*—a revamped version of the popular 1980s competition in which regular people go head-to-head in a series of battles and challenges with a crew of pumped-up male and female bodybuilders. It was my first-ever prime-time network television show, and I was all suited up with minutes to go before the cameras rolled.

Let me tell you, brother, I was nervous. It seems crazy, I know. I've been on TV a million times. I've had cameras all over my house. This was different. I'd never been a television host before.

In wrestling it was always someone else in charge of holding the mike. I'd be the guy going, "Hey, Mean Gene, let me tell you something!" I'd talk right into the camera with my Hulk voice raging while the other guy kept it all together. On *Hogan Knows Best*, you weren't even supposed to acknowledge that the camera was there. So this was new. And I couldn't even lean on my cohost, Laila Ali, the daughter of the great Muhammad Ali, for advice because she was on shaky ground, too. She'd just come off *Dancing with the Stars*, and I think the producers thought I was gonna lead *her* through this hosting thing. Boy, were they wrong.

As if the pressure I was laying on myself wasn't bad enough, the head of the network, the big man in charge, Ben Silverman, was ten feet away watching my every move. He was the guy who thought I'd be the perfect host for this show; who made the decision to hire me; who put his name on the line; who had the faith that Hulk Hogan could carry the day even after all of this bad press I'd suffered after Nick's accident.

We'd spent the day doing walkthrough rehearsals, and none of them were smooth. The stunts, the Power Ball, the Gauntlet, the rigging—here it was the eleventh hour and everybody was still scrambling to try to get the mechanics down. So nobody really paid any attention to Laila or me. Neither one of us knew where to turn, or which camera to work to.

It felt to me like we needed two more *weeks* of rehearsal, and here we had scrunched all of it into one day and had just a few minutes to go before we went live. (Not "live" live. We wouldn't be on the air. They were shooting this "live to tape," which means they try to do the whole thing without stopping so it has the energy of a live show; and if you mess up and have to shoot something over again, there's usually hell to pay.)

So there I stood. A thousand people in the stands at the Sony building in L.A. The excitement was wild. Nobody knew how hard my knees were shaking. The thing is, no one knew how much I *needed* to be on prime-time TV.

As far as I was concerned, this was the break of a lifetime. I had so much riding on it. Not only in my career, but in my life. *If this is a hit, maybe Linda will realize I'm not ready to go to the glue factory after all.* This is what I'm thinking as we're about to start the show: *If this prime-time gig takes off, maybe I can get other stuff going where I don't have to get hit in the head with a steel chair to make a living anymore. This could be the huge transition I've been waiting for. This could lead to bigger endorsements, big movie work.* And if all that happened, then maybe—just maybe—this would be the thing that could finally fix my marriage.

Even then, no one in the outside world knew that my marriage to Linda was broken almost beyond repair.

The thing is, after all these years, Linda still didn't seem to fully grasp the concept that I couldn't make a living in L.A. I couldn't walk away from wrestling. There was too much money in it. And my wrestling career was on the East Coast. Sure, I could live in L.A. and make a low-budget B movie for kids every two to three years, but that wasn't anywhere near enough to pay the rent—not the way Linda wanted to live. At fifty-three years old, what did she expect me to do to keep bringing in millions of dollars a year?

So this, a primetime gig on *American Gladiators*, a show I loved in its original incarnation back in the 1980s, with the same kind of showmanship and characters you'd find in the wrestling world, a show that shot in L.A.—just a few miles from that house Linda rented in Brentwood—this thing really got me fired up.

"What do you want to do that for?" Linda said when I first told her about the gig. "That show sucked the first time. And now it's a re-make?"

I knew enough not to take career advice from Linda. I also knew *American Gladiators* wouldn't make me millions all on its own. Not even close. But if it took off? The possibilities were endless. There was no period at the end of the sentence, no cap on top of what could come next, and that fired me up. Even with my knees shaking, I remember thinking, *I can do this. I can pull this off!*

So I stood there with the microphone. We were ready to go. Ben Silverman was on one side. The president of Sony was on the other. A few feet away I had my entertainment attorney, Henry Holmes, who had been with me for what seemed like a million years, and my business partner, Eric Bischoff, who had made me more money during my WCW years than I ever made at the WWF. They had a lot riding on this, too. They were already laying the groundwork for a wrestling-related show to sell to another network if this show worked. Lastly, sitting off to the side, sat my son, Nick. My boy who had been through so much, and who I would have done anything for just to see him strong and happy again.

"Thirty seconds!"

This was it. Time to focus. The audience went nuts. Right then, my cell phone rang. With John in the hospital and so much going on with Linda, and Nick now facing criminal charges over his accident, I kept my phone on me all the time. The only people who had the number were people I needed to hear from. I knew I had to take that call.

I looked at the screen and saw it was my financial attorney calling, Les Barnett. I told the crew to hold on, and I flipped the phone open.

"Les, what's up?"

"Are you sitting down?" he said.

"No, I'm not sitting down. Why?"

He sounded real serious. Nervous even.

"Well, you might want to sit down," he said.

"No, I can't, I'm getting ready to work, Les. What's going on? Just tell me."

"I just got served papers by your wife's attorney," he said. "She filed for divorce."

Brother, I felt like I'd been kicked in the chest by a mule. I'm telling you that couldn't hurt any worse than those words. I didn't know if I was gonna puke or faint.

The whole crowd started chanting, "Ho-GAN! Ho-GAN! Ho-GAN!" Instead of pumping me up for the big moment, the noise made me wobbly.

I flipped the phone shut.

"Give me a second," I told the crew. "I just had an emergency phone call."

Then I did something I would never do unless it was part of the plan: I turned my back on a stadium full of fans who were chanting my name. I couldn't take it. I felt dizzy. I walked over to Eric and Henry and said, "Guys, you're not gonna believe this. Linda just filed for divorce." Eric panicked. He knows me too well. He knows how emotional I can get. Henry just kept saying, "Oh my God. Oh my God."

These guys knew everything. They knew how bad things had been with Linda. They'd seen it all. They'd witnessed their share of it firsthand. They also knew this was news I never expected to hear. Not in my wildest dreams. No matter how bad it got, I was married for life. "Till death do us part."

In my mind, the fact that Linda had moved three thousand miles across the country to get away from me and our life in Florida was nothing but a major bump in the road. We'd fix it, like we'd always fixed it. I believed that. I thought I knew it for a fact.

The fact that something so devastating could happen at this moment was just unimaginable. Henry saw it in my face, and for some reason he knew just what to do. It was like a scene from *Rocky*. He became my Mick—my longtime personal trainer and coach in the corner. "Pull it together, Terry," he said. He looked me dead in the eye. "Terry! You've got to pull it together!"

He was right. *American Gladiators* was too important. I couldn't cave now. No way. I took a deep breath. I Hulked Up like I was in a title match at Madison Square Garden. I turned around and gave a nod to the crew and stepped back to my spot in front of the camera. The crowd roared. The countdown began. "And five . . . four . . . three . . ."

I stared into that lens as they rolled tape and didn't even look at the teleprompter. I fired myself into performance mode, and when they gave me the sign, I squeezed that mike tight and held it to my mouth and growled off the top of my head, "Do you wanna live forever?!"

I have no idea where that came from or why I said it. Neither did the crew. So we backed up and they made me do it again. I took a deep breath. The crowd roared. I held that mike. I looked into the lens and I said, "This is *American Gladiators*!"

I managed to get through the first segment of the show without a hitch. Everyone seemed pleased. No one but Eric and Henry had any idea how torn up I was inside. I've pushed through wrestling matches with torn muscles and even a shattered kneecap. But this was different. This was a pain that couldn't be ignored.

As soon as I got a break I went to my son. I was freaking out. I knew I had to tell him, but I didn't know how he'd react. So I just said it. "Nick. Your mom just filed for divorce."

I expected him to be upset, maybe angry, but he didn't freak out like I did. In fact, when I told him he seemed rational and calm. "Well, Dad, I thought she was gonna do it. She's been talking about doing it. She's been meeting with lawyers out here."

That surprised me. I said, "Oh, really?"

He said, "Yeah, I was just hoping she wouldn't."

The way he acted, I think Nick already knew she filed but didn't want to be the one to break it to me.

My God. How could my wife, his own mother, let him carry that kind of a secret around on top of everything else he had going on in his life? How could she do that to her own son? How could she do this to our family?

Dazed all over again, I went on and finished the show. I went through the motions. I did what everyone expected Hulk Hogan to do. The whole time I was thinking about Linda.

I knew she wasn't happy. But why now? Why in the middle of everything else we were going through?

My God. It suddenly hit me. *Now we're gonna have to go through this whole thing in public.*

Why would she want that? Why?

CHAPTER 17

The Downward Spiral

From that moment on, things started spiraling down for me. I had a real hard time getting through the days. I remember being on the set and looking at myself in the monitor and realizing how stressed I looked. I worried everyone could read it in my face, like I had just experienced a tragedy or something.

If you went back and looked at tapes of those shows now, I'm sure you'd see it. It got to where it was like drudgery being on the set. During every break, every moment of downtime, my mind would race. I started to doubt everything in my life. *I'm not a quitter. I don't fail. How could I fail at marriage?* Then I'd turn it around and keep thinking there must be some way to fix this, something I could do to make it better.

I kept trying to call Linda. She answered my calls for a while. I didn't know what to say, so I'd go, "Hey, how you doing?" Or I'd say something as simple as "It's a nice day out today," and she'd lose it. "It's not a nice fucking day. It's blah blah blah." She was completely over the edge.

As much as I didn't want to believe it, my wife of nearly twenty-three years had made her mind up that there was no talking or fixing or changing this. That was something new. Something had changed gears. She had changed. I don't know whether she was hell-bent on starting her life over or if she had already met somebody else. Whatever her mission was, she was planning to accomplish it.

For all those nights of hearing "Fuck you, Terry" as my head hit the pillow, for all those divorce threats over all those years, it never occurred to me to take the first step and leave my wife, because every new morning would be a new start. She'd show me some little bit of her old self, and it would give me hope. It would give me a reason to keep going.

Plus, I thought, after twenty-three years of marriage, what would Linda do without me? She'd been Hulk Hogan's wife for most of her life. I provided for her. I gave her everything she wanted and needed. She depended on me.

Once I realized there was no talking to Linda, there was no changing her mind, I met with a divorce attorney named Ann Kerr. Ann's been in this business forever and has seen it all—but even she had never seen anything like Linda.

I've never been to a shrink, but I think Ann Kerr played that role for me. Once I started telling Ann all the details of the state of my relationship, I just unloaded on her. When I was done talking, Ann said something that really knocked me out. She looked me square in the eyes and she said, "Terry, in my opinion, you were verbally and mentally abused."

"What are you talking about?" I said. I didn't even know what that meant.

"Terry, your wife manipulated you," she said. "It seems to me, for all these years, you've been mentally and emotionally abused."

Here I am, fifty-four years old, and this divorce attorney is telling me that it sounded to her like I'd been browbeaten throughout my entire marriage. Could that be true?

The more I thought about it, the more I thought, *Maybe so.* I mean, look at my actions: always trying to appease Linda, always trying to make her happy. When you think about an abused child, they're always seeking more affection from the parent that's abusing them. If there's one parent who's good to them and cooks them breakfast and takes care of them, that relationship is fine, but it's the parent that's abusive that the child will jump through hoops for, doing whatever he can to win their acceptance. The squeaky wheel gets the grease, right? Is that what I was doing with Linda? Just going back for more? Trying to appease her no matter how badly she beat me up? For all those years?

Oh, you're not happy here? Okay, Linda, let's move to Miami. Here's a $12 million house. Is it possible that despite all my physical strength, Linda was capable of beating me up on some mental level?

I've been trying to come to grips with that possibility ever since. That's not easy to do when every time I let someone know what was happening behind closed doors they question why the hell I stayed with her in the first place. I guess it goes back to that obsessive thing: When I'm in, I'm in—150 percent. That's just how I've always been.

When I took that vow "for better or worse, till death do you part," I meant it. In my opinion, that's the strongest, most important contract you can ever sign in this lifetime. It's a vow of total commitment.

Listen to those words: "for better or worse." There's no out clause! There's no walking away if it doesn't work. If it gets worse? Tough. You deal with it.

There was no doubt we had seen the "worse" part. As a family we were certainly in the thick of it with this whole situation with Nick. For me, though, Nick's accident was a wake-up call. I was suddenly so grateful that Nick was alive. I was so grateful for Brooke and Linda and this life we had together—as imperfect as it was. Rather than the accident putting everything in perspective for Linda, rather than it showing her what's important in life and how important it was to pull our family together and to keep our eyes on the blessings we have simply being alive and being healthy, she decided that this was the moment to cut loose and go out on her own.

I couldn't understand it. I still don't understand it. I honestly thought that no matter how bad things got, we would always be together.

I love Linda unconditionally. I mean it. It goes far beyond the marriage vows. Far beyond the legal contract. In my mind, love is forever. That's what I believe, and what this whole terrible situation made me believe more than ever: that once you love someone, if you truly love someone, love never goes away. Am I a hopeless romantic? Am I a numbskull? I don't know, but if you stop believing in that, then what else is there to believe in?

I mean, even if you argue, even if you separate, even if you can't live together and decide to get divorced, if you truly love someone you will always, *always* love them.

As soon as I got a chance, I called Brooke to talk to her about the whole situation, and my daughter told me, "Dad, Mom hasn't loved you for a really long time." As a husband, as a father, to have your own kids tell you they think it might actually be better if their mother and I don't live together anymore? It was devastating. It messed with everything I ever thought I knew about life and love and marriage. Marriage was supposed to be forever.

Knowing all of that, knowing what true love is, and knowing that Linda was openly telling her own children that she didn't love me anymore, I was left with one big question—a mind-blowing question that I've been wrestling with ever since that phone call on the *Gladiators* set kicked me in the chest. *Did Linda ever really love me?*

FACING THE MIRROR

A week and a half after I got that call, *Gladiators* went on break and I flew home to Tampa. Alone. Nick stayed at his mom's house there in L.A., and Brooke had found her own apartment in Miami.

So I walked into the big house on Willadel, this giant place that was always full of noise and energy with the kids running around, and their friends, and especially this time of year with

Linda going over the top with holiday decorations that rivaled something you'd see in Rockefeller Center in New York City. I walked in, and it was dead silent. I'm looking at all these pictures of my family. The kids. Me and Linda. I just couldn't take it.

I made it all the way upstairs and saw Linda's empty closet— this closet of hers that's bigger than most people's whole bedrooms. The whole thing was just empty.

I walked into Nick's room, and kept asking myself over and over again why he was upset with me. He kept telling me nothing was wrong. He said everything was fine. But then he'd spend 90 percent of his time with his mother, and when he was with me he had this "woe is me" look in his eyes. I just didn't get it.

I sat on Brooke's bed and asked the same questions. She had moved out and was barely talking to me anymore. What had I done?

I felt miserable, and after traveling back from California, I was so tired I was wired. Do you know that feeling? My mind was racing, and I just couldn't be alone. I couldn't take it. So I grabbed my keys and headed right back out the front door.

I wound up at a place called Oz. A strip club. I was so naive, I never even stepped foot into a strip club until somewhere around 1992. No joke. All I ever thought about was wrestling and making money, and then when I had a family all I thought about was getting home to see them in between matches on the road. Man, I had no idea what I had been missing. And when Hulk Hogan walks into a strip club it's not like any normal guy walking in. The whole place kind of goes wild, you know? The girls get all excited. "Oh, Hulk . . ."

I went out seeking company that night, and I had plenty of company at Oz. "Hulk, you're so strong!" "Hulk, oh my." I sat there and drank and drank and enjoyed the company of all these adoring young women till the place closed down. Until the house lights came up, I felt like I was the Wizard of Oz!

I had a pretty good buzz on by the time I came back to the house. Don't even get me started on how stupid that was to be out drinking and driving. Imagine if the cops had pulled me over.

After what Nick had been through? They would've thrown me in jail just to make an example out of me. I wouldn't have blamed them one bit. My mind was so messed up, every decision I made was bad. I could've killed someone. In fact, I could have killed someone in more ways than one, because I think I brought my gun with me. I think I had it in the car. Can you imagine the headlines if I'd been pulled over drunk with a gun in my lap? Why the hell did I bring the gun in the first place? Or did I? I honestly can't remember. I was really a mess.

So I walked back into the house in that ridiculous condition, and there I was confronted by the photos of my so-called happy family again. Going to the strip club, drinking, getting all that attention from the girls—it didn't solve a damned thing. In fact, it made me feel worse. I felt more alone than ever.

That's when I sat down on my chair in the bathroom. A big bottle of Captain Morgan's and an open bottle of Xanax found their way to the counter. The gun found its way to that counter, too. I can't tell you how. I can't tell you if I sat down with the intent to kill myself. I don't know the answer.

I used to keep that gun in a safe, the same safe where Linda kept some of her really expensive jewelry, but I'd have these crazy paranoid thoughts sometimes. After Phil Hartman, the *Saturday Night Live* star, was shot and killed by his own wife, I started having these visions of Linda getting all drunk or coked up and grabbing that gun and shooting me in my sleep. What's really crazy is Phil Hartman's wife was from Thousand Oaks, and when we had a home in California it was right there. Linda and Phil's wife used to drink at the same bar down at the bottom of the hill.

So I started moving that gun. I'd hide it in different places in the house and then forget where I hid it and have to search for it, worrying the whole time that Linda had it. I'd make myself crazy over this stupid gun that I'd only fired twice, ever, at a shooting range. It was nuts. So I have no idea where I picked up the gun that night, or why, but there it was. Waiting for me.

I know that some time the next morning I took a phone call from Eric Bischoff. He was real concerned. He wanted to make sure I was okay. I told him I was. I wasn't. I took a call from my neighbor Steve Chapman, too. He was real worried. I told him I was fine. The phone rang a few times after that, and I just didn't pick up. I didn't want to talk to anyone. I just sat there, popping half a Xanax at a time—not the little pills, but these big horse-pill Xanax—and washing them down with the rum.

There were times when I thought that whole bottle of pills would go down easy. A bunch of those pills with the rest of that bottle. I'd heard that wasn't a painful death—that you'd just go to sleep and that's it.

Then I noticed the gun in my hand.

I was careless with it—running it up and down my right leg. Scratching the side of my nose with it. Feeling the cold steel of the barrel as it dragged across my cheek. I'd learned years earlier to never put your finger on the trigger unless you were ready to fire. It was basic gun safety: You keep your index finger pointed straight ahead, and you don't curl it over that trigger unless you mean it. But I kept my finger pressed right to that trigger the whole time. Right on it. Firm.

Just three pounds of pressure is all it would take—nothing for these big hands of mine—and if I moved that finger like an inch in the right direction, like flicking off a light switch, I could have blown my brains out.

I remember how it tasted when I put the barrel in my mouth, and the sound it made when the metal clicked against my teeth.

It was real weird behavior—like I was psyching myself up to do the deed. Mystifying myself into thinking it was the right thing to do.

People might look at a guy like me and think, *He would never commit suicide.* But I was so depressed I just kept thinking, *This would be so easy.* I understand now how it's possible for *anyone* to get themselves into such a trance that the actual suicide could happen by accident. It's seductive. And like I said before, when I make my mind up on something, you can pretty much count on the fact that I'm gonna follow through. Whatever the cost. Whatever the pain. Whatever it takes: When I'm in, I'm in all the way.

Add to that the haze of the pills and the booze and it's some sort of miracle that the gun just didn't go off. Heck, the tips of my fingers are still numb from that Tombstone incident way back in the '90s. Which means I probably could have pulled that trigger without even knowing I'd done it.

Boom! The end.

Two days into this mess, my phone rang again. I looked at it. I didn't recognize the number, but it was a 310 area code. The Beverly Hills area. Not many people have my cell phone number. *Could it be Nick or Brooke calling from that rental house Linda's got in L.A.?* For some reason, at that second, I was real curious. So I picked it up.

"Hi Terry. It's Laila."

It was Laila Ali—my cohost on *Gladiators*.

"I just wanted to see how you're doing."

This girl I barely knew had picked up on the fact that I was having a real hard time on the *Gladiators* set. Days had gone by, and she was still thinking about it. She was thinking about me. I was floored. Why did she care?

The funny thing is, I'd met her dad a bunch of times. He was the guest referee at the very first WrestleMania—holding my arm up when I won the championship belt. Right there in the ring with me in the heart of Hulkamania. Whenever we saw each other, the greatest boxer on earth used to hug me and whisper in my ear, "You're the greatest of all time, Hogan." I got such a kick out of that—that this guy I idolized, who was truly the greatest, would say that to me. And here his daughter is calling me up out of the blue to see how I'm doing. She cares how I'm doing. She wants to know if I'm okay.

You know what? I wasn't okay. Not until that moment. For some reason, that phone call snapped me out of it. I can't explain why. Who knows why things happen the way they do? Was there a *reason* it happened? I can't help but think, *Yes.* I've never told her this, and she might not even understand the depth of the impact she had on me, but Laila Ali saved my life. With a simple phone call. By simply thinking about me, and caring enough to call me and ask me how I was doing. At that moment, that call saved my life.

Laila invited me to go to church with her—to a place called the Agape Church (pronounced "a-GAH-pay"), a place I had never heard of and that had absolutely no meaning to me at that moment. But I loved the idea that she would offer something like that. Something so personal.

At that time in my life, for somebody who was almost a stranger to say, "Hey, we love you and we miss you and we care about you, and we wanna make sure you're doing good," was just shocking. It was so the polar opposite of what I'd been hearing from Linda for so long.

She didn't stop there, either. She told me to call her back if I needed to talk. "Here's my other numbers in case you can't get ahold of me," she said. "If you get a hold of my husband, have him page me or call me so I don't miss your call." She was being so nice to me. She didn't want anything from me, or need anything from me. She just wanted to make sure I was okay. It caught me so off guard.

When I hung up that phone I broke down crying like a baby.

Maybe other people get phone calls like that every day. Maybe I've been living under a rock all these years. But for me, that was it. After I stopped crying I got up from my chair. I took a shower. I ate. I slept. That feeling of bleeding inside, that emptiness, that depression, wasn't gone, but the flow of it had slowed just enough that I could move again.

The next day I flew back to L.A. I went back to the set. I gave Laila a big hug when I saw her, and I got back to work. I never did go to church with her. We were only there for a few more days of shooting, and I just don't think I fully absorbed what a good idea it would have been for me to go with her to that church. It would take me quite a while to learn to be fully aware of the people who were reaching out to help me.

It still wasn't easy for me to be on that set, performing the way everyone wanted me to perform, but somewhere in the middle of those December days I started psyching myself up for something better.

I realized that those moments with the gun in my hand were as low as I'd ever been, but I'd been low for a very long time. Even before Nick's accident, I just felt angry or depressed or fed up all the time.

I was sick and tired of feeling sick and tired.

I was determined to change things.

I got way too close to the edge, and I told myself I would never go down that dark road again.

I was gonna get through this. Not only was I gonna get through this, I would somehow rise above it all and fix everything that had gone to shit in my life and be happy again!

Yeah, I know. Even I thought it sounded pretty ridiculous. I had absolutely no idea how I was gonna do any of that. I trusted the feeling, though. I trusted my resolve. I trusted my instincts. I trusted my gut. That's pretty much how I've made every big decision I've ever made in my whole life, and I knew that nothing had ever mattered as much as my resolve to be happy at that moment.

What I didn't know was that my will would be tested before December was even finished.

BACKING AWAY

When *American Gladiators* wrapped for Christmas break, I headed home to Tampa again.

I'll be honest: I was still worried about what might happen when I walked back into that house—when I saw those pictures again, when I laid down alone to go to sleep in that big bed that

Linda and I used to share, knowing my family wasn't there. I had made up my mind to get through this, but that certainly didn't mean it would be easy. What if I freaked out again?

I tried not to think about it as I came home from the airport. I must've had my head buried worse than I thought, because I didn't even notice that all the lights in the house were on when I walked up to the front door. I put my key in and turned the lock and pushed the door open.

I froze. What the hell was going on? The house was all decked out with greenery and Christmas lights. I walked in and saw there was a fire going in one of the fireplaces. I rounded the corner and saw another fireplace lit up, too. There were like fourteen fireplaces in that house. Were they all on?

It smelled like a turkey dinner was cooking. It smelled delicious. There were Christmas trees set up.

All of a sudden someone steps out from the kitchen. "Hi, honey."

It was Linda!

I felt like I'd stepped into *A Christmas Carol*. Was I dreaming?

It staggered me. And if this was a ghost, was it Christmas Past or Christmas Future?

Linda's hair was all hot-rolled up like she wore it in the '80s. She had an apron on, and pink lipstick, and these long pink fingernails. I couldn't figure out if she looked like the young Linda I fell in love with, or if this was more *Play Misty for Me*—like a *Fatal Attraction* moment.

She had a big smile on her face. "Merry Christmas! Welcome home!" she said, and she came over and put her arms around me. "Give me a hug," she pleaded.

I didn't hug her back.

It was weird. Like *Clockwork Orange* weird. I'm seriously thinking, *What the fuck?*

"Linda," I said, "What's going on?"

"I thought the whole family could be together for the holidays," she replied in this cutesy voice.

I finally backed up. "Whoa, whoa, whoa," I said. "Linda—wait a minute here. I've been trying to talk to you for months, and you haven't wanted to talk about anything, so—just let me regroup for a minute here."

As soon as I gave her any hesitation, that cutesy tone started to change. "What do you mean?" she said.

"Well, I need more than thirty seconds to figure this out, Linda. Just hold on," I said.

That's when she noticed I wasn't wearing my wedding ring.

"If you want to reconcile, put the ring back on your finger and let's reconcile," she said.

It was all too much. I said, "Well, we need to talk about this. I'm not just gonna—"

"God damn it. Put the fucking ring on, Terry!"

Just like that, the nasty side of Linda came flying right back out.

Now, I don't want to overanalyze the situation, but all my lawyers, everyone around me who was really close and who saw the back-and-forth and this "abuse" (if that's what you want to call it) that Linda laid on me, they all seem to agree that there could only be one explanation for why Linda did this: She never thought I would answer her divorce filing.

That's a legal term—when someone files for divorce, the spouse has to "answer" it in order for the filing to proceed. And I did. After my meeting with that divorce lawyer, Ann Kerr, I answered Linda's filing. As much as it pained me that she wanted to end the marriage, I saw that something had changed in her and she didn't want to talk about getting back together. I knew that it was truly over.

So the only thing that makes any sense as to why Linda was in that house with an apron and a smile on is that my "answering" the divorce filing caught her off guard; that she never actually dreamed that I'd go through with it. She was so used to my kissing her ass and bending over backward—"Oh, honey, we can move to Miami. Oh, honey, we'll do whatever it takes to make you happy"—that she filed the divorce as a big public "Fuck you" to get back at me somehow and make me do things her way once and for all. And if that's the case, then this whole situation must've been some kind of a move to win me back and take control again.

So I'm sure she never expected what happened next.

The old Terry, the old Hulk Hogan—that guy? I can guarantee that he would have wrapped his arms around Linda and thanked her for coming home, and probably broken down like a baby as he put that ring back on his finger, feeling so thankful that his marriage wasn't going to fail after all.

That's not what I did. When Linda started cussing, I started walking backward down this long skinny hallway behind me. She kept cussing and demanding I put the ring on. "Don't you dare walk out that door," she said.

But that's exactly what I did. Without saying a word, I walked out that door. I got in my car. And I left.

That was the last time I stepped foot in that house, and the second step I took toward gaining control of my life. This idea that I could change direction and somehow find happiness wasn't just a thought anymore. It wasn't just something I had resolved to do. I had actually taken action. I made the choice not to go backward. I made the choice not to step into a future with Linda by my side.

If I wasn't going backward, and I wasn't standing still, that could only mean one thing: I was moving forward.

And that scared the shit out of me.

PART V

TURNING THE PAGE

CHAPTER 18

A Secret Revealed

It never occurred to me how much looking back I would have to do in order to move forward with my life after Linda. From the moment I backed away from her, I started paying more attention to the things I had done and said in the past. It's almost like I needed to piece together clues from my own life to convince me, fully, that I was doing the right thing. And when I thought about some of my behavior—especially my behavior in recent years, and in the most private moments of my life—there was no question I had been yearning for a major change.

In the last years of my marriage, there were times when I'd wake up early on Sunday mornings and tune the TV to whatever religious programming I could find. I wasn't really paying attention to the sermons or anything like that, but there was something about the organ music and the whole mood of those shows that would just set me off. And I'd cry. It was just my way of venting. Just this crazy release.

I never told anyone about it, but this roller-coaster ride I was on was so dramatic, and so stressful, and so painful, it was eating me alive. I had to unlock a valve now and then just to get some relief. If I had a moment to breathe, to not be Hulk Hogan, to not hold it all together for the cameras or my kids, I'd just let it go. I couldn't help it.

I remember every once in a while my kids would catch me crying at the movies. It wouldn't even have to be a sad scene. I'd look
around the theater and nobody else would be crying, but two
people hugging on screen, or the rise of the music, some little
thing would set me off and I'd just lose it. It was kind of embarrassing, you know? All of a sudden the kids would hear me sniff a
little bit. I'd try to catch myself real quick, but Brooke would always notice, and sometimes laugh at her sensitive old man.

When friends of mine hear about some of this stuff, they ask
why I haven't gone to see a therapist. Maybe it would have done
me some good, but honestly, the idea of going to a shrink just
never occurred to me. I've always found my own way to handle
everything.

After Linda filed for divorce and then pulled that *Play Misty
for Me* crap at the house before Christmas, I started turning
strangers into therapists.

I felt like I was just bouncing around in a pinball machine for
a couple of weeks there. Sometimes I'd run into someone who
seemed like they wanted to talk, and I'd just unload on them
about everything that was wrong with my life. At the same time,
I didn't really want to be around people. Public appearances were
real hard for me at that point. To be mobbed by fans who wanted
to see that Hulkamania madness and pose for a snapshot as I
flexed my muscles was nearly impossible for me. I just wanted to
be at home.

But I couldn't go home. My wife was in our home, and now the
legal system was getting involved and deciding who went where.
So I bounced around. I stayed at our beach house for a few days,
but then there was a dispute over who could live in which house,
so I stuffed whatever clothes I could find into Hefty bags and
rented an apartment further down Clearwater Beach, in a high-
rise overlooking the ocean. It was a nice place. It had sort of a
bachelor pad feel to it, up on a top floor. But it wasn't home.

I hadn't lived in an apartment since I was in my twenties. Now,
in my midfifties, to have all of my things taken out of my hands
was such an empty feeling. My bed. My toothbrush. The chair

where I brushed my teeth. Most of my clothes were still hanging at the big house. My gym and my office—two big things I depended on for my work and my income. All of it was inaccessible to me. The real irony of it was, from the balcony on the north side of that apartment, I could look across the Intracoastal Waterway and see the red roof of the twenty-thousand-square-foot mansion that I was no longer allowed to step foot in.

I could have fought to stay in that house. In fact, I'm sure a judge would have granted that to me, while Linda could have stayed at the beach house and lived the idyllic job-free life she wanted. But I didn't want to fight. I also wanted the comfort of that house to be available to Nick.

During this time, because Nick was still a minor, he had to choose which parent to live with. Linda and I were fifty-fifty. He could choose wherever he wanted to go, and I told him I would not put any pressure on him. He said to me, "You know what, Dad? I think you're going to be okay, but I'm worried about Mom. If she's upset, I want to be there for her." I understood why he wanted to do that. I also thought it was good for Nick to sleep in his own bed, in his own room, to have access to the life he knew before this all started. I knew how tough it was for me to not have access to my normal life, my normal routines. Why should he have to suffer that same fate?

At the end of that month, I flew to Texas for an appearance, and on the way back I started into my whole "woe is me" routine with a guy sitting next to me on the plane. We were seated in first class, where there are only a few seats, and when he opened the door of conversation I just walked right through.

I went on and on about all the misery in my life, and my wife filing for divorce, and how my son's got to go through this whole fiasco in court because of these criminal charges even though he's suffered so much because his best friend is still in the hospital, and my back hurts so bad that my legs are starting to go numb if I sit too long, not to mention my feet swell like crazy every time I get on a plane now. Just on and on and on with my complaining.

All of a sudden I feel a tap on my shoulder. I turn, and this dark-skinned woman with the most peaceful face who was sitting in the row behind me says, "You should read this."

And she hands me *The Secret*.

I realize now that *The Secret*, by Rhonda Byrne, is a book that became a giant bestseller, and was featured on *Oprah*, and has all these followers and people who swear by it—so much so that there are spoofs of it, and whole groups who think it's a bunch of mumbo-jumbo and do all they can to hate it. But I had never heard of this book when she handed it to me.

"Just read it," she said. "It may help you."

Help me?

The guy next to me was sick of listening to me anyway, so I thought, *What the heck,* and I opened it up—and it hit me like a lightning bolt. It was eerie how much this book resonated with me. I get chills just thinking about it.

I'm an extremely fast reader. I can speed-read a whole script in fifteen minutes. That's how I do a lot of my reading—knowing that I can always go back and read something slowly, line by line, if I want to study it a little closer.

So I read this book as fast as I could, just devouring its revelations about "the law of attraction"—this idea that we are personally responsible for attracting *everything* that happens in our lives. It was such a simple idea.

I went back and started to read from the beginning again to see if I could get a better handle on it—this whole idea that what you think about, you bring about. That your thoughts, both conscious and unconscious, dictate the reality of your life. This idea that seemed to trace all the way back to a phrase I remember reading in the Bible at the age of fifteen: "Ask and ye shall receive." Was God really saying that everything we ever wanted or needed was there for the asking? All we had to do was ask?

Was this book suggesting that I could change this downward spiral I was on just by changing my way of thinking?

Just as it was starting to click for me, *ding!* The seat belt sign came on, and we started our initial descent into Tampa. I panicked. There was something about this book. I just kept reading, absorbing the pages as best I could, hoping I would get all the way through it again. We were at the gate with the seat belt sign turned off and I still wasn't done. I didn't want to move! The lady who gave it to me got up to get ready to leave, but she took one look at my face and saw how into this thing I was—and she gave me a great big smile.

"Keep the book," she said.

"No, no, I can't," I said. She insisted. So I thanked her, and I took it home, and I read it again and again that night.

I wish I could find that lady to let her know what she did for me by handing me that book. Because that moment right there marked the start of a whole new journey in my life. A journey that would lift me off the treadmill of misery I'd been on for far too long.

The funny thing is, I had actually started the journey much earlier without even knowing it—in those moments when I started praying for happiness; in that moment when I sat with a gun in my hand thinking life might not be worth living; in the moment I backed away from Linda at the big house before Christmas—but I'd have to get a lot further down this path before I would understand what any of it meant.

I don't want to Bible-thump you with a bunch of new age philosophy and religious teachings. I can't say it half as well as the dozens of preachers and teachers and authors who've already spent years explaining the law of attraction and how it fits into every aspect of life. These books may not have all the answers, but I challenge anyone to read books like *The Power of Now*, *A New Earth*, or *Stillness Speaks* and tell me that the ideas that thread through those pages don't stir some pretty big questions about your own life. Questions you didn't even know you had.

I'm not a philosopher. I'm not a preacher. So all I can do is tell you how *The Secret* and all of these other books I started to read at the beginning of 2008 helped *me* change my life for the better.

Let me see if I can sum it up in a way that's easily understandable. Basically, the whole idea behind all of these books is that it's up to you to choose your destination in life. You can't always choose the path. That's up to God, or the various forces of the universe, or whatever you want to call the higher spirit or energy that ties everything together. But the destination, and especially all of the little destinations along the way that help to get you to your final destination, are something that you can control. And you choose those destinations through the law of attraction—whether you know it or not.

Think of it like this: Your thoughts are like a magnet. If you worry all the time about not being able to pay your bills, guess what's going to happen to you? You're not going to be able to pay your bills. If you worry about never falling in love? Good luck finding someone to fall in love with. If all you think about is how grateful you are to live this amazing life filled with wealth and happiness of every kind? Well, that life of wealth and happiness can be yours. It might take a long time to get there, but it's coming.

It seems ridiculously simple, and I know there are people who are thinking right now that Hulk Hogan has lost his marbles. Linda accused me of joining a cult when she heard I was getting into this stuff. But indulge me just a little bit longer here.

Have you ever known a couple who were frustrated and angry and devastated that they couldn't get pregnant? So frustrated that they couldn't have a child, that they finally decided to adopt—then just as the adoption got approved, they got pregnant? Ask around. If you don't know someone directly, I guarantee that you know someone who knows someone who has gone through that exact scenario.

That's the law of attraction at work.

You might say, "Wait a second? If this law of attraction is real, and they were wishing and praying and hoping for a baby, shouldn't they have had a baby since that's all they were thinking about?" No. Wishing and hoping and praying is not the same as actually thinking about and feeling what it is you want to achieve, and if all that hoping and praying is coupled with endless negative thoughts of *Why can't I get pregnant?* or *Why can't I achieve whatever it is I want to achieve?* then it just won't cut it.

Negativity and negative thoughts can kill the whole process of accomplishing whatever it is you want to achieve.

The fact is, once that couple adopts a child, once they finally think and feel and know in their hearts that they are, in fact, going to *be* parents, that's when the law of attraction comes into play and gives them an abundance of children—the very thing they wanted most.

Roll your eyes at me. It's okay. I never would have believed any of this stuff just a few years ago. Heck, I never would have believed it just a few months before I started reading about it. By the way, you don't have to believe in it in order for it to work. It's like gravity. It's just there, whether you want to believe in it or not. But opening my eyes to the possibility that we can control our own destiny just by how we think about things and approach things in our lives was one of the most exciting concepts I've ever read.

In that beginning of 2008, I devoured book after book, and reread those books over and over. I also bought the DVD film version of *The Secret* and watched it again and again. I loved seeing these spiritual leaders and life coaches (Life coaches! What a concept!) from the book suddenly come to life on-screen. People like Michael Beckwith and James Arthur Ray. I got so obsessed, I started to put the DVD on repeat on the DVD player in my black Mercedes—so every time I got in that car it would play on the little pop-up TV screen in the dashboard.

The more I read and the more I listened, the more I started to connect the dots in my life going all the way back to my childhood. I pulled out a Bible again. I thought about what it meant to walk in the spirit of Christ. I thought about the teachings of Rev. Lindstrom at the Christian Youth Ranch. I thought about that old moral code that I used to live by—that simple, instinctive code about wanting to be good and not bad. It started to change my perspective on every single thing that had ever happened in my life. Right then and there. Almost overnight.

For far too long my thoughts had been consumed with the problems in my marriage, the pain in my body, the horror of Nick's accident and John Graziano's condition. All I thought about were the problems in my life.

Maybe I've just been hit in the head one too many times, but I'm telling you, brother, as soon as I started paying attention to the law of attraction, as soon as I started not just praying for happiness, but believing that happiness was possible again, happiness started to find me.

MY LIGHT

One day in January, with all this new perspective fresh on my mind, I walked into the Good Earth, a health food store in Clearwater. Now, it's not unusual for me to strike up conversations with people wherever I go. People feel like they know me—from wrestling, from the show, from just circling around Tampa for the last fifty years. Whatever it is, people talk to me, and I usually talk to them.

On this day, for some reason, I struck up a conversation with this statuesque blonde. There was something about her that was just so appealing. Her eyes were so clear—not all bloodshot and tired-looking like mine had been for so long. She just had this real positive energy about her. Not to mention she was seriously attractive. Mostly, though, it was the clarity of those eyes. There was a light in those eyes that I was drawn to.

Her name was Jennifer McDaniel, and apparently she had met me before. She worked for Delta Air Lines and used to see my whole family going in and out of the airport. I don't know how it's possible that I didn't remember her. She was so striking. Maybe I just wasn't ready to notice her before that moment in the Good Earth.

Two weeks later I ran into her at that very same health food store. This time, I couldn't resist. I asked her out. And from that night on we've been inseparable.

Jennifer, it turns out, was completely dialed in to the law of attraction, along with the whole idea of living positively, taking care of your body and mind, and living life for a higher purpose. All of these things I had been reading about, that were so new to me, she had been following for most of her adult life. She was only thirty-four, but she was light-years ahead of me.

Another thing I really liked about Jennifer was she barely knew anything about me. She had never seen *Rocky III*, she had never watched wrestling. I'm recognizable enough that I think you'd have to live on Mars not to have ever heard the name Hulk Hogan, or not to have caught a glimpse of this Fu Manchu mustache on TV at one point or another, but Jennifer isn't one to watch the news or pay attention to gossip pages or any of that stuff. So the only baggage I brought to the relationship as far as she was concerned was the baggage I used to heft to the airport.

We both got to know each other with a clean slate, and that felt pretty amazing.

As we spent more time together, hanging by the ocean, driving around—simple stuff—a strange thing started to happen. I started smiling again.

That may not seem like much to the average person, but I was so down for so long that it was a noticeable, double-take moment for me just to catch myself smiling for no reason at all.

Jennifer became my constant companion, and in many ways, my constant coach.

It's hard to describe what it's like to spend time with someone who stays positive all the time. Especially after what I had lived with for so long. From the very beginning, it's like Jennifer was there to help talk me through whatever negative influence came my way. When my back starts aching and I start complaining, she's quick to remind me to envision my back not hurting at all. To live like I'm not in pain. To be grateful to God for giving me the strength to heal my back.

I'm still new to this stuff. It's hard for me not to bitch and moan about everything. Like any great coach, though, she keeps me in line—and I'm not so easy to keep in line!

That whole idea of being grateful for possibilities, grateful for things you don't even have yet—let alone being grateful for the gifts we have in our lives, and the gift of simply being alive—that was the second part of this spiritual awakening of mine. Being grateful is one of the big keys to leading a happy life. I should have realized that all on my own. Whenever I was grateful in my life, I was happy. After Brooke and Nick were born, I was as grateful as I'd ever been, and my life was *filled* with happiness—but I was never consciously aware of that fact.

Now Jennifer was there to help me understand that, and to embrace it, consciously, so I could bring about that kind of happiness in my life more often.

The thing about the law of attraction is it doesn't happen overnight. You reap what you sow in life. Call it karma, call it whatever you want, but the negativity that you put into the world will come back around to bite you one way or the other. That's exactly what started to happen in February of 2008.

One day, out of the blue, I got a panicked phone call from Christiane Plante. She and I hadn't really spoken at all since the summer of 2007, so you can imagine how surprised I was to hear from her. The news she had was not good.

"I got a message from Brooke," she told me.

Apparently, a friend of Brooke's who worked at the record company with Christiane just casually decided over lunch to inform her that Christiane had been having an affair with her father. Brooke was incensed. So she called Christiane looking for answers.

I told her, "Christiane, just tell her the truth."

I had already come far enough in my new way of thinking to know that lying would only make it worse. Lying would postpone the inevitable: the heartbreak, the pain that was about to be un-leashed.

Christiane was real nervous about it, of course, and she didn't think she could keep it together and make sense of it all in a phone call. So rather than call Brooke back, Christiane decided to send Brooke a letter—a letter in which she admitted the affair and apologized for letting it happen.

At this point, Brooke was just about 100 percent in Linda's camp as far this divorce was concerned. I couldn't understand why, and I wouldn't understand until much later. What happened next made the whole situation a lot worse.

First, Brooke confronted me. She wanted to know if it was true. She wanted to know why I'd done it. I told her the truth. "There's two sides to every story, Brooke," is what I said. I tried to explain that her mother and I were so broken, and I was so lonely and hurt, that when this thing with Christiane presented itself, I almost couldn't help myself. I wasn't making excuses, I was just trying to explain where I was coming from, and how I found my-self in that situation.

Brooke wouldn't hear it. "There aren't two sides, Dad. There's right and wrong." My daughter, who had barely been speaking to me anyway for months, suddenly stopped communicating with me at all.

Two days after Brooke received that letter, a reporter from the *National Enquirer* knocked on Christiane's door. Her personal letter to Brooke had somehow found its way into that tabloid's hands. They cornered Christiane and left her no choice but to re-spond. So on February 28, my affair became national news. I don't think there's a blog or entertainment show in America that didn't run with the story of Hulk Hogan cheating on his wife.

I was humiliated. I was angry. I didn't know what to do. There was no one to sue—the story was true. I couldn't even figure out who to be angry with, except for myself for letting it happen in the first place.

Then something remarkable happened. After about a day's worth of wallowing in all this self-pity and frustration, I stopped.

I took a deep breath. I realized nothing positive could possibly come from my being angry about this. And I put it aside.

I made a choice right then and there to take the high road on this thing. I didn't want to stoop to the level of whoever gave the *Enquirer* that letter—so I decided not to respond.

Eventually I learned that Brooke had shown that letter to Linda, and Linda had turned around and faxed it off to her attorney. Do you see where I'm going with this train of thought on how that letter made it over to the *Enquirer*?

As far as I was concerned, this was the first volley in what was sure to be a giant battle of a divorce with Linda. There would be many more shots to come, and when it came to talking about my private life to the press, I knew I would have to pick my battles carefully. So I decided not to fire back.

I'm not sure if Linda was frustrated by my lack of response or what, but months later she hired a publicist and sent out a statement to the media claiming that the Christiane affair was the reason she filed for divorce. But she had no idea until Brooke showed her that letter. I couldn't believe it. From everything I've ever seen, if Linda had known about Christiane, she would've gone ballistic. She wouldn't have kept it quiet for all those months. She would have shouted it from the rooftops, just as she was doing now.

The thing I couldn't figure out was why Linda would want to drag this divorce out and turn it into a battle in the first place. Florida is a no-fault state. Even if the affair were the reason she filed for divorce, it wouldn't have any bearing on a judge's ruling on how much money or support Linda should get. So why would she want to make a big deal out of it again and drag it all out into the public eye?

Oddly enough, I would eventually find explanations for all of Linda's behavior in the middle of all of that spiritual reading I was doing. Answers that would allow me to understand that behavior, and finally learn to move past it.

———

I was so excited by the results of all the reading I'd done, and the possibilities of this whole spiritual awakening I was going through, that I started to share it with everyone I could. I bought multiple copies of *The Secret* and handed them to friends. (Yes, a few of them laughed at me.) I talked about the law of attraction and how important it was to be grateful for everything we have in this life with anyone who would listen. The person I was most grateful to have listening to me was my son.

It's hard to explain how broken up Nick was by the fact that he wasn't allowed to visit John in the hospital anymore. It had been four months since he'd seen him with his own eyes, and as scared as he was to go to that hospital, and as painful as it was for him to see his best friend in that condition, to not see John and to just live with the mystery of whether he was getting better or not was so much worse. He knew the reason he couldn't see John— because the Grazianos were preparing to sue us—but he couldn't make sense of it.

On top of it all he worried about what might happen with these criminal charges, and he was real down about the situation between Linda and me. I'm sure he blamed his accident, in part, for causing the stress that led to the divorce. Even though he was wrong, the thought that he was laying that additional guilt on himself just killed me.

So I started talking to him and reading him passages from these books whenever I could. I thought it would help to keep his spirits up, the same way it was helping me. Now that I knew about the law of attraction, I also wanted to make sure he stopped dwelling on the negative and started looking ahead to the positive things that could come out of this whole terrible situation.

One big way we did that was to pray for John to be totally healed. We committed ourselves to being grateful for John's recovery. The more positive energy we could send John's way, the better chance he'd have of pulling out of this thing. I truly believed that, and still do.

Of course, just as I started to get Nick dialed in to this positive path I was on, John's family started their negative campaign against the Hogans.

On March 24, 2008, the Grazianos finally filed their civil suit against me, Linda, and our still-minor son, Nick. Like I said, I knew that day would come. The cost of John's care is immense. There are bills to pay, insurance companies involved. They wanted to collect damages to somehow put a price tag on John. As cold as that seems, that's just the way things work. I knew that.

But the Grazianos' first priority didn't seem to be to take care of John at all. Instead, it felt like they wanted to punish Nick, punish me, and punish Linda. More than that, their primary goal, in my opinion, was to get rich from this terrible tragedy.

I tried to step back and look at the millions of dollars they were trying to squeeze out of me with some kind of objectivity, and I just couldn't make any sense of it. I kept asking myself, "Is the point of a lawsuit to bankrupt the other party so that everything they've worked for their whole lives is taken away? So that one family is no longer allowed to function while the other family suddenly gets rich? Or is the point of a lawsuit supposed to be to make sure that John has the best care possible for the rest of his life so that someday he can get back on his own two feet?"

If this situation were reversed, and Nick were the one in that passenger seat without a seatbelt, I know with 100 percent certainty that I would be seeking the latter. Just as I know with 100 percent certainty that I would want John in that hospital room every single day visiting my son and trying to help him pull through. That's what friends do. Instead, they banned us from seeing John, sued us for what I felt was a ridiculous sum of money and started making horrible statements about us to the press.

As all of this got under way, I basically started a whole new career: talking to lawyers. Since early 2008, I feel like that's been my full-time job. There were lawyers everywhere I turned. Linda's lawyers, the Grazianos' lawyers, my own divorce lawyers, the defense lawyers I put in place to help my son with the criminal charges stemming from the accident. All of them demanding my time, taking deposition after deposition. Before I knew it, my mornings, my afternoons, my evenings, and even my weekends were taken up talking to lawyers. It never stopped. All that talk has forced me to relive the events of my crumbling marriage and the horror of driving up on that accident scene over and over again. It's enough to make a person's mind explode. It's no exaggeration to think that I might not have survived without the support of my ever increasing connection to spirituality.

At one big powwow a few months down the road, as I attempted to reach a settlement with the Grazianos, I looked around the room and counted twenty-four lawyers. Twenty-four! All of them getting paid, presumably, by me. Meanwhile, as all of those people sat around earning big fat paychecks, John sat in a hospital bed with nothing.

There's no logic to it. I mean, in a sane world we would all sit down and agree to set up a medical trust fund for John with an endowment that would more than pay for the absolute best care at the best medical and rehabilitation facilities in the world, no matter how long it takes to get John back on his feet—something I still haven't stopped believing will happen someday. Instead, all I see is this crazy ongoing cycle of lawsuits and lawyering that prevents that from happening.

Tell me: How does that make sense?

CHAPTER 19

Coincidence or Fate?

The Grazianos filed their suit just a few days before I was scheduled to fly to Los Angeles to start work on the second season of *American Gladiators*. I had already decided to invite Jennifer to come with me to California, and I couldn't have been happier when she said yes. It was a big step for such a new relationship, but I felt like there was a reason we met, and I wanted her there every step of the way.

Walking onto that set felt really good that second season. Despite the new pressure of the lawsuit, I was already in a much better place emotionally than I was the season before. I knew that being happy was a choice I could make, and it was definitely the choice I was making.

After all I'd been through, it was real weird to see Laila Ali again—the girl who almost single-handedly saved my life. She was just as friendly as ever, and just as positive as ever. I'm not sure if she picked up on this change I was going through right away or not, but out of the blue she asked me again if I'd like to go to her church with her sometime.

"Where is this church again?" I asked.

"It's the Agape Church, here in L.A.," she said. "It was founded by Dr. Michael Beckwith. I could—"

"Whoa, whoa, whoa. Michael Beckwith from *The Secret*? That Michael Beckwith?"

"Yes!" she said. She seemed surprised that I knew of him.

Michael Beckwith was one of *The Secret*'s most prominent voices. He was one of the main figures in the DVD that played over and over again in my car.

"Yes!" I said. "I'd love to go!"

The coincidence was too strong to ignore. She had invited me to go to that very church when I was sitting in my bathroom on Willadel Drive with a gun in my hand. Now the teachings of the leader of that church were a major part of my life. Laila had offered me a golden ticket back then, and I mistakenly ignored it. I sure wasn't ignoring her now. I was floored by it.

That was the second remarkable coincidence that happened right around that same time.

One of the biggest revelations in the *Secret* DVD, a moment that had truly knocked my socks off, was when author James Arthur Ray asked this really weird question about gaining control over the direction of your life. "When would *now* be a good time to start?" he asked.

It was such a weird phrase, and it just blew my mind. His point was that you could change your life whenever you decided to do it. You didn't have to wait for a New Year's resolution, or put it off until you lost some weight, or until you felt better, or until you finished school. You could change your life *right now*. You could change everything this instant just by changing your perspective, changing your outlook, and changing how you thought about your life and your circumstances.

I was so blown away by that idea and by the presence James Ray had on screen that I started to think about what it would be like to meet him and talk to him in person.

Not three weeks later, Nick was in the lobby of the Beverly Hills Hotel, and who did he bump into? James Arthur Ray. Nick called me up, all excited. "Dad, I just ran into that guy from *The Secret*. Hold on. Let me see if he'll talk to you!"

Nick approached him, and next thing I know I was on the phone with James Arthur Ray. The two of us started talking pretty regularly after that. He became an adviser and friend to me, and to Nick, as we geared up for Nick's upcoming court date.

James, it turns out, was also friendly with Michael Beckwith. When I told him I was planning on going to the Agape Church, he put me on the phone with Dr. Beckwith himself. So when Laila and her husband and Jennifer and I got to the church that day, we had a parking spot right up front, and they led us right up near the front of the church for his sermon.

I hadn't been inside a church for a very long time, and I didn't realize how much I'd missed the experience. I never thought much about it in all those years. My church was Madison Square Garden, you know?

Now here I was, surrounded by this congregation of people who were all dialed in to this world I knew nothing about just two months earlier. The tradition they have at this church when a new guest comes in is they ask you to stand up, and then every member of that whole congregation points his or her palm right at you, arm outstretched in your direction, while they welcome you into the fold with words like "we love you" and "we're here to support you." Now, that's a powerful experience. Remember how I told you I would tear up just hearing the music on those religious Sunday morning TV shows? There was no way I could avoid the waterworks in this place. I wept like a baby.

It's hard to explain that feeling of suddenly having a whole church full of people vowing to support you and love you. I didn't feel so alone anymore. It dawned on me that there's a whole world full of people out there who experience life in a way that I never even knew existed.

It also occurred to me that I had been thinking about church all wrong, ever since I was a kid. You don't go to church to find God. God is already inside each and every one of us. The reason to go to church is simply to help bring God out of you, and to better help God function through you. I loved that whole concept.

Jennifer and I met with Dr. Beckwith after the service, and we went back again a few times while we were in L.A. Ever since, his assistant has been kind enough to send me CD copies of Michael's weekly sermons so I can listen to them in my car here in Florida.

Jennifer. Laila. Michael. James. From personal friends to spiritual guides, I suddenly had new people in my life that cared about my spiritual and emotional well-being. For all these years I had agents and accountants who watched out for my money and career. I had doctors who cared for my aches and pains. But this huge, important area of life had been mostly void of contact going all the way back to when I was a teenager.

It's almost like a set of support beams was added to stabilize this big crooked frame of mine—just in time for the hurricanes that were about to pummel my shore.

MY HOMETOWN

Back in Tampa, the media frenzy around Nick's accident stayed at a fever pitch from the day after the crash straight through that spring of 2008. The news would come and go in the national press, but in Tampa? It never slowed down. Mostly because one DJ on one local radio station decided to boost his career on Nick's back—a DJ that goes by the name MJ.

Now, here's where Tampa being such a small town comes into play. MJ, many years earlier, had come to me with a plan to buy the local radio station. He and his partner were the top DJs in the Tampa market, and they thought if they bought the station they could corner that market and keep all the profits. I'm not sure why they thought Hulk Hogan would be the perfect guy to put up the big money to make this happen, but that's what they thought. I turned them down. It was nothing personal. I just looked at the deal they were offering, and what my return on investment would be, and I didn't think it was a good business deal. So I passed.

Years go by, and I become really good friends with another DJ in town who goes by the name Bubba the Love Sponge. I would appear on Bubba's radio show whenever I could just to help him out. Well, as time went by, Bubba became the number-one DJ in Tampa. He just blew MJ right out of the water.

I think that caused more than a little bad blood. So when this accident happened, MJ started hammering away at Nick, non-stop, every morning, for months on end. He put a call out to listeners. "Did anyone see Nick Hogan racing that night? Did anyone see Nick Hogan drinking that night? Who out there has embarrassing stories to tell about Nick Hogan. Call in now!" He inspired all these anonymous idiots to call in with crazy stories about Nick and John and Danny and Barry—the whole bunch of them—and he did his best to hammer me, too. MJ was the guy who stirred up the whole ridiculous controversy over whether or not Nick went into the liquor store with me that Sunday in August to buy beer.

Now, you may think the words of a local DJ aren't anything to worry about. In this case? The words of a local DJ kept heat on Nick's case. It seemed the whole Tampa metro area turned against my son. All of a sudden it was a lynch-mob mentality. MJ's listeners were whipped into a frenzy thinking Nick was at fault for this accident and he should burn at the stake.

My friend Bubba did everything he could to make the counterargument. He would go on the air and talk about the fact that John was the adult in this situation, that John was the one drinking that day, that John was a marine and was certainly responsible for his own behavior. None of us wanted to say bad things about John, though, and no matter what was said it was difficult to undo the damage that MJ's listeners did to my son.

No matter how blind justice is supposed to be, it is impossible for judges to sit on a bench and not be influenced by the mob mentality and media frenzy of a case like Nick's. Think of Judge Ito displaying mugs on his desk during the O.J. trial. Think of that teary-eyed judge in the Anna Nicole Smith case. Cameras change everything. So does the sway of the local community.

It didn't help that Nick's case came up in the middle of an election year. Do you think the mob mentality shared by tens of thousands of MJ's local listeners every morning didn't have any sway? Anyone who's ever watched an episode of *Law & Order* knows better than that.

There was more. When Nick finally received a hearing date on his case, we were assigned a female judge. My lawyers were excited. They said she was one of the most reasonable, fair-minded judges around. A woman who was unlikely to be swayed by the morning DJs or the celebrity factor of this case. As soon as my attorneys walked in the room for a prehearing conference, though, that judge removed herself from the case. Turns out many years ago my attorney, Lee Fugate, was responsible for putting that judge's brother in jail for life. It was a conflict of interest.

My attorney said he forgot.

Welcome to the hillbilly circus of the Greater Tampa justice system.

Knowing how this whole thing turned out, I can't help but wonder if I should have objected to her replacement judge as well: Judge Philip J. Federico.

Years earlier, I actually helped Judge Federico's brother, Rick, break into the wrestling business. I changed his name from Rick to Rico Federico and helped launch his career. He did quite well as a wrestler, so I didn't think of it as a conflict of interest, but could there be some kind of bad blood I'm not even aware of? It's easy to drive yourself crazy second-guessing these things. Still, I can't help but think it was impossible for Nick to receive fair and impartial treatment in the small-town circus of the Tampa-Clearwater region. Unfortunately, it was the only circus in town. All of us would have to learn to accept that.

JUDGMENT DAY

The last thing any of us wanted was a long, drawn-out trial. Nick was driving the Supra that night in August, and while he wasn't driving crazy or racing the way the media still insists he was to this day, he agreed with our lawyers that the right thing to do was to stand up and take responsibility.

He wasn't "guilty." So he wouldn't plead "guilty." He would plead "no contest." In other words, without admitting any guilt, he would simply stand up and face the charges. It's an option the legal system offers, and for Nick, it seemed like the best option we had.

Our lawyers were very clear about the possibilities Nick would face. A charge of reckless driving with serious bodily injury could carry jail time. Any judge would have that option in this case. However, the legal precedent made the possibility of jail time extremely remote. According to my attorneys, no minor in the state of Florida had ever gone to jail for that charge. Ever. In fact, the standard sentence for that charge was six months' probation.

We knew Nick's sentence would be harsher than that—the case was way too high-profile to think Nick would get off easy. A longer probation, a suspended license, community service—there was a whole arsenal the judge could throw at him if he wanted. We even had conversations with the lawyers about what kind of a jail he would be sent to if this judge decided to really, really make an example of him, and they told us: a minimum-security facility, where Nick could go out in the yard and play basketball, and watch TV, and spend time reading in a library. It would not be a hotel. It would not be pretty. It would not be easy. But it would not be dangerous, and he would not be mingling with hardened criminals.

I told Nick not to worry about going to jail at all. "What you think about, you bring about," I reminded him. Unfortunately, in the days leading up to that trial, Nick spent most of his time with Linda and her family, and it was a depressing environment—even his grandparents kept on him about the possibility of it. Jail, jail, jail. "You're going to jail. You'd better get ready!" Nick told me about all of this talk that surrounded him, and it just scared me to death.

The thing was, the law of attraction had been in play throughout this ordeal. As he started to understand it himself, Nick confessed to me that the night before the accident he and John had been watching videos of car crashes on the Internet. Car crash after car crash after car crash. Call it a coincidence. Call it what you want. Whatever you call it, thoughts and actions are interconnected.

I kept focused as best I could. The lawyers insisted no judge would want to set a new precedent. So I put the possibility of jail completely out of my mind.

It wouldn't be enough.

On May 9, 2008, we all made our way over to the Pinellas County courthouse. Through Brooke and Nick, Linda and I had communicated enough to agree to sit together as a family in that courtroom as Nick stood up and entered his plea. It was the least we could do to put our differences aside for one day.

We did it, too. Linda and I didn't really talk. We said hello, but that was pretty much it. It was strange to see her, especially sitting in the front row, and watching her new attorney, A. J. Barranco, holding her hand, and rubbing her hand, throughout the whole court proceeding. That was something I felt I should have been doing, even with all the problems. That was my wife. It was creepy, although the distance between us was just as big as it had been in the final months of our marriage. Being in her presence again didn't change that.

Nick got dressed up in a suit and tie. He felt it was important to show the court that he took this matter seriously. And he did take this matter seriously. He had done nothing but take this matter seriously since day one.

Before we went into that courtroom, I looked Nick in the eye and said, "Just be grateful for whatever happens. We will definitely get through it."

I carried a copy of the book *The Power of Now* into the courtroom with me that day. I needed all the positive energy I could get. So did my son.

Not only were we placing ourselves at the mercy of the court, but the gossip Web site TMZ had somehow arranged to put a camera in that courtroom and stream the whole event live over the World Wide Web. So whatever was said that day would be broadcast for the whole world to see. The fact that the court allowed that to happen already meant that Nick's case was being treated differently than any normal, noncelebrity case. That was not a good sign.

This was just a hearing, not a trial. It was a chance for my son to enter a plea, and he did that. A plea of no contest. He placed his fate in the hands of the judge. The judge accepted Nick's plea and then moved on to the sentencing portion of the proceedings. He could have put off sentencing to some other day, but he didn't. It was all going down right now. In front of that TMZ camera.

Judge Federico opened the floor to both sides—the Hogans and the Grazianos—to speak out and make a case for why Nick should be sentenced one way or another. This was a chance for us to speak about the punishment Nick had already endured, seeing his friend in a hospital, and dealing with the guilt and shame of knowing he was behind the wheel when it happened. It was our chance to ask the judge for mercy, to talk about Nick's character, and to ask the judge to simply allow Nick to be rehabilitated and reeducated just like any other minor who makes a terrible mistake. I personally begged the judge not to let my fame or the celebrity nature of this case influence his decision on my son.

When we stood up to speak, my family spoke the truth. Brooke made a tearful plea for her wonderful brother, reminding the judge and the Grazianos how sorry we all were about what happened to John, and how close we all were to John. Linda and I both agreed that John was like a son to us. Our family was suffering, too.

Nick spoke as well, turning to face the Grazianos as he apologized to them for what happened to John. I can't imagine how difficult that moment was for him. It wasn't difficult to say he was sorry. He had said he was sorry a hundred times as we gathered at the hospital in the wake of the accident. But to do it in front of a camera? And a judge? And a room full of strangers? It made me real proud that he had the strength to do that.

We then sat and listened as the Grazianos put on a united front and told the judge how their family was shattered by the accident. Ed Graziano talked about how he spent ten-hour days visiting John in the hospital, which sounded like an awful big strech of the truth to me. John's former girlfriend stood up and went on about how she and John were still engaged, describing how Nick's recklessness had cost her and John the future they were about to embark upon. The whole thing was just weird. As far as I knew, John wouldn't even answer this girl's calls in the months before this accident happened. He would laugh about it. Then Debbie got up there and pulled the party line with her family as well—saying that Nick had never even apologized to her for what he had done to their son.

To the outside world, and especially to a judge who knew nothing about the truth of what had gone on in this family, I'm sure it was heart wrenching. And the sadness of John's condition is immense. Still, what the Grazianos did and said in that courtroom was not exactly honest. To make matters worse, because it was a hearing and not a trial, there was no possibility of refuting their statements. We simply had to sit there and take it, and pray that the judge would show Nick some mercy.

Once they were through, it was finally Judge Federico's turn to speak. My stomach clenched up like a fist. I listened closely to every word.

At first he talked about the circumstances of the accident, and Nick's age, and what the law allowed for punishment for the various charges. He talked about his duty to give a minor a chance at rehabilitation. Then he said something that shook me to my bones: He used the phrase "because of who you are." He said to Nick, more than once, that he was making the decision based in part on "who you are."

Did he really just say that he's going to treat my son differently because he's on TV? Is my son going to suffer now because of who I am?

With that, Judge Federico sent my boy to jail for eight months. A completely unprecedented ruling. He also suspended his license for three full years and gave him five years' probation and five hundred hours of community service.

I was floored. By any stretch of the imagination, this was an extremely harsh and precedent-setting ruling for a minor in the state of Florida. It made no sense.

I watched as court officers led my son to a little table to be fingerprinted. I watched as they removed his necktie and belt. I watched as they put him in handcuffs and led him through a side door off to the right of the judge's bench. Just like that, he was gone.

As I stood there flabbergasted, I expected Nick to look at me for support. I expected him to come over and hug his family before they took him into custody. But Nick didn't look back. He stood there and took the weight of that ruling on his shoulders, all on his own. Nick didn't break down. He didn't look to me for help. He didn't whine or complain about the ruling—even though in my mind he certainly had a right to. Instead, he stayed strong. As crushed as I was by the judge's ruling, I was equally proud of my son for taking it like a man and staying strong throughout that entire proceeding.

I held my head up and walked out of that courtroom and ignored the press who wanted me to comment. I also ignored the taunts from some of the members of the extended Graziano family, who wound up ranting and raving to the cameras in that parking lot.

What could I say? I wanted to stay positive. I was choosing to be a better person. I was choosing to walk on the high road. Sharing my real thoughts on that judge's decision would have been anything but positive, believe me.

Instead I kept reminding myself that Nick's a good kid. *He's strong. He'll get through this. We need to be grateful for this. There's a reason for it. I know it. Nick will learn from this. In the end, it will somehow make Nick a better person. A better man. I just know it.*

I had to believe that. There had to be something to be grateful for in this horrible ordeal.

Back at my apartment later that evening, I kept pacing the floor trying to wrap my head around everything that had happened. My attorneys told me Nick would have access to a phone at a minimum-security jail, so he should be able to make a phone call as soon as he was settled. I had no idea when that might be, so I went a little out of my skull just waiting to get word that Nick was okay. I just wanted to hear my son's voice, you know?

Finally, as the sun set out over the Gulf, my cell phone rang. It was Nick. He was anything but okay.

28 DAYS

"Dad, you're not gonna believe this. I'm in the mental ward."

I had never heard Nick's voice shake like it was shaking on the other end of that phone.

"What are you talking about, Nick?"

"They walked me in past all these other inmates and into this medical facility and they put me in a padded cell. It's like three by seven. I can touch both walls when I put my hands out. The whole length of the room is barely taller than me!"

"Wait, wait, wait. Nick, slow down. Did they say why you're there? Is this temporary?"

"No! They said I'm not allowed to mingle with the adult prisoners 'cause of my age."

"But you have access to a courtyard and everything, right? Like the lawyers said."

"No! They have to keep my door closed the whole time. They're saying this is the only cell they have available. That I'm stuck here. Dad, I can't be locked up in here like that. There's no windows, nothing. You've gotta help me."

I promised my son I'd get to the bottom of this. "Just stay strong. We'll get this fixed."

I hung up that phone with my heart pounding out of my chest. As a parent, there's hardly anything worse than getting a panicked phone call from your child. I had to help him. No matter what it took, I had to figure out what the hell was going on.

I called my attorneys, and they called the courthouse, the judge, and the jail. The best they could tell me is that this was some kind of a catch-22. Nick was sentenced in adult court, and he was sent to an adult prison, but because he was under eighteen they were required to keep him separated from the general population. This facility wasn't built to house minors like that, so the only choice they had was to isolate him in the medical ward.

"That's not what the judge ordered. He was supposed to serve eight months in minimum security," I said. But Nick fell between the cracks—and guess what? It was Friday. Everyone was headed home. There would be no way to get this fixed over the weekend.

I can't describe to you how hard my heart sank in my chest when they told me that. I was so angry and hurt, and once again totally helpless.

I had promised my son I would get this fixed. Now I wouldn't be able to. He would be stuck in that situation for most of the next seventy-two hours.

Nick called back that night, and I told him the situation. It was a finite amount of time. I told him to just stay positive. To be grateful that he wasn't mingled with the rest of the prisoners. Maybe that meant he would be safe. Maybe it was meant to be. I reminded him we had to find reasons to be grateful for all of this, no matter how hard it might be.

Nick seemed to calm down. It was only till Monday. He would be able to call me a few times a day. They would let him out of his cell and supervise him to make calls. I promised him that I would always be there to pick up those calls. Always.

It was a 100 percent commitment on my part. I would not miss a call—not because I was driving and my cell-phone service was sketchy, or because I was in the bathroom. I simply wouldn't leave that apartment or step away from that phone until Nick's situation was fixed.

I just never imagined it would take twenty-eight days for that to happen.

———

From that day forward, I sat in a straight-back chair at the glass dining room table in that bachelor pad of mine. I laid out three cell phones: the one Nick would call me on, and two others that I could jump back and forth on to lawyers and family and friends. I called everyone I could think of that weekend. Lawyers I had dealt with through the years. Friends who were prominent in the area, who might be able to call in a favor. Anyone I could think of who might be able to get my son out of that situation.

It might not seem like much to think that he would be locked up from Friday till Monday, but my lawyers made me realize what a grave situation Nick was in.

Solitary confinement is meant for prisoners who are uncontrollable. Rapists and murderers who act out against guards or other prisoners get thrown in solitary as a last-resort punishment because it's the most brutal punishment there is.

Isolation plays tricks on the human mind. After as little as forty-eight to seventy-two hours, many prisoners in solitary confinement have been known to crack. In extreme cases people have been known to start hurting themselves, scratching their eyes out, eating their own feces. True isolation is something human beings hardly ever experience in life. In the confines of a tiny cell, it's considered one of the most brutal punishments known to man.

So how on earth did this judgment against my son transform from a minimum-security sentence to the most brutal punishment in the American justice system? How is that possible?

As I promised, I was there every time Nick called. Right from the outset I tried to be calm and positive with him in every conversation. I read to him from the Bible, just trying to make sense of what he was enduring and how it would help him grow as a human being. I read to him from *The New Earth* and *The Secret*. I read to him from James Ray's books.

Monday came and went with no improvement in the situation. I was scheduled to start a media tour to promote *American Gladiators*. I was supposed to fly to New York to do Regis and Kelly, Letterman, every talk show you could think of. For the first time in my entire career, I canceled them all.

NBC was pissed. They were relying on the power of Hulk Hogan to go out and sell this show to the audience, but there was no Hulk Hogan as far as I was concerned. Right then, I was Nick's father. That was it. I had only one obligation to fulfill.

It's hard for people who don't know me to understand that I'm not just talking here. I'm not exaggerating. I did not move for twenty-eight days. Jennifer was real weirded out by how focused and obsessed I was, just sitting in that chair at that table making phone call after phone call, trying to get this thing resolved. She had never experienced this extreme side of my personality. If she brought me food, I would eat. If friends stopped in to check on me, I would talk to them about what was happening to my son. But the only time I would get up is when I had to go to the bathroom. Then once every four or five days I would take a quick shower—always with the cell phone right there on the sink where I could reach it the moment it rang. I was determined to take every phone call, and make every phone call, from that solitary spot until my boy was out of that cell.

This was the resolve of coming back to the ring after Matsuda broke my leg. This was the resolve of exploding my kneecap as I won the belt from the Iron Sheik. This was the resolve of tearing my back by bodyslamming André the Giant but continuing to wrestle for twenty-nine days with no break, no rest, and no surgery. I knew I could do this, no matter how long it took. "If I have to sit in this chair for the next eight months, Nick, I will sit right here for you," I told him. "No question."

After the first few days and all the calls I made, word spread to lawyers all over the country. All of a sudden some of the top legal minds in the world were reaching out to help me. Robert Shapiro (of O.J. trial fame) called from L.A. at 2:00 A.M. I had Roy Black on the phone from Miami. Brendan Sullivan was calling from Washington, D.C. All of them giving me advice on how to handle this thing. My own lawyers tried to make pleas to the judge and sheriff's department based on some of that advice. Nothing seemed to work.

The calls would come at any hour, and I felt I couldn't afford to miss a single one. So sleep was basically not an option. Catnaps with my head on my arms were the best I'd do.

Nick was served breakfast at 4:30 A.M., and that was the only set time when I knew for sure he would call—so I was always right there to pick up that phone on the first ring. I could hear him breaking down. I could hear the sound of his voice. I could hear him start to obsess over the guilt of this accident and what he had done and how badly he was being punished. I needed to get him out of that situation. Fast.

In the middle of that first week, Nick was finally moved from the medical ward. Someone realized that was not an appropriate spot to hold a minor on a reckless driving charge. Rather than improve the situation, though, the move made it worse.

As a minor sentenced in adult court, Nick was still caught in the middle, falling between the cracks. Without some broader resolution, there was only one other solution available that would keep him segregated from the adult population without forcing him to stay in that tiny padded cell: They moved him to solitary confinement at a maximum-security jail.

Now my son was in a building with murderers and rapists. He was locked behind a solid steel door with a slot in the bottom that was big enough to put a tray of food through. Nick would lie down on that floor just to watch the feet of guards going by, just to know that someone else was there. This cell, which was slightly larger than the padded cell, had a window. As if that would somehow appease my complaints. The window was a couple of inches wide. Up high. It let in a sliver of light, that's all.

I honestly would have rather seen Nick mingle with the murderers and rapists. He's a big strong kid. I think he would have had a better chance at fending off an attack than he would at fending off the pressure that confinement was laying on his mind.

So I sat in that chair. I did not move. I kept making phone calls. Jennifer brought me food. Friends stopped by to check on me. I refused to move from that spot and those phones. I watched the sunset each night over the water. The sunset that Nick couldn't see. It broke me down. Again and again.

I wouldn't let Nick know that. When he called, I stayed as up-beat as possible. I had to. He was unraveling.

Toward the end of that first long week, it looked like there might be a breakthrough. It looked like the judge was ready to agree to step in and allow Nick to be put into the adult population at the minimum-security prison.

Then Linda spoke up. Remember when I let Nick choose who to live with as the divorce proceedings got started? Well, officially that meant that Linda had physical custody of Nick, and therefore, she had more say than I did. So, from what I understand, she had her lawyer call the judge to object to my request to mingle Nick into the general population.

I was baffled by it. I called Linda and asked her why. She told me she did it to protect him. She told me she was taking her mother's advice that Nick would be in great danger as a minor surrounded by a bunch of adult criminals.

She clearly didn't understand the danger he was in by staying in that solitary cell. That's probably because she didn't talk to Nick as often as I did.

Brooke couldn't understand what Linda was doing. She couldn't understand why she would see the jail phone number pop up on her cell phone and decide not to answer. "How could she not answer Nick's call?" she asked me. I didn't quite know what to say. She needed to figure it out on her own.

Brooke started talking to me a lot more once Nick was in jail. As awful as the circumstances were, it felt good to have Brooke back in my life. She even revealed to me why she had been so distant since the latter part of 2007: For months, Brooke revealed, Linda had been telling her all the stories of the affairs she always imagined I was having. Brooke was now well on her way to figuring out that her mother might not have been telling her the truth.

The thought of my own daughter thinking the worst of me for all that time still saddens me. No daughter should have to think that about her dad. Thankfully, in the middle of Nick's ordeal, we started down the path toward setting things right.

Finally, on the Friday of the second week, it looked like Judge

Federico was ready to amend his original ruling and allow Nick to move into a juvenile facility until his eighteenth birthday on July 27.

Linda objected to that move, too.

I reached Linda on her cell phone that Friday around dinnertime, and she was out at a steak house with her friend Darci Morrison, drinking and having a good time. She told me Darci visited a juvenile facility about eighteen years ago and said it was the scariest place she had ever been. So Linda decided she didn't want Nick to go there.

"Linda, there are all kinds of different juvenile facilities! This one's not for violent offenders! They have Bible programs, and work programs." She didn't care. When I berated her friend for giving her such bad advice, she got really angry at me and hung up the phone.

Another weekend. I didn't move.

Another week of wrangling. I didn't move.

Now the juvenile facility decided they wouldn't even take Nick if a judge ordered it, because he wasn't tried in a juvenile court and they didn't want to set a precedent. So back to square one.

Nick was so fragile through this whole ordeal that I tried to do anything I could to refocus him on other things. We tried to talk about the good things that could happen when he got out of jail. He was still in talks with the TV execs about that reality show on drifting, and we talked about that. We talked about how much John would love to be a part of that show, and when he's healed and healthy and walking again how great it would be to have John back on the pit crew and participating in that show.

The guilt of the accident was eating Nick alive, so I kept reading to him from the Bible and the books about the law of attraction and spirituality and strength that I had discovered since January to help him find an explanation for what happened. We talked about the negative things he thought about in his own life, and how that could have drawn negative consequences. We talked about John, and how down he was after coming back from Iraq, how he talked so negatively all the time, how he talked about thinking he was going to die, and I raised the question of whether or not that might have been part of what caused John's injuries. I did anything and everything I could just to alleviate my son's suffering. Just to relieve some of the guilt and pressure he was putting on himself. I was willing to say almost anything, no matter what it was, to get him through these seemingly endless days in that solitary cell.

TALE OF THE TAPES

As we entered the third week of this nonstop struggle, my third week sitting in that chair, I suddenly received a flurry of worried calls from attorneys and friends describing something I just couldn't believe was real.

The Pinellas County Sheriff's Department released tapes of Nick's jailhouse phone conversations to the media. His conversations with me. His conversations with his mother. Even conversations with his grandmother, my mom, Ruth Bollea. Private conversations that were recorded in my son's darkest hours.

That tabloid trash Web site TMZ sifted through these twenty-six hours of tapes, found the most potentially inflammatory ten-second sound bites, cut them out of context, and pasted them on the Internet for the whole world to hear.

I knew all of our conversations were monitored and recorded. There was a reminder that came on and told me so every two minutes we were on that phone. I interpreted that the same way every other person with a family member in jail interprets that message. You can't have murderers and thieves having conversations about planning their escape or putting hits on people. The reason to monitor jailhouse conversations is safety. We all get that. Nowhere is it ever said or written or even implied that these tapes could be released for public consumption.

Have you ever heard Charles Manson's jailhouse tapes? Have you ever heard Ted Bundy's jailhouse tapes? Have you heard O.J.'s jailhouse tapes? A lot of people would find it pretty fascinating to hear those tapes, but they've never been made available. Come to think of it, have you even heard Paris Hilton's jailhouse tapes? Or any other celebrity's jailhouse tapes? No! Never before, to my knowledge, have *anyone's* jailhouse tapes been released to the media except ours down here in the hillbilly circus. It is a violation of privacy at someone's most vulnerable point, and I pray that no other parent with a child in jail is ever forced to go through something like this. The release of those tapes was unconscionable. Now all of us would have to face the music when it came to the things we said.

The most inflammatory statement of all of those sound bites was one that came out of my mouth. I was talking about the law of attraction, and I made the suggestion that God laid some "heavy shit" on John. Then Nick responded, in the spirit of talking about the law of attraction and the idea that there could be some explanation for why this accident happened to both of them that night, that John was a "negative person." We weren't just talking about the accident, of course. The "heavy shit" that was laid on John was also the horrible situation in his home life.

I've apologized for making that statement, and I'll apologize again here. Even in complete privacy, it is not for me to judge how John lived his life. I shouldn't have said it, and I'm sorry. I hope that after reading this book, people will understand that my words weren't said with any kind of malice.

Before and after that moment on that tape, we spent all kinds of time talking about the good things about John, and how much we were praying for his complete recovery. Those twenty-six hours of tapes are filled with positive, life-affirming messages that were meant to help my son survive his ordeal, but the media didn't play them, or the long passages I read from the Bible. That's just the way the media works. I accept that.

You want to know what? After we had a chance to digest it and talk about it, Nick and I were both grateful that those tapes were released. We were grateful because it woke us up. It made us realize that even as we discussed our spirituality in private, it was important to be mindful of our words.

Words are powerful things. The words I used to distract Nick from his misery, combined with the motivational words and spiritual words I used in those phone calls, helped my son to survive the cruel and unusual punishment of his confinement.

We stayed on the path of positivity—and something good actually came out of that whole ordeal. At the end of May, my friend Duane "Dog" Chapman read what I was going through with Nick and those tapes, and he had his lawyer, David Houston, give me a call. The last thing I wanted to do was explain Nick's case to yet another lawyer, but David heard me out and did something none of those other lawyers did: He hopped on a plane and flew into Tampa to take care of this thing firsthand.

First he filed a lawsuit against the sheriff's office for releasing those jailhouse tapes, asking a judge to bar them from releasing any more tapes in the future. Then David Houston came up with a way to file a motion that even Linda wouldn't object to: We asked that Nick be removed from solitary and allowed to serve his jail sentence at home with an ankle bracelet until he turned eighteen, at which time he would go back into the adult minimum-security jail as expected. It was less than two months that Nick would be on house arrest. It seemed like a very reasonable solution.

On June 3, Judge Federico held a hearing and denied the request.

After all the press attention, I think he simply didn't want to lose face. He didn't want to look like he was giving in to the Hogans. That's my opinion. He also must have realized that it was time to do the right thing, though, because two days later, in what sources at the jail told the press was a "routine review," Nick was suddenly moved out of solitary and allowed to mingle with two other juveniles who were brought into a segregated area of the adult minimum-security prison. Nick suddenly had some human contact. He had access to a television. He had access to an outdoor courtyard.

"Dad, I can even go outside at night and see the stars!" he said. My son was elated. My son was grateful beyond belief. His voice finally regained some sense of normalcy.

I knew he would survive now. I knew he would make it.

After twenty-eight days, I finally got out of that chair and walked into my bedroom. With eyes full of tears—the best kind of tears—I fell asleep the moment my head hit the pillow.

VISITING DAYS

During that twenty-eight-day nightmare, I disregarded everything else in the world. Nothing else mattered to me. In fact, had Nick stayed in solitary any longer, I actually would have given up a tremendous opportunity to move forward in a new direction with my career.

Back when *American Gladiators* first started, my old WCW pal Eric Bischoff and I started pushing an idea for a show called *Celebrity Championship Wrestling*—sort of like *Dancing with the Stars* but with body slams and choke holds. We wanted to take some well-known TV stars and teach them how to wrestle—give them the moves, the attitude, the character development, really teach them how to work a match and whip a crowd into a frenzy.

It was a chance for me to continue a wrestling-centric career without continuing to bust up my back. I would act as a judge and mentor, and I'd bring my friends in, people like "Mouth of the South" Jimmy Hart and Brutus Beefcake, to really show these celebrities the ropes.

Just as I wrapped season two of *Gladiators* and dealt with Nick's going to jail, this idea became a reality. CMT, the country music cable network, picked it up. Filming was slated to start in early June—coincidentally within a couple of days of Nick being taken out of solitary.

Even then, I didn't want to go. I didn't want to risk missing a phone call from my son. It was Nick who encouraged me to follow through with it. "Go, Dad. It'll be good for you," he said. "I promise I'll be okay."

So I flew off to California and started this new show where

I was really calling the shots (along with Eric) for the first time in my TV career.

There was only one problem: visiting days.

For the rest of Nick's stay, we were allowed to visit with him for an hour on Wednesdays, Fridays, and Sundays. They weren't in-person visits. We weren't sitting behind a screen or a piece of Plexiglas like you see on TV. The only view we had of Nick was through a video-monitor system, and we spoke to each other on an old-fashioned phone handset.

I wanted to make as many of those visits as I could. I knew how important they were to Nick, and I figured that his mother would potentially flake out on them.

That meant flying back and forth from *Celebrity Championship Wrestling*'s Los Angeles set to Tampa every chance I got. Suddenly, it occurred to me that those old crazy days of flying back home to Florida in between matches to see the kids had been training sessions for this summer of 2008. There was no way I could make every visiting day and still film this show. So Brooke promised me that she would make it to see Nick every Wednesday, and I arranged the show on a four-day schedule for myself so that I could fly to Tampa first thing every Friday, and fly back to Los Angeles every Sunday night.

The crew on the show called me Yawni, like the musician Yanni, because I yawned my way through that whole experience. I didn't have the energy I did in my thirties and forties, that's for sure—but those visits with Nick were worth every single yawn.

In the beginning Linda and I would go together. We would actually lean our heads together against the phone's earpiece so we could talk to our son and hear him at the same time. Nick just loved seeing us together. It gave him hope. But Linda stopped that after just a few visits. I have a feeling her lawyer told her it was setting a bad precedent for whatever she wanted to win in the divorce. So we decided to split the visits half and half. I would take the first twenty minutes, she would get a straight half hour, and then I would step in for ten minutes to say good-bye at the end.

It worked fine once or twice. Then there was a Friday when Linda didn't show up at all. Nick had spoken to her over the phone, and she said she was out on the boat and was going to skip her visit that day.

She was out on the boat, she said, with Charlie.

Just as I was starting to feel better about my son's condition in jail, I got hit with the news that Linda was dating a guy named Charlie Hill. A kid who went to school a year behind Brooke, and a year ahead of Nick.

My wife was dating a teenager.

Nick told me how she met this guy on the sand one day out in front of our beach house. How he started hanging around all the time before Nick's sentencing. How Linda tried to push Brooke to hook up with him before she ever did.

Brooke found out Charlie and Linda were dating by accident. She walked into the big house on Willadel one day expecting to meet Linda for lunch, and all of a sudden as she walked up to her bedroom, she noticed Nick's TV was on. Nick was in jail. Why was his TV on? She saw clothes all over the bed in his room, and three of Linda's little dogs were there staring at the bathroom door, like they were waiting for somebody to come out. So she opened the bathroom door and found Charlie and some guy hiding from her in the bathroom. She recognized Charlie right away, but thought they had broken in or something—until Charlie told her he was actually living there and had been dating Linda.

Brooke was shocked. She didn't believe him. She forced Charlie and his friend to leave the house and then called me all panicky, so I hopped in my car and went racing over there. At this point Linda was headed back to the house, too, and when she saw me driving by she called the cops. She then followed me while she was on the phone with the 911 operator, accusing me of stalking her and threatening her life and claiming that she had an injunction against me! I wound up getting pulled over—which wound up all over the TV and gossip Web sites. It was just a mess. The police apologized to me in the end. Linda didn't have any injunction against me. But the damage was done.

Apparently Linda was embarrassed to be dating a nineteen-year-old, because even after that incident, even after Charlie admitted the situation to Brooke, Linda kept insisting that Charlie was only a friend. She even said they were "just friends" in an interview with a national magazine.

A few weeks down the road she finally admitted it to Nick. Her rationale? "Don't you want me to be happy, Nick?" I can't believe she made our son respond to that question. From jail. Of course he wanted his mother to be happy—but was this really what it took to make her happy?

Linda even started bringing Charlie along for her jailhouse visits. That really freaked Nick out. I just couldn't believe the audacity of that.

People started telling me about seeing Linda on the beach, Linda on the boat, Linda hanging out with all these dock rats and young Clearwater kids at all the local hot spots and bars. It's like she was a totally different person. She hated going out on the boat. She hated the wind at the beach. She never wanted to go out to bars.

She never wanted to do any of those things with me. I kept questioning, *Why?* Was it just me? Was she trying to go back to the age she was before we met? Was she trying to relive her youth? I didn't get it, but whatever it was, it sure didn't seem healthy.

There were times during those visits when I'd take the phone from Linda to do my last ten minutes with Nick, and the handset would reek from the alcohol on her breath. She started missing those visits more often as well, and with no notice at all. Here I was flying in from California for that precious half hour, and she couldn't make it from fifteen minutes away.

I could have kept getting angry. I could have flipped out on Linda. I could have flipped out on Charlie. I didn't, though, and I thank God for that. I thank God that I put myself on a new path before any of these situations presented themselves. I think about the alternate course my life could have taken under all that stress and pressure. What if I hadn't gotten my head on straight? Is it possible that Hulk Hogan could have become just like some of these other wrestlers who've taken their own lives in recent years? Could I have turned into something worse?

Many months later I made an unfortunate comment to a magazine about this subject, suggesting that I "understood" what O.J. Simpson did. Out of context, it made me seem like some kind of a monster. All I meant by that statement was that as my life started to unravel at the end of 2007, I peered over the fence of reason and saw what insanity and rage look like. I never came close to jumping that fence. But when your whole world falls apart and you start thinking about taking your own life, there's a lot of darkness. Without help, it can get real hard to see in the dark. I was lucky enough to find some light—through Laila, *The Secret*, the Bible, Jennifer, and embracing the spirit of Christ once again—I was able to choose an entirely different path. I've walked so far down that path now that the fence separating me from any sort of insanity and rage isn't even visible in the distance anymore.

Starting that summer of 2008, I just prayed that Linda would find happiness. I really did. I started keeping a journal next to my bed that summer, and every morning when I got up I would write down all of the things I was grateful for. The lists I made included plenty of things that weren't real yet. (That all goes back to the law of attraction again.) I said I was grateful for my back being totally healed. I said I was grateful for Nick getting out of jail stronger than he ever imagined he could be. And every morning I wrote down how grateful I was for Linda finding happiness. I meant that. I still write those words down. Every day. Just for her.

FACING THE FANS

As I slowly refocused my life, becoming more aware of every action I took and every thought I had, I neglected one very important area: my public image.

I knew I was choosing to move in a more positive direction by not speaking out to the media throughout the demise of the marriage, and Nick's ordeal, and the release of those tapes. The problem was nobody else knew it.

My fans were left to come to their own conclusions about what I had become based only on the words of others. The only message the public heard about Hulk Hogan for almost an entire year had come from Linda and her attorneys, the Grazianos and their attorneys, bloggers, DJs, and Nancy Grace—the CNN *Headline News* personality who took up Hogan-bashing as a full-time job in the wake of Nick's accident.

By June of 2008, I was operating on such a different plane and acting in such a calmer, more rational fashion than I ever had before, some of my friends in the wrestling business said they didn't even recognize me. I stopped complaining all the time. I stopped bashing Linda's antics. It's like I exhaled all that bad energy and let my shoulders relax for the first time in years. Maybe the first time ever in my adult life.

"You're like a whole different person," Eric Bischoff said to me as we started working together on *Celebrity Championship Wrestling.*

"That might be true," I said, "but this is the real me."

Brutus Beefcake was so surprised by my change in demeanor that he went out and started reading *The Secret* and all these other books, too.

The public didn't know any of that. They had no clue. In fact, if you added up all the horrible things that were being said about me, you'd have thought I was nothing more than a cheating husband who stalked Linda, encouraged his kids to drink and drive, and blamed John Graziano for his own condition!

For a long time I didn't care how the public perceived me. Honestly, I knew I needed to get my head on straight before I could deal with anything outside of my own life and family situation. Then all of a sudden Eric and my publicist Elizabeth Rosenthal and Brutus and every one of my attorneys, including David

Houston—all of the people I trust to look after my image, my career, and even my family's well-being—came at me simultaneously with the very same message: "You need to respond or you won't have a career to come back to."

So finally, in early June, I decided it was time to come out of my little spiritual cocoon.

Talking about all of this, especially my son's accident, would not be easy. This was delicate territory, and the last thing I could afford to do was to make another mistake like I had on Arsenio's show in 1991. My image had already suffered too much without my direct involvement.

What I said was almost as important as where I said it. I didn't want anything to seem sensational. I didn't want to make it seem like I was somehow trying to promote myself, when all I wanted to do at this point was let my fans hear my side of the story first-hand.

I worked closely with Elizabeth, who stuck by me through this entire ordeal and somehow saved me from having to answer every tabloid headline. I also hired a crisis management PR firm in Los Angeles, just as backup in case anything got worse. It cost me a fortune, but I didn't want to take any risks this time.

In the end, I think the only thing I needed was the biggest weapon I already had in my arsenal: honesty.

I had crossed that bridge in my personal life once and for all. True open honesty was it for me now. With my kids. With my ex. In my business dealings. Everything. I knew it wouldn't be any different when it came to talking in public.

Within a couple of weeks we decided on two press outlets known for their fairness and journalistic integrity: *People* magazine and Larry King. That was it. I wouldn't go on a media tour. I wouldn't appear on late-night talk shows or early-morning broadcasts. I would let my words speak for themselves. I would give my fans the chance to make up their minds who *they* wanted to believe—the naysayers and haters who were trying to burn me at the stake, or me, the man they'd grown up with and watched and embraced both in and out of the ring for the last thirty years.

It actually felt good to talk about it all. It was cathartic in a way to finally speak out and just tell someone outside of my immediate circle what I'd been through, and what I was still going through. Plus, I felt it was so important that I shift some of the focus back to John Graziano, so the public would be thinking about his healing and sending positive thoughts and prayers his way after reading or listening to what I had to say.

I answered Larry King's questions as honestly as I possibly could. There was no acting or putting on airs. I just spoke to him, from the heart, and I think people could tell. I answered *People* magazine's questions the same way. Once I had said my piece, I went back to my life. I went back to Jennifer. I went back to making my new TV show. I went back to spending time with Brooke; we finally saw eye to eye after all we'd been through, and she even moved back in with me for a while. I went back to visiting my son every hour I possibly could for the remainder of his time in jail.

It felt good. I somehow felt like I had completed a big step in my journey. It was out of my hands now. I was grateful that those big media outlets still embraced me in a way that allowed me to say what I had to say.

In fact, the only downside to it was the effect it seemed to have on Linda. It put her on the defensive, even though I did my best not to say anything too negative about her at all in those interviews.

Right in the middle of it, her lawyer stood up and proclaimed to the world that this divorce was going to be a war. He was actually quoted saying that to *People* magazine, in a rebuttal quote they included in my story.

A war? I remember thinking what a terrible thing that was. For the two of us. For our kids. Linda already knew I was willing to give her half of everything at that point. I was happy to give her whatever a judge deemed was her share. She deserved it. We had been married twenty-three years. That wasn't enough for her. It seemed like she wanted to try to destroy me. And that just made me sad for her.

I kept asking myself, *What kind of a person wants to turn their divorce into a war?*

CHAPTER 20

Revelations

Sometimes, asking a question is all it takes for the universe to suddenly provide you with answers.

With all of these questions about Linda on my mind, I went back and reread *A New Earth*—and suddenly I saw things I had never seen before. Starting on page 129 I came across a description of something so familiar to me it felt like it was specifically written about my wife.

The basic idea is that certain people feed off of negative energy. They need it to live. The only way they can survive is to constantly create negativity in the lives of everyone around them: family, friends, co-workers—anyone they can draw into that vacuum of misery, they will.

A New Earth calls that powerful, living, breathing type of negative energy a "pain body," but I'll spare you the new age language and try to describe this phenomenon in my own words.

It all goes back to the idea that your thoughts are like a magnet. The more negative the thoughts you harbor, the more negative the consequences you bring. Certain people get caught up in that negative energy: As their thoughts get worse, the consequences get worse, and as the consequences get worse, the bitching and moaning and complaining about the circumstances of their life gets worse, which creates even more negative energy, and so on.

Sometimes these same people fall prey to addictions. Alcohol and drugs fuel the hunger, but the thing they're addicted to most is the uproar and chaos that they themselves create.

Reading those passages, realizing that what I'd witnessed in my own household had happened to other people, that it was tangible and describable—I can't tell you what a relief that was. The understanding I took away from those pages acted like a construction crane, grasping and lightening the load of that boulder I'd been carrying on my shoulders. And that made it easier to carry the whole truth of my marriage once it finally started to emerge.

"Ask and ye shall receive." I asked for answers about what kind of person would turn their divorce into a war, and in the summer of 2008 my own children opened my eyes to sides of Linda that I never even knew existed.

I still can't believe it took a divorce and my son going to jail and my daughter not talking to me for months on end before I finally took off the blinders when it came to my wife. I was finally ready to understand not only the person Linda had become, but the true person she was in all of those years when I wasn't around for days on end and she was home alone with my children.

In mid-2008, every time I saw Brooke I told her how bad I felt for all she had been through in these recent months and years. It just killed me that my daughter had been thrown on this emotional roller coaster that Linda and I created. I kept saying to her, "I just wish we could go back to the good times we had as a family."

Then one day that summer, Brooke stopped my little trip down memory lane dead in its tracks. She stopped me by asking a question: "When *was* that, Dad?"

"What do you mean?" I asked her.

"Those good times you're talking about. I mean, it wasn't really that good," she said. "Ever."

From that day forward I started to really talk with my daughter about this marriage, as *she* saw it. I guess I had never taken the time to do that—to fully imagine what life was like as Hulk Hogan's kid and Linda Bollea's daughter.

In fact, it really shook me up, because part of me never really thought all that much about what was happening in my home when I was on the road all those years. I think I made a lot of assumptions about how the kids were being raised, and the messages they were getting, and the lessons they were receiving. Linda was my wife, and I just assumed she was parenting in a way that was appropriate and compatible with my own values.

Until that summer, I didn't realize there was a whole life between Linda and these kids that I knew nothing about.

Brooke didn't want to explain it all to me, but she wanted me to understand. So one day, she told me about her diaries. Diaries she had kept going all the way back to when she was a little girl, maybe eight or nine years old. It was a shocking thing to hear my daughter open her private thoughts to me in that way, but it was that important to her.

The biggest revelation from Brooke was that Linda's drinking affected the children. Linda was especially mean when she got drunk. So mean that Brooke apparently dreaded the sound of Linda's footsteps in the hall. Brooke, my little girl, kept rosary beads hung above her bed so she could hold them and pray for the misery to pass.

All those years I had no idea.

I'll stop there. I think you get the point. Having Brooke open up to me about what was in her diaries broke my heart.

The thing is, I'm not talking about all of this to *trash* Linda. I'm talking about it because I'm trying to *understand* her, and because I want you to stop and think about what happened to me and how it might apply to you: How massive, deep-seated problems can go unnoticed in a marriage or any other relationship if you're not totally present and aware of what's going on in your own life.

It's staggering to me that I could have been blind to these things for so many years. I could stand in the ring at Madison Square Garden, totally present and aware of the mood swings and mindset of twenty-two thousand people—so much so that I could hold that entire audience in the palm of my hand—and yet I wasn't present and aware enough in my life outside the ring to notice how dysfunctional and damaging my own family had become.

FINDING FORGIVENESS

Throughout this yearlong reevaluation of everything I've ever done in my life, coming to grips with what went wrong in my marriage was the hardest part of it all.

But once I had that understanding, I had to do something more: I had to learn to let go of my anger toward Linda.

Linda's a product of the home she grew up in, a product of her parents, a product of the environment that shaped her. She's even a product of the life I gave her. A life filled with excess. A life spent living in Hulk Hogan's shadow. A life with a husband who was constantly gone.

The more I've grown to understand all of that, the more I've grown capable of forgiving her. For everything.

I will always, always love Linda. Nothing will change that. And I'm so grateful that she came into my life. I'm grateful for the time we shared together. I'm grateful for this tremendous life that she allowed me to live—and she really did make it possible. She was the one taking care of my home and children and even my money while I was out wrestling every day. So I'm grateful for that. And of course I'm eternally grateful for the children that we brought into this world.

I'm even grateful—get ready for this one, folks—for the hell that Linda put me through at the end of our marriage: the disappearing, the drinking, even the divorce itself.

If it wasn't for all of that, I never would have bottomed out in December of 2007. And if I hadn't bottomed out, I might still be walking on that treadmill of misery I called my life.

The fact is, I'm not walking on that treadmill anymore. As much as it may look like my life is nothing but pain and misery and ordeals as I continue to undergo back surgeries and the divorce gets drawn out and the Graziano lawsuit looms, nothing could be further from the truth.

The thing I've come to realize in this last couple of years is that sometimes right before your greatest success you face your darkest hours. Sometimes you have to have a tragic loss or some tragic event has to happen to you in order to make you become aware and present and grateful for your life. I've reached a point where my life is now drastically happier than it has ever been. On a minute-by-minute, day-by-day basis, I spend more time smiling than ever before.

I only wish Linda could get there, too. I pray for that to happen every day.

That's the amazing thing about negative energy: Sometimes it gets so powerful that it finally crashes and sends you careening in the opposite direction overnight. That's what happened to me when all of a sudden I grew sick and tired of being sick and tired. I just keep praying that Linda finds that feeling soon. I really do.

As for all of that other ongoing stuff in my life? Those are all just situations I have to deal with. I'll admit there are a lot of really heavy situations that are still hitting me simultaneously. It's more than a lot of people could take. Sure, it can be daunting at times. That's a good thing, though. I like a challenge, and I know now that I can survive and thrive through all of these obstacles because something better is waiting for me on the other side.

That's the power of spirituality.

I'm not some kind of hero for acting this way. There are no heroes here. I'm not doing anything other than what everybody should try to do. It's pretty simple stuff, actually.

When it comes down to it, no matter what your situation, no matter what your circumstance, just ask yourself, "Would I rather be happy or sad?"

When you wake up every morning, stop and ask yourself, "Would I rather be joyful or miserable?"

When faced with a situation in life that could go either way, just ask yourself this one big question: "Do I want to be good or bad?"

That's it. You choose. End of story.

I wish I could say that every circumstance in my life improved the moment I had this spiritual awakening and these moments of forgiveness. It didn't. I'd spent far too many years wallowing in negativity for it all to turn around just because I'd read a few books and made some new friends.

Just like it takes time for a seed to sprout through the surface of the soil, it takes time for a life to turn around and head in a new direction. My books taught me that. I see evidence of my life turning around every day now, because I'm as present and aware of what's happening in my life as any man can be.

I could go on for pages and pages here about all the crazy situations life continued to throw at me as 2008 turned to 2009. I could talk for days about how quickly all the money I've ever made is being depleted—by Linda, by lawyers, by these massive expenses I'm laying out—to the tune of hundreds of thousands of dollars each month. I could go on about the fact that at this moment, I don't have a job, which means that all of that money could truly be gone by the middle of 2010 if this cycle doesn't stop; which means there won't be any money left for me to fund John Graziano's care, let alone anything else his family wants to do with their winnings, should a judge decide to rule in their favor. I could go on about Linda trying to have me arrested when I drove near our old neighborhood. Or explain how Linda treated our kids now that I was no longer around to serve as her punching bag. I could certainly talk for hours about my wife's nineteen-year-old boyfriend who was living the high life, driving my cars, driving my boat, and sleeping in that mansion while I paid for the nonstop party he and a whole bunch of his friends were having care of Linda's wide-open wallet, and more.

Like I said, though, those are all just "life situations." They're not my life anymore.

I haven't gone soft. Don't get me wrong. I will continue to fight for what's right, and what's mine. There's nothing about this new lifestyle of mine to suggest that I should just roll over. In fact, just the opposite. I need to fight for what's right more than ever—to fight for what's "right" and not "wrong."

All I'm saying is that those things don't consume me anymore.

The things that consume my thoughts are much bigger, and much brighter.

Nick walked out of jail a free man on October 21, 2008. I don't use the word "man" lightly. He grew up a lot in those months. It's hard to imagine a way to become more present and aware and grateful for what you have in life than to see your simplest freedoms taken away, and I know Nick is stronger than ever for going through that ordeal.

The judge in my divorce finally allowed me to move back into our house on the sand in Clearwater Beach. So I gave Nick that bachelor pad to stay in till he decided where he wanted to live. (There was a real motivation for him to move to California—to escape the Tampa media madness, for one, and to have a shot at getting his license back sooner, so he could try to find work and establish a life and career for himself now that he's turned eighteen. In 2009, that's exactly what he would do.)

Living on the beach turned out to be a dream. I wasn't allowed to change Linda's putrid decorating experiments—the house was still a "marital asset," so the tartan-plaid carpet and paisley wallpaper she installed on the ceiling have to stay until the divorce is finalized and we decide who gets what property. Still, waking up and looking at that white sand every day, dipping into the ocean whenever I feel like it—it's an idyllic life that I appreciate now more than ever.

I follow a pretty simple routine most days. In fact, I recently had a pretty good laugh when I realized that part of the routine I follow is something I've been preaching for a very long time: I train at the gym, I take my vitamins, and I say my prayers. Every day.

Jennifer—my light—has continued to stay at my side through every twist and turn, and the two of us started to do things that Linda would never allow. I reconnected with some of my neighbors on Willadel Drive, and we actually went out to dinner with them—and had a good time. What a concept! We took some time off to get away to Key West. Just the two of us. I started inviting friends over, without any fear that they'd suddenly feel the need to flee. My old friend Brutus "the Barber" Beefcake actually spent a few weeks staying with us at the beginning of 2009. He never would have dared to do that in the old days, he admitted—he just couldn't be around my wife. That's changed now.

A lot has changed now. We haven't tag-teamed in the ring for quite a while. In fact, I've renamed him Brutus "the Barbecue" Beefcake because he mans a mean grill. I'm telling you, you haven't tasted steak and lobster until you've tasted Brutus's.

If it sounds a little bit like a retirement, it's not. Not by a long shot. Remember, talking to lawyers is almost a full-time gig for me now. That makes it difficult to get the next phase of my life under way. But I'm definitely in transition—and that's exciting.

I'm constantly talking to Eric Bischoff about new projects, potentially mind-blowing projects that could rock the world of sports entertainment. I'm toying with the idea of letting cameras into my life again, imagining how different a show could be now that I'm living with a positive mindset. I'm looking past all of that to some bigger ideas that go way beyond just my "career," too.

There's one thing I know: If everything goes south on me with these lawsuits and the divorce, if I wind up broke, I'll be cool with it. I'll live in a van by the beach and be happy. I really will. That may sound like cheap talk, but it isn't. I've been there before, and I can go there again. I know it like I know that I'm standing here living and breathing today.

Don't get me wrong. I would love to keep my cars and my

houses and a chunk of this money that I gave up most of my life and half of my body to get. I'm still spending hours and hours talking to attorneys to try to make sure I get to keep what's mine. At the same time; I know that I can live without any of that material wealth if that's what God has in store for me.

Even if I'm forced to start over from scratch, I know I will rise and prosper again, because this time my mind will be focused on something higher than just my personal goals. I really want to help people. I want to find a way to let all the Hulkamaniacs in the world start profiting from their devotion. I keep having visions of myself and Eric Bischoff and Brutus and all of my lifelong friends filling stadiums full of fans. Not necessarily to watch wrestling. For something else. For something that gives back to all of those wrestling fans who were so loyal to all of us for all those years. Something that will change people's lives for the better.

I can't quite put my finger on what it is yet, but I was put on this earth to do something more than wrestle. I know that now. All of these tests I'm going through? All of these life situations that keep hitting me again and again? They're the proof. They're preparing me for the greatness that's waiting for me, just up ahead around the corner.

OLD BUSINESS

I know some people are going to laugh at me for continuously talking about all of this positive-energy/positive-thinking spirituality stuff. Especially as I continue to hit bumps in the road going forward. That's okay. I just want to point out one extreme example of what happens to someone when they're living life to the opposite extreme.

In February of 2009, Ed Graziano—John's father, the man John feared was out to kill him, the man who stretched the truth in a court of law in an attempt to further punish my son for that car accident, the man who fought with his own family at the hospital as their son lay struggling for life—was arrested for allegedly attempting to hire a hit man to kill his wife, Debbie. According to police, he tried to get the job done with a couple thousand bucks and a gift card to a local pizza joint. No joke. According to everything I read in the papers, he wanted it set up to look like his wife had died in a car accident.

That man's negative energy is so strong that it deeply affected every member of that family.

I pray for them to bounce back from all of this. I do. Just as I continue to pray for John's recovery, and will keep praying for John's recovery for as long as it takes.

Another strange thing happened early in 2009: I started getting calls from Vince McMahon Jr. He was putting together his massive plans for WrestleMania XXV. I could hardly believe it had been twenty-five years since the original WrestleMania set the world on fire; twenty-five years since Muhammad Ali held my arm up in the air and I took home that championship belt.

I have to say, it was hard to imagine the twenty-fifth anniversary of WrestleMania going down without Hulk Hogan in the ring. Still, I didn't say yes to Vince right away. He kept calling me and calling me, but for some reason I hesitated.

I thought about the bad blood between us in the past, but I was such a different person now. I considered the fact that Vince still owned so much of the Hulk Hogan legacy, and that he and the whole WWE organization were still unwilling to share that. I built that empire with Vince. We were partners in this game. Yet I'm not allowed to post old videos of my matches on my own Web site because Vince owns the exclusive rights to them all. So I had issues, both business and personal, with the whole concept of jumping into that particular ring. Even so, I couldn't help but get excited about it. To this day, every time I walk by a ring I get chills. I salivate just thinking about getting back in there. I started to think about how big a comeback this could be for me. Think of the story arc: I was down and out, and beat up in the press, and now I'd show up in that ring and blow the audience away and be right back on top!

But life wasn't going to let that happen. As April approached, a string of ongoing back surgeries kept me from even entertaining the possibility of hitting that ring. Doctors finally discovered that the bottom of my spine is shaped like a J now—the result of 20 years of dropping the leg drop on my opponents, landing full-weight on my left butt cheek. I was really disappointed. I felt miserable about it. I wanted to be able to make that choice myself and not have it dictated by doctors.

Of course, once I stepped back and looked at it through my new eyes I realized that I did make that decision myself. I brought these back surgeries into my life, and everything happens for a reason. *These new doctors I've seen and new techniques they're using should leave my back feeling good in the very near future*, I told myself. *I can feel that tremendous relief already, and I'm grateful for it.* Plus, for me to go participate in that kind of one-off wrestling spectacle was much more a part of my old life than of the life I'm living now. *My new life is going to hold so much more.*

In all practicality, maybe I'm simply too old to keep doing this to my body. If I'd forced myself to go into that ring, maybe something really terrible would have happened. Who knows? I've just learned to be grateful for whatever circumstances arrive in my life. Right now, I am grateful to stay home.

A NEW HOPE

There's a lot to be grateful for in my new life, but almost nothing can compare to how grateful I am to have solid relationships with both of my growing children.

Brooke is still pursuing her music, and finding TV success on her own (even though the old man continues to make a few cameo

appearances). Her show *Brooke Knows Best* drew even bigger numbers than *Hogan Knows Best* on VH1. I couldn't be more proud.

More important, I'm just real proud of Brooke for how far
she's come, and how positive she's managed to stay after going
through all of this with our family. She's so wise sometimes it
blows my mind.

And Nick? Nick's state of mind after all that he's been through
can be summed up in one small moment I was lucky enough to
witness.

One night, just before Nick made the move to California, Jennifer and I, along with Brutus and some friends and neighbors
from just down the beach—all these real positive people I sur-
round myself with all the time now—were gathered at the beach
house getting ready for dinner, and we had just watched the sun
drop down behind the dunes, throwing the most amazing colors
up into the Florida sky. A few minutes later, Nick came walking in
through the front door.

"Did you guys catch that sunset?" he asked. "It was beautiful!"

He was right there. In the moment. Paying attention to life as
it unfolded around him.

That night, we sat around the kitchen eating some of Brutus's
barbecue and talking about Nick's big plans. He was so excited to
make the move.

At one point Nick asked me what I thought of that Mickey
Rourke movie, *The Wrestler*. He hadn't seen it yet, and he wanted
to know if it was worth the price of admission.

I told him I could do better than that. I had a DVD copy of the
film right there if he wanted to watch it.

As some of our guests filtered out, and others settled in to
watch the movie, I went to the sofa with my boy. Just as we were
sitting down I placed my hand on his head and tousled his hair.
It's just one of those things parents do with their kids, and as I did
it I realized I hadn't done it in ages. For some reason it struck me
how big his head was now. He was no longer that little boy I used
to line up peas for at dinnertime, you know?

As the movie started, I told him it was accurate in a lot of ways, but the real stories of wrestling were so much bigger. This film was like watching wrestling on a TV with the color saturation turned way, way down. When Mickey cut his forehead in the ring, I reminded him of the way I used to pull blade jobs all over my head. He had heard some of my stories of the injuries and the crazy shit that went down in and out of the ring in my early days, but not many. It's funny how little our kids really know about the people we were before they came into the picture. This movie gave me a really cool excuse to walk him through memories of my life before he was born.

Not to spoil the movie for you, but there's a real sad twist at the end of *The Wrestler*. After all of these down-and-out years, Mickey Rourke's washed-up character goes back into the ring for one last comeback. Just *one more match*, you know? And he dies. He dies right there in the ring, and all of his dreams die there with him.

I kept glancing over at Nick as that scene played out, his face lit in the blueish light of the big-screen TV. All of a sudden this real worried look washed over him.

"Dad?" he asked. "Could that happen to you?"

Honestly, a few years ago, it might not have been all that far-fetched. If I look inside at the person I was, and what my priorities were, and what I was doing with my life, I have to admit that the thought of a washed-up Hulk Hogan going down in the ring was one possible outcome for my life.

Now? After all I've been through and how far I've come? Knowing that I still have so much to do, and how grateful I am just to wake up every morning, completely aware and alive? The answer came real easy.

"No," I said to my son that night. "That is not how I'm gonna go down."

I'm choosing to live life differently in the second half of the game, and the fact is, my future looks brighter now than at any point in my whole life. That may sound crazy coming from a guy who already had such an amazing run.

But I'm telling you: It's the God's honest truth.

AFTERWORD

Expect the Unexpected

Just before this book went off to the printer, something happened that took a lot of people, especially the media people here in Tampa, by surprise: Linda and I reached an agreement and settled our divorce.

I wasn't surprised. I knew it would happen. In my mind, in my heart, it had already happened. Like I said, all the craziness stopped consuming me many months ago. I moved past it. I was grateful for reaching a truce with Linda and grateful for Linda finding happiness long before any of this happened. Remember: "What you think about, you bring about" really works. And maybe this sudden outbreak of peace in the Hulk vs. Linda war will serve as a little bit of proof to those who doubt it.

I can't reveal the terms of the divorce settlement. We both agreed to keep that between us. But I do want to share the story of how this resolution finally came to pass.

The thing is, as dirty and crazy as everybody thought our divorce proceedings were—and I swear, especially here in the Tampa area, people were ready to put us in the history books alongside Burt Reynolds and Loni Anderson, as if our split made Alec Baldwin's and Kim Basinger's divorce look like a squirt-gun fight—I can tell you now that we hadn't even taken the gloves off.

This thing was set to go to trial in October of 2009, and it was about to get really, *really* nasty.

I didn't want it to get nasty. I didn't want to slam Linda. But as she and her attorney and her publicist kept amping up the drama, and amping up the accusations in the press, I felt I had no choice but to unleash my lawyers and a team of investigators to fight for what's right. That meant interviewing people all over Tampa and Clearwater about everything they knew about Linda and her young boyfriend, Charlie Hill, and the nonstop party I felt they had been living at my expense.

Finally, in July, we sat down for a big day of depositions with the man himself: Charlie. We started at 7:45 A.M., and for the first time ever, he and I were face-to-face, just across a table from one another, and I had a chance to stare him down. I knew I'd never hurt Charlie. As I've said all along, even the thought of getting into a violent confrontation makes me feel sick inside. But Charlie didn't know that. And boy did he look nervous.

The depositions started like most, going through Charlie's work history, just establishing who he is. Before we got into the heavy stuff, we took a break. I stood up, and was probably the last one to leave the room—just 'cause it takes me an extra minute to get my legs moving after I've been sitting for a while—and as I started walking down the hall, I had my head down. I was looking at my cell phone, not paying attention to where I was going, when all of a sudden I looked up and almost ran smack-dab into Charlie.

We were way down the end of a hallway, face-to-face, with no one else around—and I guess he felt trapped because, man, he was shaking!

For ages people had told me that Charlie was worried I was gonna kill him. I heard it from friends, from strangers, from Nick. And here I was towering over him in the corner of this hallway, and I thought he was gonna faint.

"Calm down," I said. "I'm not gonna kill you. I don't want to hurt you. You don't have to be scared of me."

All of a sudden Linda came power-walking toward us, and before she could say a word I said, softly, "Linda, I was just telling the kid that I would never hurt him."

Right then and there, something shifted. Linda put her hand on my chest and started crying: "I thought you were gonna kill Charlie," she said.

My response? "Linda, you *know* me. I would never do anything like that. Twenty years ago I might have *threatened* it, but I never would have done it. You know that. You know *me*."

She nodded. She agreed. And for the first time since all this craziness started in 2007, I saw an opening. "Linda," I said, "what are we doing? After all this fighting we're in the same place we were eighteen months ago, only now there's a lot less money. This is just ridiculous. We need to put a stop to this."

For a moment, she paused. "Okay," she said.

That's how we started talking. And that's how our lawyers started talking, in earnest, about reaching a settlement instead of dragging out this thing that Linda herself had once called a "war." A couple of weeks later we put the paperwork in high gear, and I sat with my attorneys, David Houston and Ann Kerr, and Linda's attorney, and hammered this thing out over the course of five fourteen-hour days.

When we walked into court on July 28 to present our settlement to the judge, Linda kissed me on the cheek. She chatted with Jennifer. And when the gavel came down, I gave Linda a big hug and said, "Have a good life." After reading this book, I hope it's clear to you that I meant it. Heck, I even told her to call me if she ever needs my help with something. You know what? It's not that big a deal, brother. When you're living like I'm living now, the bitterness all goes away.

Linda's getting what she's wanted for a very long time: She's moving to California with enough money to be set for life. I'll be moving back into the big house on Willadel, at least for the time being, and eventually we'll sell our properties and start our new lives without any of that old baggage attached.

"The war is over," Linda told a reporter that morning. As I

write this, two days later, my cheeks still haven't come down. They're stuck in a permanent smile. I'm free.

The "life situations" aren't over for us. Not by any means. The civil suit from the Graziano family is still moving forward. Finding a way to provide the right kind of care for John will still be a challenge, and my days spent talking to lawyers are sure to last for a long time. But when people ask if I'm worried? I think about everything I've been through, everything I've learned, and I smile because I know the answer: That lawsuit is already taken care of. It's going to turn out however it's going to turn out, and I'm grateful for whatever happens.

The good stuff in life, the intense stuff, the crazy stuff—all of it happens for a reason. And now, more than ever before, I see the big picture and keep it all in perspective, which means that the future can only get brighter from here.

To put it another way: The best is yet to come, brother. The best is yet to come.

INDEX

Afa (Wild Samoans, wrestling team), 74
Agape Church, 235, 258–59, 260
aggression, steroids, 140–44
Alabama wrestling circuit, 67, 73–74, 75
Albano, Capt. Lou, 82
alcohol, 65–66. *See also* drugs; steroids
    Claridge, Linda (wife), 179–81, 191, 213,
      290
    Graziano, John, 201–2
    Hogan, Nick, 206–9
    negativity, 289
Alfonso, Martha (sister-in-law), 23, 114
Ali, Laila, 221, 222, 234–36, 258–59, 260,
    261, 283
Ali, Muhammad, 221, 297
Allentown, Pennsylvania, TV recording
    studio, 81, 83, 89, 103, 105
Alley, Kirstie, 149
Altomare, Tony, 82, 85–86, 106
American Gladiators (TV show), 221–25,
    234, 258, 271–72, 279
Anavar (steroid), 64, 142
Anchor Club (Cocoa Beach, Florida),
    62–63, 65, 67
Anderson, Pamela, 159–60
André the Giant (wrestler), 12, 33, 86, 89,
    101, 134, 135, 272
androgen, 64
Anheuser-Busch, 41–42
AOL, 165
Arsenio Hall (TV show), 143–44, 145, 155
Atomic Leg Drop, 89. *See also* leg drop
attraction, law of, 247–56, 277
Augusta, Georgia, 11

Backlund, Bob, 86, 103, 104
Backstreet Boys (band), 170
Ballast Point Baptist Church, 28–29
Ballast Point Elementary School, 17–19

Barnett, Les, 224
Barnum, P. T., 107
Barris, Bob, 20
Barris, Gary, 20
Barrymore, Drew, 159
Barselo, Anthony, 42, 44
baseball, 15–16
Baywatch (TV show), 145, 159
Beckwith, Michael, 249, 258–59, 260–61
Bee Gees (trio), 182
Belleair neighborhood, Clearwater,
    Florida, 149–51
Belushi, John, 110
Bennett, Scott, 177
Benoit, Chris, 33
Betty Ford Clinic, 180
Bischoff, Eric, 146, 150, 151, 155, 223, 224,
    225, 232–33, 279, 280, 284, 295
Black, Roy, 272
blade jobs, 134–35, 300
Blair, Brian, 55, 59, 60, 61
Bockwinkel, Nick, 101
Bollea, Alan (brother), 12
    death of, 116–17, 119, 124, 165
    drugs, 21, 23, 24, 99
    finances of, 115
    Hogan and, 98–99, 115–17
    personality of, 14, 15, 22–25, 30, 114
    shooting of, 25, 36
Bollea, Brooke (daughter). *See* Hogan,
    Brooke (daughter)
Bollea, David (nephew), 99
Bollea, Kenny (half-brother), 25–27
Bollea, Linda (wife). *See* Claridge, Linda
    (wife)
Bollea, Marsha (sister-in-law), 99, 115–17,
    119
Bollea, Michael (Horace Hogan, nephew),
    114

Bollea, Nick (son). *See* Hogan, Nick (son)
Bollea, Peter (father)
  career of, 12–13
  death of, 27, 165, 191
  Hogan and, 53, 117
  personality of, 13–14, 191
  religion, 28
Bollea, Ruth (mother), 12, 13, 276
  Bollea, Kenny, 25–26
  health of, 190
  Hogan and, 117
  personality of, 13–14, 35
  religion, 28
Bollea, Terry Gene, birth of, 11. *See also*
  Hogan, Hulk (Terry Gene Bollea)
Boulder, Terry "the Hulk," 77. *See also*
  Hogan, Hulk (Terry Gene Bollea)
Boulder Brothers (Terry and Ed Boulder),
  73, 75, 76. *See also* Hogan, Hulk
  (Terry Gene Bollea)
bowling, 15
Bridges, Whitey, 62, 65, 66–67, 68
Brisco, Jack, 45, 56, 62, 80, 81
Brisco, Jerry, 56, 62, 80, 81
Broadman, Steve, 18
"Broadway," 59
Brooke Knows Best (TV show), 299
Brutus "the Barber" Beefcake (Ed Leslie),
  22, 63, 64, 65–66, 67–68, 73–75,
  77–78, 123–24, 160, 199, 279, 284,
  295, 299
Bubba the Love Sponge (Todd Alan Clem),
  160, 262
bullies, 14–15
Bundy, Ted, 276
Byrne, Rhonda, 246–47

cable television, 102
celebrity. *See also* fan base; Hulkamania
  Hogan Knows Best (TV show), 178
  Hulkamania, 109–11, 151
  Miami, Florida, 181–82
Celebrity Championship Wrestling (TV
  show), 279–80, 284
celebrity exhibition matches, 164–65
Cena, John, 140
Channel 9 television (New York City), 101
Chapman, Duane "Dog," 278
Chapman, Steve, 212, 233
Charles, Ray, 12
Cher, 159
children, role models, 112–13
Christian Youth Ranch, 29, 31–32, 39, 249
Chrysler Corporation, 109
Church of Scientology, 149
cigarette smoking, 65
Claridge, Gail (mother-in-law), 147–51, 180
Claridge, Joe (father-in-law), 180
Claridge, Linda (wife)
  alcohol, 179–81, 191, 213, 290
  Brooke Hogan and, 172–73, 174, 177,
    185, 186, 187
  celebrity, 110–11
  courtship, 96–98

divorce, 1, 4, 7–8, 158–59, 161, 186,
  214, 224–26, 238–39, 254, 256–57,
  280–83, 286–87, 300–04
finances, 149–50
Graziano lawsuit, 265, 274–75
marriage to Hogan, 99–101, 121,
  122–30, 137, 145, 147–52, 158–61,
  236–39, 289–90
personality of, 13, 123, 148, 159–60, 174,
  177, 179, 181, 183–84, 186, 191–93,
  216, 254, 288–89
son Nick's car crash, 4–6, 206, 210, 214,
  220
television, 177–78
Clark, Sue, 22
Clearwater, Florida, 149–51, 301
Clem, Todd Alan (Bubba the Love Sponge),
  160, 262
Clinton, Bill, 143
CMT music cable network, 279
CNN *Headline News* (TV show), 284
CNN television network, 178
cocaine, 111–13, 117
Cocoa Beach, Florida, 63, 64–66
Colt, Buddy, 33, 57
Conroy, Jeannie, 39
construction work, 42

Dancing with the Stars (TV show), 221
Daytona 500, 185
death, attitude toward, 200
Deca-Durabolin (steroid), 64
Disney Studios, 145–46
divorce
  Claridge, Linda (wife), 1, 4, 7–8, 158–59,
    161, 186, 214, 224–26, 238–39, 254,
    256–57, 280–83, 286–87
  Hogan, Brooke (daughter), 230, 245, 274,
    281–82, 289–90
  Hogan, Hulk, 193, 214, 224–26, 227–32,
    238–39, 244–45, 256–57, 280–83,
    286–87, 289, 291–92, 295–96
dockworker, 42, 43, 80
driver's license, 28–29, 35
drugs. *See also* alcohol; steroids
  Bollea, Alan (brother), 21, 23, 24, 99
  cocaine, 111–13, 117
  high school, 21
  Japan, 94
  marijuana, 65, 66, 94, 104, 111, 117, 127,
    128–29
  negativity, 289
Duff, Hilary, 171
Dynabol (steroid), 64

Ebersol, Dick, 110
elementary school education, 17–19
entertainment, wrestling, 15, 50–51
ethnicity, 85
Everson, Cory, 160
Everson, Jeff, 160
"Everything to Me," 171
"Eye of the Tiger" (theme music), 96
eyewitnesses, 205

fakery, 51
fan base. *See also* celebrity; Hulkamania
  building of, 78, 79, 86–87
  celebrity, 112–13, 138
  ethnicity, 85
  Hollywood Hogan persona, 161–62,
    166–67
  Hulkamania, 95–96, 103, 119–20
  Japan, 90
  relationship with, 283–87
  steroid scandal, 151–52, 155
fatalism, 71
Father of the Year Award, 191–93
Federico, Philip J., 263, 266, 267, 274–75,
  278
Federico, Rick, 263
Ferrigno, Lou, 76–77
Flair, Ric, 138, 146, 150, 151, 155
Florida Championship Wrestling (TV
  show), 32–33
Florida wrestling circuit, 50–62
Folio modeling agency, 94
football, 17–18, 29, 39
Ford Motor Company, 109
Fort Homer Hesterly Armory, 34, 50
Fox News television network, 178
Fugate, Lee, 263
Funk, Dory, Sr., 34
Funk, Terry, 80

Gagne, Verne, 95, 101, 103, 105
Gail Claridge Interiors, 151
gay wrestlers, 57–60
General Motors, 109
gimmick, New York wrestling circuit, 74–75
Gold's Gym (Los Angeles, California), 98
Grace, Nancy, 284
Graham, Billy (the Superstar, wrestler), 33,
  44–46, 48, 50, 54, 67, 82
Graham, Eddie, 33, 51, 52, 81, 88
Graham, Mike, 33, 49, 51, 52, 88
Graziano, Debbie, 199, 210, 212–13,
  215–16, 219–20
Graziano, Ed, 199, 211–13, 219–20, 267,
  296–97
Graziano, John, 201–3
  car crash, 3, 4, 6, 206, 208–9, 284
  family life of, 198–200, 201–3, 213
  injuries to, 210–11, 215, 216–18, 255,
    257
  lawsuit, 8, 219–20, 256–57, 304
Graziano, Michael, 210, 216
Great Malenko (wrestler), 33

Hackman, Gene, 110
Hall, Arsenio, 143–44, 145, 155
Hall, Scott, 162
Hart, Jimmy, 279
Hartman, Phil, 232
hazing, 57–60, 62
Headline News (CNN TV show), 284
Hector's Gym, 37, 38, 42
Hell's Angels, 98–99, 115
Highlander (film), 159

Hill, Charlie, 281–82, 301–03
Hillsborough Community College, 40
Hilton, Paris, 277
Hogan, Brooke (daughter), 13, 124
  birth of, 125–27, 156, 252
  car crash, 5, 206, 210
  divorce, 230, 245, 274, 281–82, 289–90
  family life, 163, 199, 220, 252–54
  Graziano lawsuit, 266, 274
  health of, 181
  home-schooling, 174
  music and recording career, 168–69,
    170–71, 173, 178, 181, 185, 197–98,
    298–99
  personality of, 176, 186
  television, 171–73
Hogan, Horace (Michael Bollea, nephew),
  114
Hogan, Hulk (Terry Gene Bollea)
  birth of, 11
  career of, 41–43
  childhood of, 11–27, 168
  divorce, 193, 214, 224–26, 227–32,
    238–39, 244–45, 256–57, 280–83,
    286–87, 289, 291–92, 295–96, 300–04
  education of, 17–19, 40–41, 53
  finances of, 61, 73, 78, 79, 82, 100,
    110–11, 115, 116–17, 125, 130, 140,
    148–51, 155–56, 222–23, 293, 295–96
  future prospects, 295–96, 300
  Graziano lawsuit, 8, 219–20, 256–57,
    261–81
  Hollywood Hogan persona, 161–62,
    166–67
  injuries to, 135–40, 162–63, 197, 298
  introspection, 243–46
  Madison Square Garden debut (1979),
    83
  marriage and family life, 99–101, 121,
    122–30, 137, 145, 147–52, 158–61,
    163–64, 168–75, 178–84, 191–93,
    213–15, 222–23, 229–30, 236–39,
    252, 289, 291–92
  McDaniel, Jennifer, 250–52, 260, 261,
    273, 283, 295, 303
  merchandising, 155–56, 167
  music, 19–22
  name change, 85
  personality of, 11, 14, 35–36, 47, 78–79,
    80, 163–64, 250, 291–92
  physical appearance, 15–16, 38, 41, 42,
    63, 64, 67, 73, 74, 76–77, 81–82, 83,
    144
  popularity of, 86–87, 88–89
  religion, 28–32, 247–50, 259–61
  romantic life, 21–22, 83–85, 87–88,
    96–98, 157–59, 185–88, 252–54
  sexual assault allegations against,
    157–59
  spirituality, 247–50
  suicide, 1–2, 4, 6–7, 232–35, 259
  weightlifting, 37–38
  wrestling, 15, 18–19, 32–36, 40, 44–49,
    74, 89, 91, 106–8, 136, 298

Hogan, Linda (wife). *See* Claridge, Linda (wife)
Hogan, Nick (son), 13, 124, 201, 203
  arrest of, 218–20
  birth of, 129, 252
  car crash, 1–4, 206–9, 214, 255
  childhood of, 130
  family life, 163, 225–26, 245, 255, 299–300
  Graziano lawsuit, 256, 261–69
  home-schooling, 174
  imprisonment of, 269–81
  motor sports, 169–70, 198–99
  reckless driving, 204–5
  release of, 294
  Secret, The (Byrne), 259–60
  television, 176
Hogan Knows Best (TV show), 7, 175–84, 185, 186, 188–89, 192, 197–98, 199, 203, 221, 299
Hollywood Hogan persona, 161–62, 166–67
Holmes, Henry, 153, 223, 224, 225
homosexuality, 57–60
Honda Civic, 170
Houston, David, 278, 284–85, 303
Hulkamania, 27, 107. *See also* celebrity; fan base
  celebrity, 109–10, 151
  fan base, 95–96, 103, 119–20
  the Iron Sheik match, 103–5, 136
  lifestyle and schedules, 118–21
Hulk Hogan's Pastamania (restaurant), 157–58
"Hulk" nickname, 77, 85, 95–96
human growth hormone, 142
Humperdink, Oliver, 45, 47–48, 49

Incredible Hulk, The, 76–77
Infinity's End (band), 20
(Inside)Out: Hulk Hogan, Stage Dad (TV show), 171–73
Iraq war, 200
Iron Butterfly (band), 21
Iron Sheik, The (wrestler), 75, 103–5, 136, 272
Ito, Lance Allan, 262

Jacobs, Danny, 198, 201, 203, 205
jailhouse tapes, 276–77, 278
Japan, 89, 90, 91, 93, 94–95, 96, 114, 118
Jarrett, Jerry, 74–75, 76, 77
Jeannie Conroy Show (TV show), 39
Jericho, Charles, 33
Joe Louis Arena (Detroit, Michigan), 109, 138
Johnson, Dwayne "the Rock," 166–67
Johnson, Rocky, 166

Kansas City wrestling circuit, 62
Kearn, Steve, 88
Kennedy, Kate, sexual assault allegations by, 157–59
Kerr, Ann, 228, 303

Kidwell, Nelson, 96, 97
Kimmel, Jimmy, 178
King, Larry, 178, 285, 286
knee injuries, 135–37, 162–63, 181
Koloff, Ivan (the Russian Bear, wrestler), 33

Lachey, Nick, 171
Lanza, Blackjack (wrestler), 116
Larry King Live (TV show), 178, 285, 286
Late Night (TV show), 65–66
Lauper, Cyndi, 109
Lawler, Jerry, 74–75
law of attraction, 247–56, 277
Law & Order (TV show), 263
Lawrence, Barry, 198, 201
Lay, Charlie, 50, 53–54, 61
LeDuke, Jos (the Canadian Freight Train, wrestler), 33
legal issues
  divorce, 1, 4, 7–8, 158–59, 161, 186, 214, 224–26, 238–39, 254, 256–57
  Graziano lawsuit, 8, 219–20, 256–57, 261–81
  steroids, 141–44
leg drop, 74, 89, 136, 298
Lennon, John, 35
Leno, Jay, 164–65, 178
Leslie, Ed (Brutus "the Barber" Beefcake), 22, 63, 64, 65–66, 67–68, 73–75, 77–78, 123–24, 160, 199, 279, 284, 295, 299
Letterman, David, 65–66
life coaches, 249
Lindstrom, Hank, 29, 30, 31–32, 249
Little League, 15–16
Little League World Series, 15
Little Mermaid, The (animated film), 168
Locklear, Heather, 151
Lohan, Lindsay, 171
Longoria, Eva, 182
longshoremen's union, 42, 80
Lopez, Jennifer, 182
Los Angeles, California, 96, 98

Madison Square Garden (New York City), 33, 81, 83, 87, 88, 89, 102, 103, 104–5, 113
Make-A-Wish Foundation, 112
Mall of America, 157
Manson, Charles, 276
marijuana, 65, 66, 94, 104, 111, 117, 127, 128–29
marines, 200, 202
marks, 50, 55, 59, 62, 75
Mashburn, Sherry, 21–22, 87–88
masturbation, 22
Matsuda, Hiro, 51–53, 54–56, 57, 61, 62, 63, 88, 134, 272
Mayo Clinic, 139
McDaniel, Jennifer, 250–52, 260, 261, 273, 283, 295, 303
McMahon, Vince, Jr., 81, 101–4, 106–8, 109, 142–43, 144–45, 146, 151
  trial of, 152–55

WrestleMania XXV, 297–98
WWF, 165
McMahon, Vince, Sr., 33, 80, 81, 82, 83, 84, 85, 86, 88, 89, 90, 92–93, 94, 101, 103, 104, 105–6, 136, 137, 159
Memphis wrestling circuit, 74–77
merchandising, 155–56, 167
Metabol (protein), 66
Miami, Florida, 181–82
Minnesota wrestling circuit, 95–96, 97–98, 100, 101, 102, 103–4, 108, 111, 157
MJ (DJ), 261–63
Mobile Civic Center, 76
Monday Night Raw (TV show), 162
Monday Nitro matches (TV show), 158, 162
Morrison, Darci, 275
motor sports, Hogan, Nick (son), 169–70, 198
Mr. Nanny (film), 145
Mr. Wonderful (wrestler), 99
MSG Network (television network), 89, 90, 110
MSNBC television network, 178
MTV, 171
MTV/*Rock 'n' Wrestling* phenomenon, 109
Muscle and Fitness magazine, 160
music. *See also* Ruckus (band)
    Hogan, Brooke (daughter) and, 168–69, 170–71, 173, 178, 181, 185, 197–98, 298–99
    Hogan, Hulk and, 19–22, 29, 31–32, 35, 39–41, 43, 44, 53, 60, 66, 109, 158
My Chemical Romance (band), 185

Nash, Kevin, 162
National Enquirer (newspaper), 253–54
National Wrestling Alliance, 114
NBC television network, 110, 272
neck injury, 138–40
negativity, 288–89, 293, 296–97
New Earth, A (Tolle), 247–48, 271, 288
Newlyweds (TV show), 171
New World Order (nWo), 161–62
New York, New York, 110
New York wrestling circuit, 74–75, 81–83, 102, 154
No Holds Barred (film), 107, 145, 154
North Pensacola Beach, Florida, 73–74
'N Sync (band), 170

Oklahoma! (musical), 39
O'Neal, Shaquille, 182
Ono, Yoko, 35
Oprah (TV show), 246
Orndorff, Paul "Mr. Wonderful," 55, 61
Orton, Bob, 46
Orton, Randy, 46
Osbourne, Ozzy, 171
Osbournes, The (TV show), 171, 175

paralysis, 139
Patterson, Pat, 57–58, 105, 142–43
pay-per-view television, 102, 109, 150

Pearlman, Lou, 170–73
People magazine, 178, 285, 286
Pettit, Vic, 15, 20–21, 28, 32, 34, 35, 79
physical education class, 17–19
PinkSneakers, 175–76
Pitt, Brad, 95
Plante, Christiane, 185–88, 193, 252–54
Plastic Pleasure Palace (band), 19–20
Playboy magazine, 159–60
Power of Now, The (Tolle), 247–48, 265
Presley, Lisa Marie, 149
Preston, Kelly, 149
Price, Doug, 139

Ray (film), 12
Ray, James Arthur, 249, 259–60, 261, 271
real estate, 151, 182
reality TV, 171–73, 175–84, 188–89
Redford, Robert, 86
religion, Hogan and, 28–32, 247–50, 259–61
Reynolds, Burt, 12
Rhodes, Dusty, 33–35, 45, 47, 48, 76, 88, 134
Robin Hood: Men in Tights (film), 159
Robinson High School, 40
Rock 'n' Wrestling phenomenon (MTV), 109
Rocky (film), 89–90
Rocky II (film), 90
Rocky III (film), 90–93, 95, 96, 97, 251
Rodman, Dennis, 165
Rolling Stones (band), 94
Rosenthal, Elizabeth, 284–85
Rourke, Mickey, 134, 299–300
Ruckus (band), 44, 45, 49, 56. *See also* music
Rundgren, Todd, 40, 44
running, 55
Russian Bear, The (wrestler), 75

Satterwhite, Don, 28, 29
Satterwhite, Ron, 28, 29
Saturday Night Live (TV show), 110, 112, 232
Scientology, 149
Scorpion King, The (film), 166
scripting, of wrestling, 165–67
Secret, The (Byrne), 246–47, 249, 255, 259–60, 271, 283, 284
Sergeant Slaughter, 75
Shapiro, Robert, 272
Shaw, Bill, 151
Shea Stadium (New York City), 89
show business, wrestling, 50–51, 89
Sicilians, the (wrestling team), 82
Sika (Wild Samoans), 74
Silverman, Ben, 221, 223
Simpson, Ashlee, 171
Simpson, Jessica, 171
Simpson, O. J., 262, 272, 276–77, 283
SkyDome (Rogers Center, Toronto, Canada), 166–67

Smith, Anna Nicole, 262
Smith, Butch, 15
Somers, Suzanne, 110
songwriting, Hogan, Brooke (daughter), 169
South Florida, University of, 40–41
Spears, Britney, 214
spirituality, Hogan and, 28–32, 247–50, 259–61
Sportatorium, 50, 51, 53, 57, 61, 81
sports entertainment, 133
Stallone, Sylvester, 89–93, 94, 96
Steel Cage Matches, 101
Steppenwolf (band), 21
steroids, 45–46, 63–66, 74, 81, 112, 115, 125, 127, 128–29, 140–45, 151, 153–55, 162. See also alcohol; drugs
stevedores' union, 43, 80
Stewart, Rod, 94
Stillness Speaks (Tolle), 247–48
Sting, The (film), 86
Storch, Scott, 178
Studio 54 (New York City), 110, 112, 114
Suburban Commando (film), 145
suicide, 1–2, 4, 6–7, 232–35, 259
Sullivan, Brendan, 272
Superstar. See Graham, Billy (the Superstar, wrestler)
surgery, 137, 139–40, 162–63, 181, 298
Survivor (band), 96

Tampa, Florida, 11–13, 39, 87–88, 189–91, 261–63, 300, 301
Tampa Bay Buccaneers (football team), 84
Tampa Electric Company, 41, 43
television
    American Gladiators, 221–25, 234, 258
    Hogan, Brooke (daughter), 171–73
    Hogan Knows Best, 175–84
    pay-per-view, 102, 109, 150
    reality TV, 171–73
    Thunder in Paradise, 145–47, 149, 150
    World Championship Wrestling, 146
    wrestling, 32–33, 76–77, 79, 81, 83, 89–90, 101, 102, 103, 109, 110
testosterone, 65, 142
Thornton, Scott, 37
Thousand Oaks, California, 151
Thunder in Paradise (TV show), 145–47, 149, 150
Tillet, Louie, 67, 73, 74, 75
Time Warner, 165
TMZ Web site, 265–66, 276
Tolle, Eckhart, 247–48, 250
Tombstone, the (wrestling move), 138–39, 162
Toyota Supra, 169–70, 198, 205, 208
Travolta, John, 110, 149, 165
Turner, Ted, 32, 146, 151

Ultimate Fighting Championship (UFC), 54
Undertaker, The (wrestler), 138–40, 162

United States Air Force, 26
USA Today (newspaper), 157

Vale, Fernando, 212
Valium, 142
Venice Beach, California, 120
Ventura, Jesse, 95, 157
VH1 (TV network), 171–73, 178, 186, 299

War on Drugs, 141
weightlifting
    Hogan and, 37–38, 42, 55
    steroids, 64
West Haven, Connecticut, 82, 85
Whitey and Terry's Olympic Gym (Cocoa Beach, Florida), 63, 64.67
Wild Samoans, 74
World Championship Wrestling (WCW), 146, 151, 154, 155, 158, 162, 165, 166, 279
World Wide Wrestling Federation (WWWF), 32, 33, 81, 84, 85
World Wrestling Entertainment (WWE), 32, 297
World Wrestling Federation (WWF), 26, 32, 101, 102, 103, 106, 108, 142, 143, 144, 145, 146, 150, 155, 162, 165, 167
WrestleMania (TV show), 109
WrestleMania III (TV show), 89, 134, 137
WrestleMania XVIII (TV show), 166–67
WrestleMania XXV (TV show), 297–98
Wrestler, The (film), 134, 299–300
wrestling
    Alabama wrestling circuit, 67, 73–74, 75
    apprenticeship in, 50–60
    blade jobs, 134–35, 300
    business of, 73, 78–79, 85–87, 93, 106–8, 133
    cocaine, 111–12
    Florida wrestling circuit, 50–62
    Hogan, Hulk, 15, 18–19, 32–36, 40, 44–49
    Kansas City wrestling circuit, 62
    Memphis wrestling circuit, 74–77
    Minnesota wrestling circuit, 95–96, 97–98, 100, 101, 102, 103–4, 108, 111, 157
    New York wrestling circuit, 74–75, 81–83, 102, 154
    pain, 133–39, 145, 162–63, 197
    pay-per-view television, 102
    Portland, Oregon wrestling circuit, 77–78
    scripting of, 165–67
    steroid use, 140–45

Young, Peter, 90
Young, Rhonda, 90

Zahorian, George, 115, 142–43, 154